EPIC
HIKES
of
EUROPE

Explore Europe's most thrilling treks and trails

CONTENTS

Easy   Harder   Epic

INTRODUCTION

Europe can perhaps thank the Romantic artists for its excellent network of hiking trails. That wild bunch of aesthetes from the late 18th and 19th centuries extolled the power, beauty and exhilaration of nature, and through their poetry, paintings, music, and even early guidebooks, inspired generations to get outside for the simple, rejuvenating pleasure of it. Two centuries later and the continent is covered in a web of well-organised waymarked trails, ranging from easy Alpine day hikes that are helped along by a cable car or two, to the legendary Grande Randonnées and European long-distance paths, which cross the entire continental landmass from several compass points.

With such a huge choice of hiking options available, we wanted to do more in this book than list a selection of our favourites; we wanted to showcase hikes that would inspire Romantic-style exaltations: emotions such as joy, satisfaction, awe, and a decent frisson of spine-tingling fear as well. To help with our task we commissioned some of Europe's most seasoned hikers and nature writers to recount their most thrilling experiences on foot. Phoebe Smith, adventurer, wild camper and author of *Extreme Sleeps*, writes about the Arctic Circle Trail, an eight-day hike in the empty wilds of Greenland that she undertook alone, with just reindeer for company. Jasper Winn, slow travel evangelist and author of *Water Ways*, tells us about the surreal experience of 'sludging' (sliding and trudging) across the mudflats of the Wadden Sea, with one eye on the incoming tide. Jini Reddy, travel journalist and author of *Wanderland: A Search for Magic in the Landscape*, describes a five-day trail through Slovenia's Karst region, a sensuous walk that is as much about delicious tastes, as sights and sounds.

Each hike in this book is epic in some way, whether because of the dramatic landscape, the commitment (and pay-off) involved in taking a week or more to cross a country on foot, or for other meanings more personal to our writers. 'Epic' for Oli Reed, for example, was the anticipation of tackling the formidable Striding Edge, a ridge in the English Lake District that had fascinated him since childhood. For Sarah Baxter, 'epic' meant overcoming a fear of heights to attempt a vertiginous cliff-hugging path through the Cares Gorge in Spain. For radio DJ and President of The Ramblers, Stuart Maconie, the term was appropriate for a coastal loop in Scotland's Shetland Islands accompanied by the shadowy shapes of swooping kittiwakes and immense sea stacks.

Time is a consideration for anyone planning a trip away from the nine-to-five, and the hikes here include a mix of time frames. Some of the experiences in this book last just a few hours, and there are plenty of day hikes, while other hikes are a week- or even month-long undertaking, requiring planning and special equipment.

Europe is a veritable hiker's adventure playground in terms of the variety of terrain, climate and landscape that can be found in such a compact area, not to mention the fascinating cultures and people you can meet along the way. Above all, however, whether it's bogshoeing in Latvia, following in the footsteps of the Ancient Greeks to Delphi, or summiting Montenegro's highest peak, we hope that the hikes in this book will inspire you to reach for your boots and strike out somewhere new.

HOW TO USE THIS BOOK

The main stories in each chapter of the book feature first-hand accounts of fantastic hikes in that region of Europe. Each includes an orientation toolkit to help plan the trip – when is the best time of year to hike, how to get there, any special equipment required. But beyond that, these stories should inspire other ideas. We have started that process in the 'more like this' section following each story, which offers other ideas along a similar theme, or in the same region or country. On the contents page, the hikes have been colour coded according to their difficulty, which takes into account not just how long, remote and challenging they are but their logistics and local conditions. The index collects different types of hike for a variety of interests.

It's important to note that many of the routes in this book are challenging. Whether you're a seasoned hiker or a novice embarking on your very first trek, please ensure that you're adequately prepared and have taken appropriate safety precautions to help prevent dangers to yourself and others.

Clockwise from left: snowshoes and poles at the ready; big skies over Hadrian's Wall; autumn colours in Slovenia's Julian Alps

Opening spread, clockwise from left: on the Peaks of the Balkans Trail; hikers setting out; Capileira – a typical white village in the Alpujarras; sundews growing on the Great Kemeri Bog. Previous page: the St Olav Ways

© SolStock | Getty Images

NORTHERN EUROPE

EARTH, WIND AND FIRE: LAUGAVEGURINN

Iceland's back country feels like an elemental place ruled by elves and Arctic energy, and a walk between its volcanoes and glaciers is a symphony of wind, stone, fire and ice.

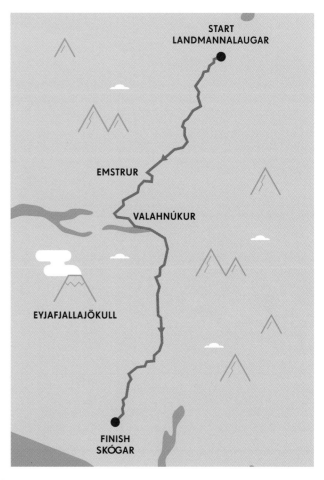

Want to hear every guide's favourite joke to tell visitors to Iceland? Here it is: 'How do you find your way out of an Icelandic forest?' 'Stand up.'

Not the best joke in the world then, but as a guest you're obliged to give it a polite giggle. Every time.

My guide, Siggi, grew up among the island's treeless recesses. His home town, Hvolsvöllur, is known for having the country's biggest abattoir; its backyard the setting of *Njál's Saga*, an epic pre-medieval legend enumerating the Shakespeare-style demise of its leading characters. And while the landscape is as bleak as its reputation, there's an uncanny beauty to the area's wilderness that lures countless travellers from every corner of the globe.

They come to complete the Laugavegurinn, Iceland's premiere hike, which tackles a sequence of lunar landscapes over the course of several days. The name translates into 'Hot Spring Rd,' which seems appropriate, especially at the trailhead, Landmannalauga, where Siggi and I scamper over to soak our legs in a bog-ridden brook gurgling with steaming sulfuric water before setting off on our hike. The first time Siggi and I hiked the trail, we finished the traditional four-day adventure to Thórsmörk in only two, with enough energy to continue on through to the epic portion of Fimmvörðuháls, a volcanic spur leading all the way back to the coast. And to us, the entirety of the course has remained our true version of Laugavegurinn ever since.

Now, 10 years later, Siggi and I wade in the warm swampy waters and continue to reminisce about our first adventure together. I remember the flecks of shimmering pebbles (Siggi called them 'raven stones') at the beginning of the hike; a field of shattered obsidian reflecting and refracting the Arctic sun.

Over the last decade we've tackled various parts of the hike together in different directions and in different seasons; Siggi often using his Spidey sense to take us off-route to explore the neighbouring hills. But completing the traditional trail from start to finish is an undeniable act of pilgrimage we undertake with a certain amount of reverence. And it's not just us; every person who calls this giant seismic rock home feels the call to complete the journey at some point in their life.

The decision to tackle the hike in a southerly direction may seem rather arbitrary considering there's only a slight descent in elevation throughout, but on the walk towards Álftavatn – as the vista opens up to the looming Tingfjallajökull mountain range – one begins to understand the dramatic reveal of Laugavegurinn's second act.

The Álftavatn hut and its summertime orbit of neon tents mark the halfway point of the traditional trek and is where everyone – regardless of speed or stamina – takes a well-deserved break from the elements. It's like some kind of Nordic Burning Man fuelled by weariness and Snickers bars instead of hallucinogens and ayahuasca.

The walk through the third section, Emstrur, feels like an acid trip unto itself, with ribbons of red, ochre and fluorescent blue scarring the ground and hillside; a reminder of the intense geological activity creeping up from below the planet's surface. As the path

"The Álftavatn hut and its summertime orbit of neon tents [are]... like some kind of Nordic Burning Man fuelled by Snickers bars instead of hallucinogens."

curls down into a valley shot through with fingers of glacial melt, the final leg of the trek comes into view. While most of the journey has followed a more subtle undulation of scorched stone, the rise up on to the volcanic crest at Fimmvörðuháls is markedly more dramatic. A series of steps hoists hikers up on to a turfy plateau sprinkled with arctic flowers, and as the trail hugs the mountain's edge, cascading boulders hem the pass like flying buttresses, clerestories, and other architectural elements of gothic brick.

Often thought of as an add-on, the trek through Fimmvörðuháls can feel especially challenging after several days on foot, but it's also considered the most rewarding part of the trip. While the walks through Álftavatn and Emstrur will have you wondering what it might have been like to be the first person to find soothing hot springs during Viking times, the basin of ash at the top of the pass is, quite literally, history in the making.

When the slumbering volcano hidden under the Eyjafjallajökull glacier erupted in 2010 it created a mega-geyser that vaporised

KELDUR'S LIVING HISTORY

Iceland's southern swath of moonscape is the backdrop to a Viking saga as brutal as anything in *Game of Thrones. Njál's Saga* is a gruesome story of family rivalry that ends with almost every character in the ground. Remnants of those settlement days still feature on that ground – the most authentic being Keldur, a turf-roofed farm once owned by Ingjaldur Höskuldsson, one of the major players in the saga.

Left to right: Skógafoss waterfall; there's only one way to go at the River Krossá. Previous page: crossing the colourful Landmannalaugar

tonnes of frozen water and shot mounds of tar-like, liquefied ash down both the sides of the peak. Born from the embers were two brand new baby mountains, Magni and Móði, which both belch plumes of steam for passers-by to admire. Once you clear the fields of desolation caused by the recent eruption, a mossy carpet unfurls anew. Each step is slightly lower than the last, passing a parade of waterfalls (22, to be exact) that diminuendos down to a final chute – Skógafoss, plunking you right back on to the country's main drag, the Ring Rd.

But before tackling the last day-long walk back to Route 1, the valley beneath awaits. As we leave the coloured earths of Emstrur behind, Siggi explains that the area below is known as Godaland, or 'Land of the Gods'. Tucked beneath a halo of glacial peaks, the enclave is like some kind of ancient reliquary filled with mounds of shale resembling troll fingers and elven churches. The air is different here, too – calm – guarded from the quixotic elements that wreak havoc on the landscape above.

And without the perilous Arctic wind, the valley is also home to a dense thicket; Siggi and his Icelandic brothers call it Thórsmörk – 'Thor's Wood'. It's here, under the shade of a tree in the midnight sun, that we set up camp for the night. 'Turns out not every Icelandic forest is the brunt of a joke,' Siggi mutters as we settle in for the night in this unexpected spot, nestled deep within this divine land. **BP**

ORIENTATION

Start // Landmannalaugar
Finish // Skógar
Distance // 77km (48 miles)
Duration // Four days
When to go // July to mid-September.
Where to stay // Midgard (www.midgard.is) has comfy rooms, a restaurant and plenty of guides. Hike options are camping or reserving a bed in one of the huts.
What to take // Plastic bags to keep wet and dry clothes separate, a swimsuit for hot springs, and a GPS.
What to wear // 'Cotton is killer' are good words to live by as you dress for your trek. Go for wool layers, and be prepared to encounter all four seasons.
More info // www.fi.is, the homepage for the Iceland Touring Association, which runs the cabins on the trail.

© Pyty | Shutterstock; © Kelly Cheng | Getty Images

*Opposite: dramatic Hornbjarg cliffs at
the Hornstrandir reserve*

MORE LIKE THIS
ICELANDIC HIKES

HORNSTRANDIR

If it weren't so hard to get to, the protected
reserve of Hornstrandir would be Iceland's
most popular hiking expanse. Like little
lobster claws nipping at the Arctic
Circle, the northernmost peninsulas of
Iceland's Westfjords are brutally lonely,
save for colonies of cawing guillemots
and the occasional Arctic fox. In summer
(early July–mid-August) the preserve is
blanketed in a glittering green carpet as
travellers walk from cairn to cairn. For the
full experience, take the ferry from the
townships of Bolungarvík or Ísafjörður up to
Veiðileysufjörður, a glacially carved fjord,
and spend four or five days hiking up to
Hornvík and the bird cliffs at Hornbjarg
before venturing down the mountain
pass to Hloduvík and on to the cluster of
abandoned cottages at Hesteyri to wait for
the return ferry.
Start/Finish // Bolungarvík or Ísafjörður
Distance // Variable
More info // www.safetravel.is

FIMMVÖRÐUHÁLS

The more traditional version of the
Laugavegurinn hike ends in Thórsmörk;
our perfect version continues all the way
to Skógar through what we consider the
most scenic part of the journey. That final
stretch connecting Thorsmörk to the Ring
Rd is called Fimmvörðuháls, and can be
undertaken as its own hike – generally
tackled in the reverse direction. The day-
long walk is divided into three distinct
sections. The first starts at the massive
waterfall in the village of Skógar and passes
over 20 additional chutes as you make your
way to a field of ash – the site of the 2010
Eyjafjallajökull eruption – before descending
into a secret valley dotted with wild Arctic
flowers and hemmed by large cathedral-like
rock formations. The terminus of the hike
at the Básar site is known to Icelanders as
Godaland, or the 'Land of the Gods', for its
ethereal terrain – it's the perfect place to
base oneself for some quiet camping and
going on additional short walks.
Start // Skógar
Finish // Básar
Distance // 23km (14 miles)
More info // www.fi.is

HELLNAR TO ARNARSTAPI

An epically easy walk undertaken at any
time of the year, the coastal stroll from
the ancient farmstead of Hellnar to the
village of Arnarstapi in western Iceland's
Snæfellsjökull National Park is especially
dramatic on an inclement day when the
rock formations act like blowholes, shooting
a mix of rain and sea spray into the gusty
air. The short walk passes a series of frozen
lava flows and eroded stone caves that are,
of course, quite pretty on a sun-filled day
as well, and columnar basalt, ravines and
grottoes ensure plenty of off-trail exploring.
Reward yourself afterwards with a steaming
bowl of fish soup, which is available at
either end of the walk.
Start // Hellnar
Finish // Arnarstapi
Distance // 2.5km (1.5 miles)
More info // www.nat.is

A WALK WITH PURPOSE: THE ST OLAV WAYS

This ancient Norwegian pilgrimage snakes through picturesque villages and national parks, and along rugged coast into quiet farmlands – ending at Trondheim's famed Nidaros Cathedral.

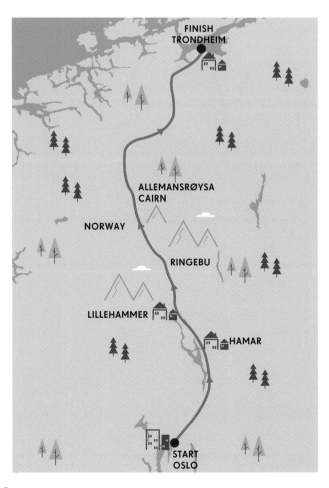

We were huddled underneath a tarp Matthias had somehow remembered to bring. A small rock in my pocket pressed into my leg as I curled into a ball, my weight on the tarp's edge keeping it from whipping in the wind – the rain was coming down in sheets. We had started hiking through Dovrefjell-Sunndalsfjella National Park about an hour ago, the clouds dark and heavy in the sky, the park more isolated, more humanless than any I had ever seen.

The sky had no chance of stopping us. We needed to hike 20km (12 miles) that day, all through the largest continuously protected area in Norway. I had been looking forward to this section of the St Olav Ways for months: here, there are no power lines. No roads. No farms. Not a single trace of humanity but yourself and the alpine trail in front of you.

At least, that is, when you're not crouching under a tarp.

As for that rock in my pocket, I picked it up in the Gudbrandsdalen Valley, leaving behind my 700-year-old accommodation at Sygard Grytting. I knew Allemansrøysa – both a cairn of stones 3m (9.9ft) high and a display of human courage – was coming. My thoughts were on it often.

To participate, hikers carry a rock along the trail, symbolising something they carry with them that they'd like to be rid of. At Allemansrøysa, they add to the cairn tower, leaving their rock – and what it symbolises – behind. While the St Olav Ways were once trekked to honour St Olav, one-time King and the patron saint of Norway, now they're wandered for many reasons: a physical challenge, spirituality, time in nature, forgiveness, fun, or to partake in this purposeful act of strength. You'll have your own reason; I had mine.

The rain let up 30 minutes or so later, the sky still bleak and dramatic, ground now slick, though the grasses provide traction and the hills are mercifully gentle. I'm on the most popular of the St Olav routes, the Gudbrandsdalsleden, which goes through central Norway and the more eastern, gentler side of Dovrefjell. Other routes tackle other terrain, but here, it's about distance, not elevation. We're trying to cover 20 to 25km (12.5 to 15.5 miles) a day.

The markers along the way – like little jagged gravestones with bright neon-blue crowns painted on – give you a sense of distance. Outside the park, they're often red and white; a combination of the St John's Arms and the St Olav's Cross. Get close to Trondheim, and the markers start counting down the distance to Nidaros, though I don't know this yet. I'm still in Dovrefjell, famous for its reindeer and musk oxen, somewhere in an open alpine expanse that's unending, waiting to see Allemansrøysa.

Slowly, the massive stone pile I'm looking for comes into undeniable view. It rests on Hardbakken, the highest point of the route – 1320m (4331ft) above sea level – shimmering wet in the patchy sunlight. I walk up to it gingerly, attempting to fathom each stone, some clearly would have been quite a burden to carry. I place my rock a metre or so up the small tower, and while I don't immediately feel lighter, I do feel a bond. Every hiker before and after me will have a sense of my carried weight, and I theirs.

Prior to Allemansrøysa, the trip had already felt more spiritual than I was prepared for. The Cathedral Ruins of Hamar – enclosed in a glass pyramid – felt like a spaceship to a previous era, a peek into an unknown world. I stepped mindfully across the ruins' threshold, touched its nearly 1000-year-old walls, and sat in a room once reserved for a few chosen men; my ancestors, had they made the trek from nearby Lillehammer, would not have been allowed in. They would've held their ears to the door, praying for a whiff of godliness. In places like Hamar, the age, the heft, and the meaning of the trail are as tangible as any pocketed rock.

The same can be said for Ringebu Stavkirke, one of only 28 remaining stave churches in the country. Dating back to 1220, runes inscribed on the walls can only be spotted by trained guides. Massive, three levels, and constructed without a single nail, 1000 or so of these churches were erected after Christianity swept the nation – though few matched Ringebu's size, beauty, and level of detail.

But in the end, Ringebu and Hamar pale in comparison to their similarly aged soapstone counterpart: Nidaros Cathedral, the northernmost medieval cathedral in the world. Every pilgrim's first aerial glance of this Romanesque and Gothic giant comes on the Hill of Joy, or Feginsbrekka, just outside Trondheim; I stuffed a pastry in my backpack to celebrate the moment. Around this point, stone markers tease you with remaining distances – 14km, 12km, 10km. Knowing the end was near, my feet felt safe to start aching; the hills on the outskirts of the city felt colossal.

Then, at Nidaros, in front of the massive, elaborately carved stone edifice, the last marker reads the unthinkable: 0km. Legend has it that those hiking the St Olav Ways should walk around the

THE WAYS

Eight pilgrim routes make up the St Olav Ways, each ending at the Nidaros Cathedral in Trondheim. Of the eight, the Gudbrandsdalsleden is by far the most popular and historic route – the final 100km (62 miles) trace the route King Olav II's body was carried after the Battle of Stiklestad. Upon being exhumed, Olav 'smelled of roses', leading to his canonisation, the building of Nidaros Cathedral, and the formation of the St Olav Ways.

Clockwise from left: Ringebu
Stavkirke; a St Olav Ways passport;
Allemansrøysa. Previous page from top:
on the trail; Budsjord pilgrim farm

ORIENTATION

Start // St Hallvard Cathedral Ruins, Oslo
Finish // Nidaros Cathedral, Trondheim
Distance // 643km (399 miles)
Duration // Allow around 32 days
Getting there // St Hallvard is a 15-minute walk
from Oslo Central Station.
When to go // April to September.
What to wear // Layers and worn-in trekking shoes.
Where to stay // Over 160 official accommodation options
dot the route, from minimalist hostels to luxurious B&Bs.
Where to eat // Hostels and B&Bs offer dinner and packed
lunches.
Things to know // Register at the Pilegrimssenter Oslo to
receive your passport; it not only gets you the Olav Letter
upon completion, but it's good for discounts at tourist spots
and accommodation. Make lodging reservations in advance.
More info // www.pilegrimsleden.no

*"Every hiker before and after
me will have a sense of my
carried weight, and I theirs."*

cathedral three times before entering, though if your feet – like
mine – don't allow it, that's okay.

In lieu of a few last laps, I made a slow, staggering line for the
nearby National Pilgrim Centre to obtain the final stamp in my
trail passport. With that ink on the page, I then received proof of
my journey: the prized Olav Letter. I took it, sat down outside the
cathedral, and breathed. One of only 1000 or so to make the trek
that year, I, without my rock, had finally arrived. **JK**

Opposite from top: sunrise at Mont St-Michel, France; vaulted interior of Canterbury Cathedral

MORE LIKE THIS
EUROPEAN PILGRIMAGES

PILGRIM'S WAY, ENGLAND

When Archbishop Thomas à Becket fell at the hands of Henry II's knights, he was built a lavish shine in Canterbury Cathedral's Trinity Chapel. Once one of England's foremost pilgrimage sites, the shrine was razed in 1538 during the Reformation. All that marks the spot today is a single burning candle – and depressions in the stones from thousands of pilgrim knees.

The trek – honored in Chaucer's *Canterbury Tales* – follows the route Henry II walked seeking absolution for Becket's death; it's an ancient thoroughfare that dates back to the Stone Age. The path roughly follows the North Downs, a ridge of chalk hills, and wanders through picturesque villages, countless hop fields, and pretty valleys. Be sure to collect your Wayfarer's Dole (a cup of beer and a piece of bread) at the Hospital of St Cross and stop at Jane Austen's house in Chawton.

Start // Winchester Cathedral, Hampshire
Finish // Canterbury Cathedral, Kent
Distance // 246km (153 miles)
More info // www.pilgrimsway canterbury.org

LES CHEMINS DU MONT ST-MICHEL, FRANCE

Legend has it that the archangel Michael appeared three times to the bishop Aubert of Avranches, asking him to build a church on the summit of Mont Tombe. A small sanctuary was thus built in 708: Mont St-Michel, as we know it today, would evolve through the 16th century, becoming both a Gothic feat rising above the sandbanks and one of Christianity's most beloved sites.

Similar to the St Olav Ways, Les Chemins du Mont St-Michel are really six different paths, though the main route to the Benedictine abbey is from the city of Rouen. From here, hikers follow a medieval route through the Roumare Forest, cross the River Seine, dip up and down valleys, skirt along fortified castles, and end at the bayside village of Genêts – though many will continue on to the abbey itself.

Make sure to check the tide calendar to determine the abbey's accessibility.

Start // Rouen
Finish // Genêts
Distance // 360km (224 miles)
More info // www.lescheminsdumont saintmichel.com

VIA DI FRANCESCO, ITALY

One of the world's most-loved saints, St Francis of Assisi eschewed his wealthy upbringing, wandering Italy to help the poor and live a life closer to nature and God. The Via di Francesco connects places central to his life – some happen to be Italy's most historic spots.

The path starts at the Basilica di Santa Croce, the largest Franciscan shrine in the world; it then closely follows the western slopes of the Central Apennines, wandering through olive groves, dense forests, and to medieval hilltop towns – including Assisi, the hometown and burial site of the saint. The route includes Piediluco, where he preached by a lake; Foligno, where he sold his father's silks; and Bevagna, a site of one of his many miracles. The route finally ends at St Peter's Basilica in Vatican City, a stunning landmark, regardless of religion or belief.

Crossing difficult terrain, this trek is recommended for experienced hikers.

Start // Basilica di Santa Croce, Florence
Finish // St Peter's Basilica, Vatican City
Distance // 550km (342 miles)
More info // www.viadifrancesco.it

DANISH DESIGN- SPOTTING IN AARHUS

Denmark's second city has been a bastion of Scandinavian design since the Viking era. On a walk through the city, journey through its past and into the future.

I'll admit it: before I went to Aarhus, I didn't have any grand expectations. I certainly hadn't been dreaming about the day I would finally go, the way I fantasised about Paris for years before studying there. Aarhus wasn't really on my radar at all, until I visited Copenhagen and fell in love with Danish culture and design. But Denmark's second-largest city is so wonderfully liveable that I immediately felt at home.

Imagine a city with a harbour on one side, forest on the northern and southern edges, and a dynamic urban landscape in the middle. The interior is a lively, walkable mix of historic buildings that date back to the Middle Ages, striking mid-century architecture, and sleek modern design. There are cobblestoned streets; charming neighbourhoods full of independent boutiques, restaurants and cafes; civic landmarks; museums; parks; and a university with a thriving student population. The historic city centre doesn't feel like a tourist trap and the juxtaposition of buildings spanning the centuries doesn't seem jarring.

Sound a bit like an urban utopia? Well, that's what I found when I visited Aarhus.

'It's a mission in the city to strive for quality in our architecture,' says Jacob Bundsgaard, the Mayor of Aarhus. When I met Mayor Bundsgaard, an avid runner, he had just started offering locals and visitors the chance to go jogging with him. Not much of a runner myself, I joined him for a walk instead, letting him lead me to some of the city's key sights and tell me about its past, present and future.

Our walk was concentrated in the centre, but both the forest and the water were crucial to the city's founding by the Vikings, so to get the complete picture, we started in the northern forest and ambled south along the harbour. 'There's a small forest in the

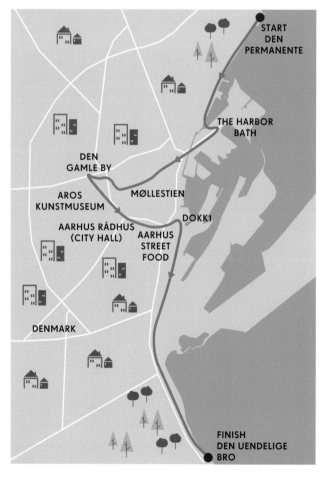

northern part of the city centre that has a bit of a hidden gem: an old harbour bath, which dates from the early 1900s and has just been renovated,' Mayor Bundsgaard told me.

Denmark has some of the cleanest harbours on the planet and Danes take full advantage of this fact in the summer, diving into the water and swimming around. The harbour baths – historic ones and new, modern ones – are essentially free open-air spas. The new Harbor Bath designed by famed Danish architectural firm Bjarke Ingels Group is an essential stop on any walk through Aarhus. It's located in a district called Aarhus Ø (Aarhus Island), which is currently being developed with a host of boundary-pushing design projects. I stopped to marvel at the Iceberg, an apartment complex composed of jagged white forms, whose architects received accolades and awards for their vision of the future.

Of course, there's more to Aarhus than just the forests and the waterfront. To experience it, I headed inland for a leisurely stroll through the Latin Quarter, where cobblestone streets are lined with boutiques selling everything from handmade ceramics to fashionable clothes and leather goods. While most of the Latin Quarter deftly marries the old and the new, Møllestein felt like a real blast from the past. This charming little street is lined with colourful homes that date back to the 18th century. Small and quaint, they looked to me like something out of Grimm's fairy tales.

To dig deeper into the history of Aarhus, I detoured to Den Gamle By. The open-air museum spans four centuries of architecture and design, starting with a recreation of a 16th-century neighbourhood and ending with an apartment building from the 1970s. I popped into the bakery for some biscuits, looked around the apothecary, and stopped for a traditional Danish lunch in the garden.

'One of the places that I would recommend people visit is actually my work place, the city hall, which is a very important part of Danish architectural history,' Mayor Bundsgaard remarked. Designed by Arne Jacobsen and Erik Møller, with furniture by Hans Wegner, it was completed in 1941 and is considered a prime example of Scandinavian modernism. The functional, minimal look that we associate with Scandinavian design today has roots in this period and, along with Copenhagen, Aarhus was one of the most important centres for it. The city's architecture school is still one of the most renowned in the region.

As I walked around the centre and continued south, I began to see a much more modern vision of Danish architecture. I stopped at ARoS, the landmark art museum with exhibits by such leading contemporary artists as Elmgreen & Dragset, Olafur Eliasson, and James Turrell. Though the museum has lots of great exhibits, my favourite part was Eliasson's permanent installation *Your Rainbow Panorama*, a huge ring-shaped walkway on top of the museum that let me gaze out at the city through glass windows in every colour of the rainbow. An expansion of the museum is underway and will add a semi-underground installation by James Turrell.

From there, a ten-minute walk down Sønder Allé brought me to Aarhus Street Food, a collection of food stalls in recycled

MOESGAARD MUSEUM

The Moesgaard Museum is a bit off the beaten path, but worth the detour. The strikingly modern building features a sloping green roof that provides a unique viewpoint and contains interactive exhibits about the Vikings. The main attraction is the Grauballe Man, an amazingly well-preserved bog man from the Iron Age, discovered nearby in 1952. Stay for lunch at the cafe, which serves Nordic dishes made using local ingredients.

Clockwise from top: 'The Infinite Bridge'; Aarhus Street Food; colour and cobblestones; the Iceberg apartment block. Previous page: 'Your Rainbow Panorama' at ARoS

"The interior is a lively, walkable mix of historic buildings that date back to the Middle Ages, striking mid-century architecture, and sleek modern design."

The Infinite Bridge © Johan Gjøde | Gjøde & Partnere Arkitekter

shipping containers selling everything from Danish comfort food to Vietnamese *báhn mi*. It's close to Dokk1, the futuristic library designed by Danish architecture firm Schmidt Hammer Lassen. 'If you have a perception of what a library is, you need to visit this because it will be completely different than you imagined,' Mayor Bundsgaard said, explaining that it's more like a public square with a roof on top than a repository for books. Inside, there are lots of different seating areas where locals congregate as well as areas dedicated to kids. In the middle of the building, there's a massive bell that rings every time a baby is born at the hospital in Aarhus. I wanted to linger with a good book, but was on a mission to see more of the city.

Continuing south along the waterfront, I walked past the industrial harbour, which is now home to film studios and creative offices. Passing by the yachts and other boats parked in the marina, I kept going toward the forest. There I found a curious art installation. Called *Den Uendelige Bro* (*The Infinite Bridge*), it looks like a wooden pier, but rather than starting on land and ending in the water, it forms a circle so you begin on land, walk over the water, and loop back around to your starting point. 'It was part of an art exhibition that has taken place in Aarhus over the years and people fell in love with the idea and the concept, so it's permanent now,' Mayor Bundsgaard explained. As I walked on its wooden planks, gazing out to sea, I thought it was a perfect metaphor for the city itself: a never-ending loop where nature, architecture, and humanity coexist harmoniously without a beginning or an end. **LI**

ORIENTATION

Start // Den Permanente
Finish // *Den Uendelige Bro (The Infinite Bridge)*
Distance // 10km (6.2 miles)
Duration // Allow a couple of hours for the walk, but all day if you want to spend time at the sights, shops and cafes.
Getting there // The train from Copenhagen takes about three hours.
When to go // April to October.
Where to stay // There are plenty of nice, good-value hotels, such as Scandic Aarhus City (www.scandichotels.com), which is centrally located near the Latin Quarter.
Where to eat // Choose from casual cafes to Michelin-starred restaurants. For a caffeine fix, stop by La Cabra (www.lacabra.dk), a sleek coffee shop with Scandinavian minimalist design that serves third-wave coffee and excellent pastries.
More info // www.visitaarhus.com

MORE LIKE THIS
URBAN DESIGN HIKES

BILBAO, SPAIN

The Guggenheim Bilbao designed by Frank Gehry was such a game-changer for the small city, it inspired others to build eye-catching museums in the hopes of replicating the so-called 'Bilbao effect'. In recent years, over a million annual visitors have travelled here to see Gehry's landmark museum, which transformed this once-declining industrial city in Spain's Basque region into a tourist destination. Immerse yourself in art and then stroll along the river to the Casco Viejo, the historic centre where locals and visitors hang out at the tapas bars lining the squares. Along the way, you'll see the ultra-modern La Salve Bridge and enjoy a scenic stroll along the riverbank.

Start // Guggenheim Bilbao
Finish // Casco Viejo
Distance // 1.8km (1.1 miles)
More info // www.bilbaoturismo.net

VALLETTA, MALTA

At first glance, the capital of this island nation in the Mediterranean seems like a fortified city preserved in amber, but look closer and you'll discover architectural influences from its various rulers, which include the Romans, Greeks, Arabs, Normans, Sicilians, French, Knights of St John of Jerusalem, and the British. Most recently, Italian architect Renzo Piano left his mark with the City Gate, which comprises the entrance to the city, the Parliament, and an open-air theatre in the ruins of an old opera house. Admire the sea views from the Upper Barrakka Gardens, visit the Co-Cathedral of St John (home to Caravaggio's only signed work), tour the Casa Rocca Piccola (the 16th-century palace of a present-day Knight of Malta) and take a leisurely stroll through the streets of the city centre, where stone steps make for atmospheric photo ops.

Start // City Gate
Finish // Fort St Elmo
Distance // 1.2km (0.75 miles)
More info // www.visitmalta.com

MILAN, ITALY

Italy's design capital has enough things to see and do to keep you busy for days. From the Quadrilatero della Moda (aka the upscale fashion district) to the Navigli, where fashionable bars and restaurants line the canal, you'll find endless attractions that engage all the senses. Start your day at Pasticceria Marchesi (now owned by Prada) for espresso and a pastry, visit the Triennale Milano (Italy's first museum dedicated to design), tour the stunning Villa Necchi Campiglio designed by Piero Portaluppi in 1932, and admire the gothic Duomo with its imposing facade. End the day with an aperitivo and dinner in the Navigli area, where you have your pick of lively places to drink and dine.

Start // Marchesi 1824
Finish // Navigli
Distance // 7.2km (4.5 miles)
More info // www.italia.it

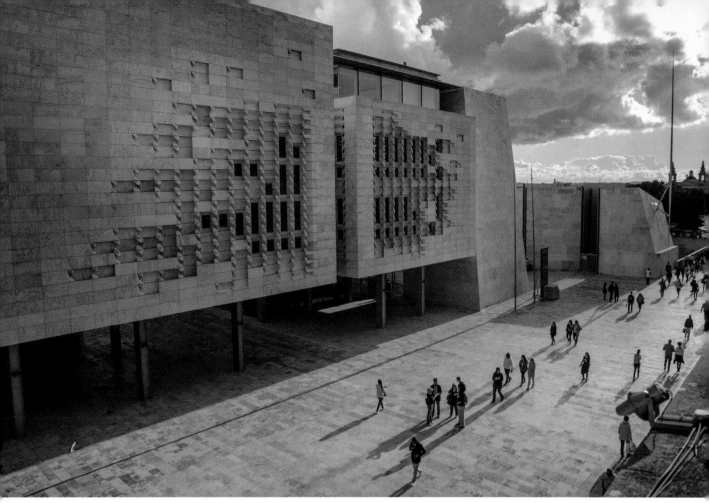

Clockwise from top: Valletta's City Gate designed by Renzo Piano Building Workshop; on the streets of Milan; elegant facades in Bilbao

WILD NORTH: THE KARHUNKIERROS TRAIL

Savour the scent of the forest while crossing fells and delving into the shadows of the taiga on Finland's remarkable Karhunkierros Trail.

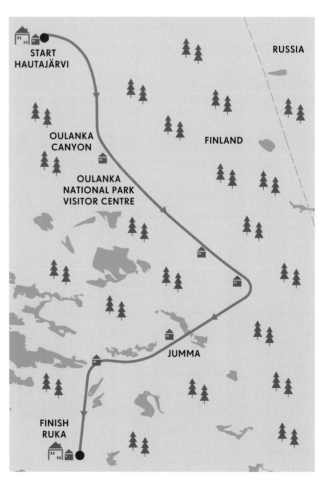

The Karhunkierros Trail (Bear Trail) turned out to be something of a misnomer. There are certainly brown bears out there in the darker recesses of these vast forests of northern Finland, but they're highly elusive and on my trip I saw neither hair nor terrifying hide. In some respects, this was a little disappointing – it has always been something of a personal dream to see a bear in the wild – but mostly it was a relief. After all, I was alone, and had a toothy member of the *Ursus* genus come tracking me down, I'm not sure my Swiss Army knife would have put up much of a defence.

Running through the heart of Finnish Lapland's Oulanka National Park, the Karhunkierros Trail is an 82km (51-mile) route widely regarded as Finland's best long-distance walking trail. It takes most people four to six days to complete the hike, which wends alongside icy-cool rivers, climbs up moorland fells, and burrows deep into old-growth forests. With temperatures ranging from -30°C (-22°F) in winter to +30°C (86°F) in summer, this is a landscape of extreme climatic change. During the eternal darkness of the polar winter, the trees are covered in a thick coat of snow that bends and contorts them into bizarre shapes. And when those snow-covered trees are lit up by the Northern Lights, the whole landscape turns into a fairy tale. But, even if you're not here in the dead of winter (and the extreme Arctic conditions mean that few people are capable of tackling the Karhunkierros Trail at this time of year), the park has an enduring beauty. Spring brings the first brave flowers, and summer has the lingering light of the Midnight Sun. But it has to be the autumn months that see the park at its finest. Gone are the mosquitoes and midges that are the bane of walkers in spring and early summer. And gone too are the

FOREST FLORA

Oulanka National Park sits on a biological crossroads of habitats, and its many microclimates nurture an unusually diverse range of plant species. The park is home to several that are unique to the area, and species such as the *Atla oulankaensis* and *Verrucaria oulankaensis* lichens that have only recently being discovered. The floral star, though, is the spring-flowering calypso orchid, or fairy slipper: a shy and delicate pink flower that favours an undisturbed forest floor.

"The tang of the cold dawn air, laced in rivers of morning mist, made me buzz with life. The flight of waxwing birds, with their cockatoo head crests, filled me with a sense of pure contentment."

high-summer crowds of fellow hikers. In their place are quiet trails and bushes bursting with blueberries and cranberries. And then there's the autumn colour show, when the leaves on the birch trees turn a searing orange and the hills are a visual treat of red-tinged flowering heather.

The lack of bears was something I very quickly forgot about. And who wouldn't when faced with all this... space, all this... wilderness, all this... Arctic. The Karhunkierros Trail is Europe at its most raw and most intoxicating. And just how much wilderness are we talking about? Well, for the most part, the Karhunkierros Trail runs through the ancient forests that make up the taiga (boreal forest). And the taiga is big. In fact, it's so big that it stretches in a complete circle right the way around the colder, northern parts of the globe. It's far and away the single biggest forest on the planet and, for the most part, it's almost completely uninhabited by people.

Before I left home I'd worried that I might be nervous walking the trail all alone, that nights spent in silent log cabins far from other

people in an unimaginably vast forest would make me jittery. But in fact, it was quite the opposite. The dull night hoot of the Great Grey Owl sent tingly thrills down my spine. The tang of the cold dawn air, laced in rivers of morning mist, made me buzz with life. The flight of waxwing birds, with their cockatoo head crests, filled me with a sense of pure contentment that I've rarely felt in places where people crowd in. But perhaps it was those creatures that I couldn't see or hear that gave me the biggest glow of excitement. There were those bears of course, but there were also plenty of wolves out there in search of their very own Little Red Riding Hood. Plus there were elegant lynxes, Europe's only big cats, and stocky wolverines who are so tough and ferocious that all other creatures in the taiga give way to them. While most of these are rarely seen, there's a certain creature that is far less elusive (and doesn't require the defensive actions of a Swiss Army knife). Reindeer. And by day two of my solo walk I'd seen dozens of Santa's favourite helper. In fact, forget Bear Trail, this could have been called the

© wmaster8go | Getty Images; © ePhotocorp | Getty Images; © Tsuguliev | Shutterstock; © Alex Robinson | AWL Images Ltd

Clockwise from top left: the beauty of the taiga in autumn; a pink orchid flowering in Oulanka National Park; a herd of caribou reindeer; wild lingonberries and bilberries. Previous page: an early start on the Karhunkierros Trail

Reindeer Trail. I'd barely finished lacing up my hiking boots at the start of the walk on day one when the first group of reindeer emerged out of the forest and ambled over to see what kind of animal I was. Disappointed that I was just another dumb human, they quickly wandered off in search of lichens to chew on.

On the last morning of my walk, change was afoot. The sky, which had been a searing autumnal blue for the past four days, was suddenly less welcoming. Low clouds, carried on a cold northwesterly wind, skidded over the top of the hills and a few flakes of sleety snow began to fall. Standing atop a hill, I could make out the lights of the ski resort of Ruka where the Karhunkierros Trail ends. The icy wind made my hands and face sting with cold. The seasons were changing and soon humanity would be gone and the reindeer, wolves, owls, and bears, would become kings of Oulanka National Park. And that, I thought, is how it should be. I pulled on a thicker jumper, put my head down and set my sights on the end of the trail. **SB**

ORIENTATION

Start // Hautajärvi
Finish // Ruka
Distance // 82km (51 miles)
Duration // Four to six days
Getting there // From June to August buses run from Kuusamo to Hautajärvi and from Ruka to Salla and Kuusamo.
When to go // June to October. From late May to early July clouds of midges and mosquitoes are the bane of hikers.
What to wear // In high summer T-shirt and shorts are fine, but always bring clothing to cope with extreme cold.
What to pack // Food, water, gas stove, good quality waterproof hiking boots, waterproofs, torch, sleeping bag.
Where to stay // There are mountain huts at regular distances. In summer they are often full. Bring a tent.
Tours // Finnature (www.finnature.com) offers wildlife-watching tours around Oulanka National Park.
More info // www.nationalparks.fi

Opposite from top: taking in the dramatic views of Svalbard; a hiking companion on the Musk Ox Trail

MORE LIKE THIS
NORDIC ADVENTURES

LITTLE BEAR'S RING, FINLAND

If the Karhunkierros Trail is too long and tough, but you still want a flavour of the taiga, then the Pieni Karhunkierros (Little Bear's Ring) could be for you. This one-day, clearly marked circular walk dips into the southern section of Oulanka National Park, taking in some fantastic scenery as it follows a river valley. Pass gushing rapids, cross a hanging bridge, walk through sheltered forests and perhaps have a campfire at one of the designated spots to round off your wilderness experience.

A popular hike, this trail is regarded as one of the best short walks in Finland and is also available to hike year-round; it's an excellent winter snowshoe option.

Start/Finish // Retki-Etappi cafe, Juuma
Distance // 12km (7.5 miles)
More info // www.nationalparks.fi

THE MUSK OX TRAIL, NORWAY

What most people don't realise is that despite its formidable size and appearance, the musk ox is in fact a type of goat. Granted, this massive, half-tonne prehistoric-looking relic from the last Ice Age, is a very grumpy and powerful goat that does have a tendency to charge at people it doesn't like, but it is still just a goat. And this is something you might want to keep in mind when hiking Norway's Musk Ox Trail.

Lying in the shadow of Mt Snøhetta (2286m/7500ft) and within the sublime Dovrefjell-Sunndalsfjella National Park of central Norway, the Musk Ox Trail runs through some of the most imposing mountain scenery in Europe. High Arctic tundra, lichen-nibbling reindeer, bleak mountains and a biting cold throughout the year, this day-walk combines genuine adventure alongside incredible encounters with Europe's only musk ox.

Start // Kongsvold
Finish // Grønbakken
Distance // 15km (9.5 miles)
More info // www.moskusriket.no/
moskusstien

ISFJORD TREK, NORWAY

Svalbard. This is a land where human beings are temporary visitors. This Norwegian archipelago, high up in the Arctic Ocean, is closer to the North Pole than it is to Oslo. A terrain of superlatives and home of the polar bear, walrus and other high-Arctic wildlife, Svalbard is one of the last true wildernesses in Europe, and the Arctic as you always imagined it to be.

Hiking in Svalbard is different to anywhere else in Europe. There are no set, marked trails, no comfortable mountain huts, and all walks here must be done in the company of an armed (polar bears represent a real danger) and qualified guide. Svalbard specialist operators offer all manner of summer hikes and winter snowshoe treks, but a multi-day summer trek along the Isfjord coastline is one of the best – and most accessible.

Start/Finish // Longyearbyen
Distance // Varies
More info // www.poliarctici.com

SENJA'S
PIN-UP PEAK

Traverse Arctic bogs and dwarf forests en route to a rock-top eyrie
providing the most dramatic views across Norway's second-largest island.

The debate about the title of World's Most Beautiful Mountain is a fierce one. Tallest? No quibbles: Everest wins by a furlong. But most spectacular? Well, there's no shortage of runners, each with its passionate proponents. The nigh-perfect cone of Mt Fuji? The Matterhorn's razor-edged pyramid? The sky-piercing pinnacle of Cerro Torre in Patagonia? All very different peaks, with diverse scenic merits and geological origins – but one thing unites them: the best way to enjoy their magnificence, I'd contend, is not to climb them but to admire them from a short distance.

That's certainly true of the most aspirational peak of Senja. Norway's second-largest island, lying some 300km above the Arctic Circle, is awash with scenic drama: it's a jumble of jagged peaks and rugged peninsulas, scoured and sculpted by ice and the elements over millions of years. With its colourfully photogenic fishing villages and skerry-speckled fjords, it's been dubbed the 'new Lofoten'; but, thus far, it remains remarkably peaceful. Whereas scenic hotspots on the Lofotens periodically bulge with cruise-ship coach tours, even on a sunny summer's day you'll encounter few tourists on Senja's winding roads, bar a handful of camper vans with Norwegian plates – domestic tourists, still low in number, far outstrip incoming visitors.

There's one sight, though, that's become a magnet for Instagram-hungry hikers: Segla (The Sail), a soaring 639m-(2096ft)-high sheer-sided fin that looms over the Mefjorden inlet in the island's far north. Every other tourist board ad depicts this unmistakable outcrop, so it's unsurprising that the hike to its summit is surely the most popular on the island. Yet here's a paradox: to get that perfect photo, you need to be not atop the peak, but admiring it from one side. That's why locals in the know shun the track leading up Segla, instead tackling the path climbing Barden, the adjacent mountain just to the south. Not only is the trail quieter, but the summit itself is loftier, at 659m (2162ft) – the ideal perch from which to ogle its shapely neighbour.

There are two routes up Barden; I'd been advised that my best chance of avoiding soggy toes was to take the one from Fjordgård, one of the aforementioned rainbow-hued fishing hamlets north of the peak, on the sheltered southern shore of Ørnfjorden.

The sun was beaming resolutely as I laced up my hiking boots in the car park at the top of the village; that's not a given in these

*"I was alone amid a landscape that
demands to be described as magical."*

parts, even in June – though it never dips below the horizon between mid-May and mid-July, unpredictable weather means it frequently retreats behind a veil of cloud. Today, though, the snow-dusted crags ringing the fjord sparkled as brightly as the waves.

The Barden hike shares a trailhead with Segla's summit path, so I was joined for a short stretch by several other hikers. Soon enough, though, my route veered away left and south, and I was alone amid a landscape that demands to be described as magical. Alone, save a solitary rock ptarmigan, resplendent in its white-and-brindled spring plumage; it peered at me curiously over its rock roost before flitting away, startled.

Away from the fjord, the breeze faded to a whisper then died altogether, and the air rang instead with a shimmering choir: the soprano voices of dozens of small waterfalls and cascades. The snow was rapidly melting from the peaks above, feeding countless streams that watered the sphagnum moss marshes blanketing the broad valley; the path, occasionally boggy, was for the most part lifted above the quagmire on wooden boardwalks that became shallow ladders on steeper sections.

Gradually the trail climbed through 'forests' of stunted silver birch, in early June just beginning to bud in preparation for the brief summer season of intensive photosynthesis. As I approached the base of Barden proper, the trees thinned and the trail wound between clusters of lichen-blotched boulders. Patches of low-lying

snow blocked the path, and more than once I sank knee-deep in crisp drifts. After an hour or so, the trail faded and the way steepened. Before long I was no longer walking but scrambling and rock-hopping in zigzags up the peak's increasingly precipitous eastern slope.

Perhaps that effort was a blessing: it forced me to fix my gaze on the route ahead, rather than glancing back or across the valley. So the vista, when it spread before me at the summit, had even greater effect. Below glinted patches of azure, small lakes reflecting that clear northern sky, and stepped waterfalls striped the valley walls. A snaking line of peaks and ridges meandered north towards the pole, sandwiched by mirror-like inlets. Boats bobbed at harbour alongside Husøy, the curious fishing citadel island afloat in Øyfjorden to the right, while across the Mefjorden to the left rose the barbed line of rock fangs dubbed the 'Devil's Jaw'. And straight ahead jutted the imperious summit of Segla, its left flank a vertiginous cliff plunging into the glittering fjord.

Reclining on a conveniently flat boulder, I soaked up the sunshine and swept my gaze across the epic panorama, sporting a grin as wide as the vista. Sure, I could have joined the line of snap-happy hikers winding up to Segla's summit – but then I wouldn't have been here on Barden, alone with the most perfect view of the most beautiful mountain on the most spectacular island in Norway. **PB**

ECHOES OF SAMI LIFE

Sami people, formerly reindeer herders from Sweden, settled on Senja from the late 18th century. For insights into their self-sufficient lifestyle, visit the open-air museum in the birchwoods of the Kaperdal valley, where, from the early 20th century, Nikolai Olsen Kaperdal built a traditional *gamme* (turf house) with branches and bark. Learn how he survived by keeping a few animals, growing potatoes, foraging berries and watercress, hunting game and catching fish from the river.

Clockwise from top left: an awesome landscape; a village and harbour on Senja; Norwegian reindeer; island flora: silver birch. Previous page: the thrilling thrust of Segla peak

ORIENTATION

Start/Finish // Fjordgård (a longer, boggier and tougher route leads from the trailhead near Mefjordbotn).

Distance // 5.5km (3.5 miles)

Duration // Four to five hours

Getting there // Fjordgård is a two-hour drive from Tromsø, including the ferry from Brensholmen to Botnhamn. Three times weekly, a ferry from Tromsø to Lysnes meets a bus to Fjordgård (www.tromskortet.no).

When to go // May to September is warmest and driest.

What to wear // Sturdy boots – either quick-drying or waterproof – are essential, as are a waterproof jacket, warm layers and a hat.

Where to stay // Mefjord Brygge (www.mefjordbrygge.no) is a simple but welcoming hotel with an excellent restaurant.

Tours // Inntravel (www.inntravel.co.uk) offers self-guided walking holidays.

More info // www.visitsenja.no

*Opposite, from top: the legendary
Suilven is one of the most distinctive
mountains in Scotland; admiring the
views of La Palma*

MORE LIKE THIS
GEOLOGICAL DRAMA

STÓRURÐ, ICELAND

Wander among Iceland's otherworldly
landscapes – the volcanoes and
geysers, waterfalls and calving glaciers,
kaleidoscopic rhyolite mountains and
opalescent lakes – and you'll quickly
understand why belief in *huldufólk* ('hidden
people' or elves) remains widespread.
Nowhere is that more true than around the
series of wild, windswept inlets in the far
northeast, particularly Borgarfjörður Eystri,
where hikers can encounter puffin colonies
and traditional fishing villages, such as
Bakkagerði, but also Borghildur, queen
of the elves, ruling the Álfaborg (Elf City)
rock. Dozens of trails lace the hills, the
most remarkable of which heads south from
the lake on the Vatnsskarð Pass, climbing
towards the forbidding, cleft-riven ridge
mountain Dyrfjöll and Stórurð, where a
jumble of giant round boulders sit alongside
a turquoise moraine lake in a landscape to
give Tolkien a run for his elf gold.
Start/Finish // Vatnsskarð Pass
Distance // 15km (9.5 miles)
More info // www.borgarfjordureystri.is

SUILVEN, SCOTLAND

Viewed edge-on from the east, the
monolithic Torridonian sandstone mountain
Suilven appears as a sheer, unconquerable
pinnacle – its name derives from the Old
Norse meaning 'pillar'. Even from the west,
among the glacial cnoc- and lochan-lumpy
lowlands of Assynt, it's dome-like and
forbidding. Yet in truth this 731m- (2398ft)-
high spine is an achievable challenge for
experienced hikers, and a worthy one,
rewarding with far-reaching panoramic
vistas. Take the route from Lochinvar,
which approaches Suilven from the north
and zigzags up steeply to the ridge and
on to the main peak, Caisteal Liath ('The
Grey Castle' in Scottish Gaelic), for
dramatic views back to the spire of Meall
Meadhonach and, on a clear day, across
to Skye and the Western Isles.
**Start/Finish // Parking area on Canisp
Rd east of Lochinver**
Distance // 20km (12.5 miles)
**More info // Check deer-stalking
arrangements between July and
October**

CALDERA DE TABURIENTE, LA PALMA, SPAIN

The northwestern-most of the Canaries, La
Palma is, it's claimed, the world's steepest
island. The volcanic speck soaring from the
Atlantic Ocean is also a verdant dream
for hikers, laced with some 1000km (620
miles) of waymarked trails. In its centre
rises Caldera de Taburiente National Park,
dominated by its namesake crater – an 8km-
(5-mile)-wide cauldron filled with Canarian
pines, laurels, flowers and birds, and venue
for La Palma's most memorable hike. From
the viewpoint at Mirador de los Brecitos,
the trail curls around the crater's inner rim,
delving into a spectacular ravine past a
once-sacred rock outcrop; a worthy detour
accesses the bijou multi-hued waterfall
known as the Cascada de Colores.
Start // Mirador de los Brecitos
Finish // Las Viños car park
Distance // 14km (9 miles)
**More info // Book a taxi to the Mirador
from the nearby town of Los Llanos de
Aridane**

ARCTIC CIRCLE TRAIL

Tracing the invisible line of 66° north, Phoebe Smith tackles Greenland's remote long-distance hike, and finds wilderness, wildlife and an adventure of a lifetime.

Before I spotted the creature, I knew I was being watched. Something in my bones told me that I wasn't alone, despite having been on the Arctic Circle Trail (ACT) for more than eight hours and not encountering a single soul. My spine tingled, my senses piqued and I found my eyes inexplicably drawn to the mountainside behind me, scanning its earthy flanks looking for someone... or rather, something.

Encountering wildlife in the outdoors is a magical experience. So much so, in fact, that I often head into the wilderness to seek these moments out – from wild camping in the Rothiemurchus Forest in the Cairngorms to spy Scottish wildcats, to spotting

wolves in the interior of Sweden at twilight, the animals lit only by the moon's muted glow.

But coming face-to-face with a wild animal while walking in Greenland is a different experience, especially as it is famed for polar bears. I had been told by locals in Kangerlussuaq – the settlement at the start of the walk – that the white members of the Ursidae family were safely confined further north, due to the lack of sea ice this far south. But still, as this was only day one on my eight-day crossing of the 160km (99-mile) trail, I was unconvinced.

I'd left the Polar Ice Cap above the town the night before, walking amid the prehistoric-looking, long-haired musk oxen as the sun began

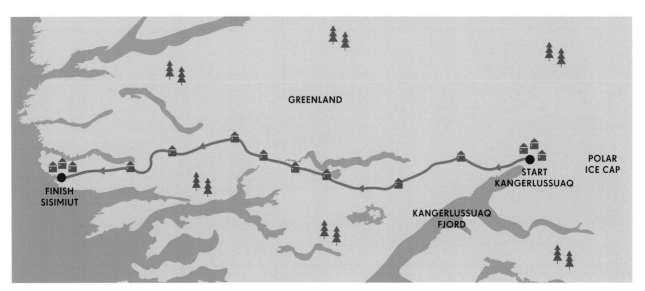

to set, turning the sky salmon pink, and transforming the thick frozen tundra into a mottled shade of grey. The following morning, after picking up final supplies, I then followed the marker cairns (denoted by red semi-circles from the Greenlandic flag and usually adorned by reindeer antlers) up to the settlement of Kellyville, population seven, before stepping foot on the ACT proper. I felt my stomach fizz with excitement and apprehension for what would be one of the most remote undertakings of my life. I was completely alone.

The sky was overcast as I took the plunge into the wilderness, and began ticking off the kilometres. The ground was spongy beneath my boots, and the hillocks that surrounded the slate-coloured lakes reminded me of the Outer Hebrides. I soon fell into the wonderful rhythm found only on a solo hike. I was absorbed in the landscape, not thinking about anything in particular, when I suddenly got the feeling I was being watched. Despite the reassurances about polar bears, I couldn't help but feel a chill of fear wash over me. Every rock looked suspicious, every tuft of grass seemed to move – then I spotted my spies: a couple of reindeer. I breathed a sigh of relief. And took a moment to enjoy watching the two doe, watching me back, in complete silence. Then the giant antlers of a male appeared behind them and they all began walking my way together.

At first I was overwhelmed with their beauty, then I realised quite how big they were and I slowly began to retreat behind a large

> ## "It was an apt introduction to a trail on which I would meet more wild animals than people."

rock, while waving my walking poles to make myself look big. Yet still them came – and there were more of them. Finally, in an effort to convince them I was a human and not a rival to his harem, I dropped my poles and began to sing. They all stopped. And by the time I reached the chorus of the pop ditty I was wailing, they retreated and I was alone once more.

It was an apt introduction to a trail on which I would meet more wild animals than people. At the first hut that night – there are a series of several that offer shelter as an alternative to camping – I ate my stove-warmed meal while Arctic hares, already in their white coats readying to camouflage themselves in the snow come winter, walked within a couple of metres of my feet.

The next day I saw my first hikers (it's estimated that only around 200 to 300 people walk the trail each year), as I bypassed the next hut in favour of a wild camp at Kangerlussuaq Fjord. They were a party of eight Germans out for a challenge, but their numbers were soon dwarfed by the sheer volume of eagles hovering overhead as I ploughed on.

At night I bathed in the water, and in the morning rose to a biting wind but blazing sunshine as I hiked to a high point looking down on a perfect lake edged by spits of golden sand – which,

TRAIL'S END

If you want a memento of your walk once you complete it, call into the Hotel Sisimiut, which you'll pass on your way into the town, and ask for a certificate. They are free of charge and signed by the mayor, dating the start and finish of your hike. Afterwards, head to the coffee shop – Café Sisimiut – where you can get a well-deserved hot drink and pastry; the perfect way to celebrate your success.

© Ben Haggar | Visit Greenland; © Lisa Germany | Visit Greenland; © Peter John Watson | Shutterstock

Clockwise from left: wild camping on the Arctic Circle Trail; admiring Kangerlussuaq fjord; waymarkers of cairns with reindeer skulls dot the route. Previous page, from top: lakeside trail hut; an Arctic fox

had they been any more accessible, would easily be crowded with tourists. Gazing upon the serene scene, the landscape perfectly mirrored in the water, the only sound I could hear was my own intake of breath.

At the next hut – a small wooden shack perched on huge boulders – I witnessed my first Arctic fox. He was still sporting his ashen coat, blending in perfectly with the pewter rocks, while he scavenged for scraps left over by boot-clad visitors.

The next couple of days passed by in blissful solitude and offered a hearty helping of amped-up wilderness. I camped alongside a stream where you could fish for Arctic char, their red bellies shining like rubies beneath the crystal-clear water. I walked within inches of near-invisible rock ptarmigan, whose feathers blended beautifully into the moss-covered jumble of cracked granite. And I crossed glacial rivers and navigated yawning glens, breathing in air so pure I felt alive with exhilaration.

By the time I reached the hut on my final night, I got the feeling I was being watched once more. It was another herd of reindeer with a stag the size of a horse slowly heading my way. But instead of being worried and blurting out song to scare him off, the only singing I was doing was to myself, celebrating the joy at having being accepted into their world. I felt like I was being seen off by an old friend, before I had to rejoin the manufactured world that lay beyond the final bend. Rather than an observer in this wild place, my hike had seen me become part of it and that memory still makes my heart sing today. **PS**

ORIENTATION

Start // Kangerlussuaq
Finish // Sisimiut
Distance // 160km (99 miles)
Duration // Eight to ten days
Getting there // All flights to Greenland go to Kangerlussuaq from where daily flights connect to Sisimiut.
When to go // June to early September. Mosquitos and midges can be an issue in high summer.
What to wear // Layering is key: merino base layers, a fleece, waterproofs. Take a hat and gloves too.
What to pack // A warm sleeping bag, camping mat, lightweight tent, walking poles, dry bag and a duvet jacket, camping stove, fuel, map and compass.
Where to stay // Either camp or stay in huts.
Where to eat // There are no shops or settlements on the trail, so take everything you need before heading out.
More info // www.visitgreenland.com

MORE LIKE THIS
REMOTE ISLAND TREKS

SUÐUROY NORTH TO SOUTH, FAROE ISLANDS

Flung out in the North Atlantic, halfway between the UK and Iceland, the volcanic archipelago of the Faroes is a rugged cluster of dramatic stone-strewn isles perfect for exploring on foot. The southernmost of the 18 major islands is Suðuroy, and here you can undertake a complete crossing of it; from the northern tip to the southern end, using a collection of old village trails and a stone-laid 'Priest's Path'. Starting at the literal end of the road, the route follows an ancient thoroughfare between the villages and settlements, including Sandvík (one of the oldest in the Faroes). Along the way, you'll take in rolling green hills, the Turkish Graves (said to be the site of many a pirate invasion), views of neighbouring small islets covered in birds, deep gorges and mountain ridges, and the area of many *Huldufólk* (Hidden People) sightings. These are the supernatural elf-like beings that hide among the rocks and tussocks.
Start // Sandvík
Finish // Akraberg
Distance // 42km (26 miles)
More info // www.visitfaroeislands.com

THE GR132, LA GOMERA

Mention the Canary Islands to most travellers and they naturally think of the resorts and beaches of Tenerife and Gran Canaria. But this collection of seven islands, located just 100km (62 miles) from Morocco, though officially part of Spain, offer myriad hiking opportunities. The best is found on the second smallest of them all. La Gomera's circumference-chasing trail, the GR132, offers a sizable week-long adventure. Circling the island in a clockwise direction, you follow the coast through the diverse terrain and collection of microclimates that belie its modest size. From crumbling cliffs, to ancient cloud forests and palm-studded valleys – all of which often sport a blanket of swirling mist – it really feels like an island that time (and tourists) forgot.

Each day on the trail offers a stop in one of the settlements – vital for picking up supplies and, importantly, water – as well as the chance to spot dolphins and whales.
Start/Finish // San Sebastián de La Gomera
Distance // 122km (76 miles)
More info // www.lagomera.travel

CYPRUS COAST-TO-COAST

Forming part of the much longer (think 10,000km/6214-mile) European Long Distance Route the E4, the Cyprus Coast-to-Coast offers a more digestible slice of adventure and is the perfect way to take in the best of the country. You can walk in either direction, but going east to west means you start with a sunrise at the Cape gazing over the Mediterranean Sea, and end with a blistering sunset on the Akamas Peninsula. The walking takes in yawning bays, harbour towns – replete with freshly caught seafood to snack on along the way – as well as traditional villages. And of course the Troodos National Forest Park where you can look out for the Cypriot golden oak tree, and the Troodos Mountains, where Mt Olympus stands at the heart of its volcanic centre. Bird life is a real highlight, as is reaching the lighthouse at the end of this unforgettable hike.
Start // Cape Greco
Finish // Akamas Peninsula
Distance // 250km (155 miles)
More info // www.justaboutcyprus.com

Clockwise from top: along the Suðuroy coast in the Faroe Islands; Paphos lighthouse, Cyprus; hiking on La Gomera

FIVE DAYS ON THE KUNGSLEDEN

Bogs, big skies, and naked hikers – out on the trail of Arctic kings,
Mark Stratton experiences a very Swedish epic.

After Everest, K2, and other hypoxic giants of the Himalayan 'Dead Zone', you'd imagine a world-renowned mountaineer might find a trek across the Swedish Arctic tame by comparison.

'Aye, it's definitely different,' says my hiking buddy, Alan Hinkes, a steely 66-year-old Yorkshireman and the only British mountaineer among an elite group to have summited all 14 of the world's 8000m (26,247ft) summits. 'But the vastness of the Arctic appeals to me. You wouldn't imagine such wilderness exists in a modern country like Sweden,' he says, as we stride onto the sodden summer permafrost of the Kungsleden Trail.

Whatever the Kungsleden (King's Trail) lacks in death-defying verticality, it's a rare piece of true wilderness in Europe. A place you can walk all night in the midnight sun and squelch across wetland where carpets of moss are grazed by Sami reindeer. And when the mood takes it, the Arctic weather can flip from summer warmth to cold downpours quicker than it takes a camping stove to boil your kettle.

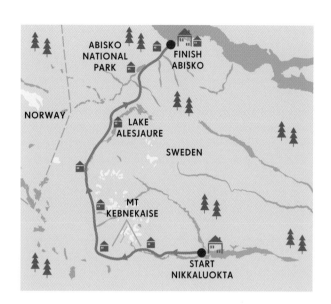

The Kungsleden has been around some time, devised by the Swedish Tourist Association (STF) in the 1900s to mark the coming of the iron ore railway from Kiruna to Abisko in northern Lapland. The trail now stretches 460km (286 miles) to its southern trailhead at Hemavan Ski Resort. We join it deep inside the Arctic Circle for the arduous final five-day route northward from Nikkaluokta to Abisko.

We enter the trail via the Ladtjo Valley, a flourishing biome of Arctic tundra habitat. Birch trees corkscrew from the black acidic soil, and dashes of rosebay willowherb and harebells sparkle in a demure landscape of pastel greens. I pick bilberries and eat them on the go, valuable Vitamin C with days of camping rations ahead.

From the start, expect to feel positively small walking within gargantuan U-shaped valleys. Not least around Kebnekaise, Sweden highest mountain. The mountain rises beyond Láddjujávri Lake where the valley broadens into a largely treeless expanse framed by rounded granite valley walls, and folds of lingering snow create a zebra-striped patterning. This landscape has been gouged by millennia of glaciation, leaving a legacy of mountainsides scalloped by cirques and writhing snakes of moraines. Kebnekaise only shows its face when a rare lick of sunshine starbursts through an enveloping drizzle to reveal the glint of its summit glacier.

Near Kebnekaise, our first STF hut comes into view. Throughout they become beacons of joy, causing us to quicken our stride upon sight. Besides dormitory accommodation and well-provisioned stores, these modern huts host restaurants serving hot cinnamon buns and coffee, a welcome fortification against the elements. They also have – and what could be more Swedish? – saunas. They seem like a good idea, yet my courage falters seeing naked hikers spill out from the wooden cabins. We watch one guy chopping logs for the fire. 'He wants to be careful with that axe,' says Alan.

Typically, we camp away from the STF huts, as you can pitch tents anywhere in accordance with *allemansrätten* – Sweden's right-to-roam. On the first night we hammer tent pegs into the soil under the peachy glow of midsummer sun at around 11pm. And after a night listening to a lullaby of grasses bristling in squally winds and the rain's pitter-patter on canvas, I awake to find reindeer grazing around the tents, pawing at the damp moss, their summer coats damp with droplets of rain, their breath frozen in the early chill. Sweden has some 15,000 ethnic Sami people who range across the Arctic, living off herding reindeers in isolated communities where temperatures in winter may sink to -40°C (-40°F).

Beyond Singi, the Kungsleden veers due north on course for the High Arctic. Tjäkjajåkka Valley is now wider than the eye can process. The weather is wild, swirling and Heathcliffian. The going tough underfoot. Slippery anaerobic mud and wet grasses necessitate boardwalks running several kilometres to guide you through Tjäkjajåkka where a quicksilver river meanders in braids, like an unkempt plait of a Viking warrior.

A memorable moment awaits early on the third morning during a 26.5km (16.5-mile) day. Tjäktja Pass (1150m/3773ft) is the highest point of the entire Kungsleden, and we reached it via a scramble

ALL CHANGE! SWEDEN'S HIGHEST PEAK

For the suitably equipped, a popular day excursion from the STF hut at Kebnekaise is to climb Sweden's highest peak. At least, the southern peak of Mt Kebnekaise, was, at 2097m (6880ft), Sweden's highest the last time I hiked this trail a few years back. Now, however, and a testimony of global warming, the glaciated southern peak of Kebnekaise has melted to 2095m (6873ft), a metre lower than the mountain's northern peak, Sweden's new highest summit.

Clockwise from top: cloudberries on the trail; taking advantage of Sweden's right to roam (and wild camp); reindeer. Previous page: the big skies and boardwalks of the Kungsleden Trail

"Whatever the Kungsleden lacks in death-defying verticality, it's a rare piece of true wilderness in Europe."

alongside a waterfall, passing blocks of quartz gleaming under a thunderous jet-black sky. From the pass, Alan and I share a vista stretching across a landscape steamrollered by glaciation's unstoppable force. 'That's a proper gnarly view,' Alan says, nodding appreciatively. 'I didn't always get time to admire the views on top of Himalayan peaks, as I just wanted to get down alive.'

It's another day until Lake Alesjaure, its placidity disturbed only by splash-landing ducks. The rain falls steadily, creating transient rainbows and swollen streams, so it's boots off for the shock of a glacial wade with bare feet. Later, we descend a treacherously slippery track through a skimpy birch stand and thereafter relish the shelter provided by the lichen-tangled forest of Abisko National Park. We camp in a sheltered glade that night, but I can't sleep for thoughts of dry feet and a hot meal the next day.

Several turbulent rivers surging towards Lake Torneträsk are the last obstacles to Abisko Fell Station, which offers comfortable accommodation. There's an element of attrition involved with tackling the Kungsleden. Battling against the elements I felt a sense of resilience knowing I was able to survive this Arctic challenge, where the smallest sightings like fly agaric toadstools and distant Arctic hares are to be cherished and admired for their own perseverance in these harsh wilds.

Alan interrupts my reverie. 'Let's see if we can get a hot brew,' he says, with the same matter-of-factness I imagine he displayed after scaling Everest. **MS**

ORIENTATION

Start // Nikkaluokta Fell Station
Finish // Abisko Fell Station
Distance // 103km (64 miles)
Duration // Allow five days
Getting there // During summer a twice-daily bus travels between Kiruna and Nikkaluokta, taking around 80 minutes.
When to go // Between the snowmelt from midsummer (July) to winter's onset (late September).
Where to stay // Along the Kungsleden, STF maintains 16 huts with dormitory accommodation, restaurant and bar, shops and sauna.
What to pack // Even in summer take a four-season sleeping bag, gaiters to go with waterproof boots, and the best quality rain gear you can muster.
Things to know // The full Kungsleden is around 440km (273 miles) and begins in Hemavan.
More info // www.swedishtouristassociation.com

Opposite from top: the ultimate high of Trolltunga; a valley path on Scotland's West Highland Way

MORE LIKE THIS
GLACIATED LANDSCAPES

WEST HIGHLAND WAY, SCOTLAND

Scotland's most popular multi-day walk is a snapshot of the very archetypal Highlands and Glens scenery. It's typically walked from south to north to help acclimatise your legs as the route becomes more challenging heading into the Highlands. The start is reached by train from Glasgow. Thereafter you'll be immersed in the splendour of Caledonian forests, valley-glens of golden heather, and mighty sea-loughs gouged out by past Ice Ages. A particularly beautiful section crosses the spartan Rannoch Moor to the scenic Glencoe Pass. There's ample accommodation along the route with B&Bs, hostels, and campsites, while a scenic train ride links Fort William back to Glasgow.
Start // Milngavie
Finish // Fort William
Distance // 154km (96 miles)
More info // www.westhighlandway.org

TROLLTUNGA, NORWAY

The 'Troll's Tongue' is Norway's most recognisable landform. A rock ledge protuberance dangles 700m (2279ft) above the serene Lake Ringedalsvatnet on the edge of the Hardangervidda mountain plateau. A return hike to Trolltunga requires 8 to 12 hours depending on fitness, including an ascent of 1100m (3609ft), which takes you through passes of alpine flora and across bald rock faces, incised by fast-flowing streams. It's only viable from June to September, if you want to do it without a guide. And rather than attempting the ultimate daredevil selfie, it's probably best to simply admire the view on top rather than edging too far onto the ledge itself, which could prove lethal in bad weather.
Start/Finish // Skjeggedal
Distance // 28km (17 miles)
More info // www.visitnorway.com

LUIROJÄRVI LAKE TRACK, FINLAND

This beautiful wilderness adventure is set in Finland's second-largest national park, called Urho Kekkonen, located in Northern Lapland. Allow four to five days plus time for a few wrong detours, as the old track to the pristine Luirojärvi Lake is without signage so requires map and compass navigation. Yet those adventurous enough for the challenge will love the pristine evergreen and birch forests and the shimmering lakes. It's best walked in summer after the snow has retreated and the forest is alive with birdsong and the occasional Sami reindeer herd. There are also huts along the trail.
Start/Finish // Kiilopääs' Gate, Saariselkä
Distance // 80km (50 miles)
More info // www.nationalparks.fi

GREAT ĶEMERI BOG

A primeval landscape hidden in the heart of Latvia offers a rare chance to try out bogshoeing — the next best thing to walking on water.

Hiking maps are of little use in the Great Ķemeri Bog. The land is turned into a labyrinth by thousands of small lakes and ponds, and despite the open horizons, disorientation is a real risk. I use 'land' in a loose sense here, since much of the solid surface is actually a floating mat of peat and sphagnum moss. Its dubious ability to support the weight of a human adult is the other reason I am not setting out alone on this early morning in autumn.

There are two ways that visitors can experience the strangeness of this landscape, which covers more than 90 sq km (35 sq miles) – a quarter of Latvia's Ķemeri National Park. They can tread a looping wooden boardwalk that sidles around the waters of the bog to reach an observation tower. Or they can strap on some 'bogshoes' and stick very closely to a dedicated bogshoeing guide.

Kristaps Kiziks is one of the few people who know their way on foot around this terra-not-so-firma. As the son of two geographers who both enjoy hiking, and in a country that has some of Europe's finest specimens of this under-appreciated environment, it was an obvious next step for him to lead bogshoeing tours.

I am already relieved to know that the bogshoes Kristaps unloads from the back of his car, as we prepare to set off from a forest track, are essentially snowshoes. This latticed, lightweight footwear straps over your boots at the toes, and leaves the heel free to move. I have at least a beginner's experience with snowshoes, and still remember the exhilaration of the first time I walked in them as a kid, through snowdrifts in an Alpine forest that would otherwise have swallowed me to my waist.

It turns out to be easier here to move my feet in a way that feels almost natural, and not like a Latvian chapter of the Ministry of Silly Walks. We pass through the pines and set off along some artificial channels, left over from peat extraction abandoned in the 1970s, two decades before the national park was set up. As I get into my stride, Kristaps explains the reverse traffic-light guidance offered by types of sphagnum moss at different thicknesses. 'The red moss you can even walk on in normal boots,' he says. 'For yellow, snowshoes are ok. If it's light green, snowshoes are fifty-fifty. If it's dark green, don't go.'

I start to eye the ground obsessively. For a practical demonstration, Kristaps leads me onto an expanse of yellow-green moss, which wobbles queasily as we walk. Standing in

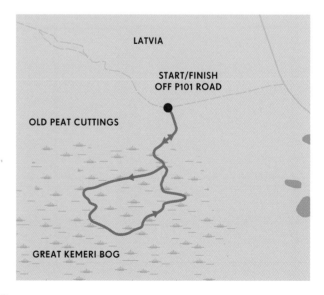

SUNDEWS

It takes a special kind of plant to thrive in a bog, and perhaps the most extreme examples are the Drosera, or sundews. These carnivorous plants sport upright, paddle-shaped leaves, from which stick out dozens of fine, red hairs capped by beads of sticky 'dew'. When an unfortunate insect lands on a leaf and gets trapped, its struggles only encourage the leaf to curl round it. The sundew then takes from its prey the nutrients it can't have from the soil.

Left to right: surveying the terrain; bog heather in the evening sun. Previous page, from top: testing bog shoes; the Great Ķemeri Bog

place, he alternately raises and presses down with his feet, sending rolling waves through the matted moss. I don't dare to copy him with the same vigour.

The waters are quite still, rippled only by the breeze. There is not enough dissolved oxygen for fish to live here, although bubbles of methane rise up when our footsteps set the borders of the pools a-shivering. 'Some people call it "Coca Cola Lake", and maybe it's just as acidic,' says Kristaps. 'I came with visitors from Sweden and they went swimming. Your hair afterwards feels like it's had conditioner on it.'

Dividing the squelchier parts of the bog are spines of more consolidated ground, where a few plants other than moss grow, such as wild rosemary (also known as marsh Labrador tea, though it's actually a kind of rhododendron). It releases a sweet turpentine scent as we tramp across it. 'This plant is poisonous, and hallucinogenic,' says Kristaps. 'The Vikings used it before going into battle. If you were walking in the bog all day you might have a headache from it.'

"Indeed, the whole landscape does look rather like an accidental Japanese garden – but laid out by Dr Seuss."

More welcome are the cranberries that in this season lie dotted around on the moss. I had completely overlooked them until Kristaps stopped to pick up a few to have on our coffee and breakfast break. All is still as we pass the Thermos around, save for a skein of geese flying overhead. Kristaps points to a diminutive tree on its own little island in a lake: 'See this pine? It's like a bonsai tree.' Indeed, the whole landscape does look rather like an accidental Japanese garden – but laid out by Dr Seuss.

The pines, stunted by the scarcity of nutrients, could be up to 300 years old. And the bog as a whole has existed for up to seven

millennia. Every year, a centimetre of moss is compacted and transformed into peat, and the bog gets a millimetre higher. It moves slowly, like a glacier, towards the Baltic Sea, and the lakes are the areas where the bog splits.

Bogs act as giant sponges, protecting against floods, and they can benefit us in other hidden ways. 'A bog is like a big archive,' says Kristaps. 'You can find all kinds of history in a bog: core samples can show pollen from thousands of years ago, and dust from Icelandic volcanoes. If an animal died here it will still be here. We can know what the first people in Latvia ate.'

I'm prepared to keep bogshoeing on for longer, risk of wild rosemary headaches aside, but it's time to return to certain ground. Latvians might be well accustomed to the peat bogs found all across their country – though every year in berry season, there are always a few who stride out confidently into the watery maze and need rescuing. For me, it has been a revelation to discover, just an easy drive from the capital, a landscape that feels both ancient and like a world in its waking days. **RG**

ORIENTATION

Start // Off P101 Rd, Ķemeri National Park

Distance // Approximately 3km (2 miles)

Duration // Two to four hours

Getting there // The small parking area where you meet your guide is a 45km (28-mile) drive west from Rīga.

When to go // Excursions run year-round. September to November can be a particularly atmospheric time to visit, with morning mists and cranberries dotted around the moss.

What to wear // Comfortable walking shoes or boots.

What to pack // Swimwear if you want to brave a dip, and perhaps mosquito repellent in summer.

Where to stay // Valguma Pasaule is a forest retreat once exclusive to Soviet party bosses and now a hotel-restaurant with an artistic bent (www.valgumapasaule.lv).

Tours // Find details of guided bogshoeing hikes in Ķemeri and other bogs in Latvia at www.purvubrideji.lv.

More info // www.kemerunacionalaisparks.lv

MORE LIKE THIS
WALKS AROUND THE BALTIC

BALTIC COASTAL HIKING, ESTONIA/LATVIA/LITHUANIA

Hug the eastern shore of this almost tideless sea on a hike that links two Baltic capitals with Unesco World Heritage-listed historic centres, Rīga and Tallinn, and which from 2021 will also be marked out along the Lithuanian coast. The boundary of land and sea is rocky and indented in the Estonian stages to the north, with smoother shores to the south, and ultimately the miraculous Curonian Spit – a sand dune curving almost 100km (62 miles) between lagoon and sea. Along the way you'll pass fishing villages, a former closed town from the Soviet era, and the seaward portion of Ķemeri National Park. The route forms part of the E9 European long-distance path, and should the urge to continue prove unstoppable, you can follow the coasts of the Baltic, North Sea and Atlantic all the way to Portugal's Cabo de São Vicente.

Start // Nida, Lithuania
Finish // Tallinn, Estonia
Distance // 1390km (864 miles)
More info // www.baltictrails.eu

SOUTH FYN ARCHIPELAGO TRAIL, DENMARK

Funen (Fyn in Danish) is Denmark's third-largest island, and together with its herd of 55 smaller islands to the south, is the home of the Archipelago Trail (Øhavsstien) – a route that's chillaxed enough to branch off, double back and conclude with a separate, ferry-accessed stage on the island of Ærø. On the east coast of Langeland, the path passes a beech tree, which in 1819 is said to have been the place where Adam Oehlenschläger composed the Danish national anthem, *'Det er et yndigt land'* ('There is a lovely country'). You will surely nod in agreement as you pad through pastoral settings dotted with half-timbered old farmhouses and crow-stepped church steeples, along forest trails and down to unspoiled sandy beaches.

Start // Faldsled
Finish // Søby
Distance // 220km (137 miles)
More info // www.visitfyn.com

HIGH COAST TRAIL, SWEDEN

If you feel yourself standing a little taller by the end of this walk, that'll be thanks in part to local geography. Sweden's Unesco-listed Höga Kusten (High Coast) is one of the world's best examples of post-glacial rebound: the land continues to rise steadily, more than 9000 years after it was freed from the burden of the great continental ice sheets. Along a 13-stage trail, granite cliffs rear up to give views over an untamed landscape of deep forests and island-studded Baltic horizons. Visit in late August or early September, and you might be dared to try *surströmming* – a fermented herring dish that's the most notorious speciality of Sweden's northern coast.

Start // Hornöberget
Finish // Örnsköldsvik
Distance // 129km (80 miles)
More info // www.hogakusten.com

*Clockwise from top: the Curonian Spit;
wild berries in Latvia; St Catherine's
Passage in Tallinn, the last stop on the
Baltic Coastal Hiking trail*

WESTERN EUROPE

PEMBROKESHIRE
COASTAL PATH

Hugging Wales' wild Atlantic coast, this two-week ramble dips and rises over cliff, bluff and headland to coves, prehistoric standing stones and dune-backed bays of astonishing beauty.

D ark storm clouds are bubbling up on the horizon and a fierce wind is buffeting the cliffs, threatening to blow me right off them and straight into the storm-tossed depths of the Irish Sea. The Welsh weather is a fickle beast, that's for sure, but even the threat of an imminent downpour can't detract from the savage beauty of Dinas Island. An island that is not an island, in fact, but a headland.

The circular path rimming this peninsula is one of Pembrokeshire's most unforgettable. The Atlantic deals a vicious blow to cliffs that rise sheer and rugged, pitted with caves, and the perfect thumbprints of smuggler's coves. Peregrine falcons screech and wheel overhead. The summertime eruption of rosebay willowherb, heather and gorse has sprayed the hedgerows pink, purple and gold. Briny smells waft up from the sea. This is a place that sets all the senses on high alert, with its rapidly changing light and wide-open views, iodine and oxygen. A place that feels hopeful.

At Needle Point on Dinas Island, I linger to watch puffins returning to their summer shores – their rapid wingbeat is unmistakable, despite the fact I've left my binoculars behind.

I'm striding into my third day of hiking the Pembrokeshire Coastal Path, the 299km (186-mile) trail that wraps itself around one of Britain's most dramatic coastlines. This is where southwest Wales slings its hook into the perilous Atlantic Ocean. Heading over stile and through kissing gate, dipping through coastal woodlands and meadows, over moors and clifftops, the trail stitches together 15 stages and takes roughly a fortnight to complete. I'm walking it from north to south, starting at St Dogmaels, on the shores of the Teifi Estuary, and ending – with any luck – at Amroth in the county's south.

Designed to show off the Pembrokeshire Coast National Park from its most flattering angles, the path is more than the sum of its dune-backed beaches and hidden bays. The region is richly dotted with vestiges of the past: Iron Age hill forts, standing stones and cromlechs (dolmens) guard almost every hillside. And the starkly eroded Precambrian rocks and folded strata that shape the coast are a geologist's fantasy. The oldest date back 600 million years: rock formations that have been around since dinosaurs walked the earth.

Saints and pilgrims have made their mark on these shores over millennia, too. The trail passes through St Davids, Britain's smallest city and the 6th-century birthplace of Wales' patron saint, capped off with an imperious medieval cathedral. On a particularly wild and steep stretch of the coast path near Bosherston, much further south, a tiny chapel wedged into the cliff face is where the hermit St Govan sought solace. On Dinas Island, the ruins of St Brynach's church in the Cwm-yr-Eglwys bay stare silently out to a lonely sea.

The following day brings more highs as I ramble along a narrow cliffhanger of a path meandering northwest to lighthouse-topped Strumble Head. It is just me and the roaring sea on this remote stretch of coastline. Below are skerries and rock stacks, off limits unless you happen to have a boat or kayak handy. My heart soars as I glimpse a half-moon bay, lapped by inky green-blue sea, where an entire colony of seals barks a welcome. I've been tipped off about sightings of dolphins, whales and porpoises on heather-cloaked Strumble Head, but today they are a no-show, so I content myself with a blustery picnic and moody views instead.

As I inch slowly south in the coming days, it becomes clear that the coast path is no walk in the park. Despite the lack of heart-pumping climbs, the constant up-and-down rhythm is not to be underestimated – the total ascent and descent amount to 10,668m (35,000ft), the equivalent of climbing Mount Everest. But effort is rewarded. My hike reveals such wonders as Carreg Samson, a 5000-year-old Neolithic dolmen in a farmer's field looking out to sea, and the Blue Lagoon at Abereiddy, a surreal turquoise pool in a flooded slate quarry.

PUFFIN WATCH

Tag on an extra day to allow time to boat across to one of the nearby wildlife-rich islands. Top billing goes to Skomer (www.welshwildlife.org), a real puffin fest of an island, dramatically rimmed by sea cliffs. This is home to 24,000 puffins as well as the world's largest population of Manx shearwaters (350,000 pairs). The island is open from April to October. Arrive early (8am latest) at Lockley Lodge in Marloes to get the first boat across.

Clockwise from top: the flower-lined path; a ruined chapel looks out to sea; meet coastal puffins. Previous page: hiking the Pembrokeshire Coastal Path

"This is a place that sets all the senses on high alert, with its rapidly changing light and wide-open views. . . A place that feels hopeful."

Forged from old volcanic rock, St Davids Head stands out, too. Here my walk takes in the fin-shaped outcrop of Carn Llidi and the Neolithic burial chamber of Coetan Arthur. Tucked between boulders and cliffs, the bay of Porthmelgan on the headland looks freshly minted for a *Famous Five* novel. The water is too cold for a proper swim, but I manage a quick paddle, delighting in the low-tide details of its limpet-encrusted, seaweed-entangled rockpools. Across the water, Ramsey Island reclines like a sleeping dragon.

As I push on further south, the path brings me to Solva at roughly the midway point. This fishing village is pure fudge-tin stuff, with boats bobbing in a deeply riven harbour and ice-cream-coloured cottages. It's a deliciously old-fashioned taste of the seaside, and I order a platter of local lobster and crab to eat by the water.

On the home stretch, the trail continues to hold me in its thrall. There is the wild seclusion of Druidstone Haven, where a waterfall spills over dark, ragged cliff faces to a beach of smooth, rust-gold sand. There is Marloes Sands, with its giant jigsaw of rock stacks and coves to explore, and a shipwreck visible at low tide. There is Barafundle Bay, a pristine arc reached through dunes and pinewoods, and Broad Haven South, a generous sweep of beach overlooking Church Rock – a limestone stack that distinctly resembles a church at high tide.

I linger on the beach as the pinkening sky renders Church Rock to silhouette. It is as though nature has found its own means of worship here. And I say a silent prayer that I will one day have the chance to return – to walk this path again. **KW**

ORIENTATION

Start // St Dogmaels
Finish // Amroth (or vice-versa)
Distance // 299km (186 miles)
Duration // 12 to 15 days
When to go // March to May for wildflowers and fewer crowds; June to August for birdlife (including puffins on Skomer) and warmer weather; or September for quiet trails.
What to pack // You'll need hiking boots and waterproofs, and a tent and stove if you're planning on camping.
Where to stay and eat // You're never far from a B&B or campground on the path. Many towns and villages have pubs as well as shops for stocking up on essentials.
Getting around // Want to skip a stage? Pembrokeshire coastal buses serve the entire path. Visit www. pembrokeshire.gov.uk for details on routes and timetables.
More info // www.visitpembrokeshire.com; www. nationaltrail.co.uk

MORE LIKE THIS
COASTAL PATHS

SELVAGGIO BLU, ITALY

Rambling across Sardinia's incredibly lovely east coast, this hike is the big one: a tough four- to seven-day trek and wild camping trip along the Golfo di Orosei. This gulf is pure drama, shaped by sheer cliffs, caves, wooded ravines and hidden coves where bone-white pebbles are polished smooth by a startlingly turquoise sea. Neither for the fainthearted nor the inexperienced, you'll need to know how to use a compass and rope for this challenging coastal jaunt, which involves scrambling, via ferrata (fixed-rope routes) and abseiling. A guide is a must for all but the very experienced, as the trail is not properly signposted and there is no water en route. Enrico Spanu's *Book of Selvaggio Blu* is a handy companion. Weather permitting, it is hikeable from April to October.
Start // Pedra Longa
Finish // Cala Sisine
Distance // 45km (28 miles)
More info // www.selvaggioblu.it; www.corradoconca.it

SOUTH WEST COAST PATH, ENGLAND

Towering cliffs, wave-lashed smuggler's coves, gorges and heather-misted moors sweeping down to fossil-strewn bays, prettily whitewashed fishing villages – this long-distance coastal romp wraps the lot into one hefty 1014km (630-mile) trail. Many choose to walk it chunk by chunk rather than devoting seven to eight weeks to complete it. But if time and energy are not an issue, it's quite something to say you've hiked the whole thing. Most hikers walk anticlockwise (north to south), beginning in Minehead in Somerset and ending in Poole Harbour in Dorset. Highlights are many: from the lonely wilds of Exmoor to the ragged rock stacks of Lizard Point in Cornwall, Britain's most southerly place; from Plymouth's rich nautical history to dinosaur traces on the Jurassic Coast.
Start // Minehead, Somerset
Finish // Poole Harbour, Dorset
Distance // 1014km (630 miles)
More info // www.southwestcoastpath.org.uk

FISHERMEN'S TRAIL, PORTUGAL

The Atlantic is your constant companion on the Rota Vicentina, a 13-stage trail that teeters along the clifftops of Portugal's wild southwest coast. Bookended by the coastal towns of Sines (in the north) and Lagos (in the south), the trail dives straight into the Parque Natural do Sudoeste Alentejano e Costa Vicentina, a nature park protecting the secluded dune-backed beaches, cork-oak forests, jagged, stratified cliffs and rock formations that define this remote, little-visited swathe of the Algarve. Sleepy fishing villages, castle-topped towns and surf resorts dish up a mix of respite, culture and action en route. The highlight? Watching the sun set from the vertiginous cliffs of Cabo de São Vicente, Portugal's southwesternmost point, nicknamed the 'End of the World' by the great explorers that once set sail from its shores.
Start // São Torpes
Finish // Lagos
Distance // 226km (140 miles)
More info // www.rotavicentina.com

Clockwise from top: walking the
Cornish section of the South West
Coast Path; the Fishermen's Trail; a
Sardinian shepherd's hut

TOULOUSE TO CARCASSONNE ALONG THE CANAL DU MIDI

Oliver Berry follows the banks of France's most famous canal, from the pink city of Toulouse to the fairy-tale castle of Carcassonne.

'Péniches, that's what we call them,' explains Agnès Montand, as she leads me on a tour around her vintage narrowboat, painted in the jaunty colours of the funfair: bottle green, sunflower yellow, cherry red, cornflower blue. Potted plants and two vintage deckchairs are arranged on the deck in front of the wheelhouse; the boat's name, *Hirondelle* (The Swallow), has been elegantly traced in serif letters along the prow. 'When we bought the boat it was a wreck, but we've spent the last five years restoring it. Once upon a time there were hundreds like this, but now they're becoming quite rare. For me, they're the soul of the Canal du Midi.'

I thank her and step off onto the towpath, watching as the narrowboat putters round the bend behind a screen of tall plane trees. Gradually the sound of the motor dies away, and silence reigns again along the waterway; the only sounds are the warble of birdsong, the rustle of leaves and the slap of water against the canal banks.

It's my first day walking along the Canal du Midi, the queen of French waterways. Stretching for 240km (149 miles) between the pink-stoned city of Toulouse and the port of Sète, it's the oldest working canal in the world. It was commissioned in 1666 by Louis XIV and built by tax-inspector-turned-engineer Pierre-Paul

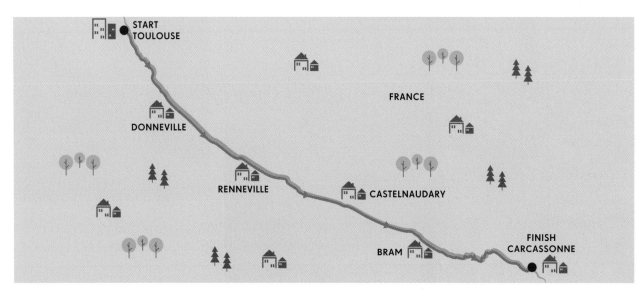

PLANES

Plâtanes, or plane trees, are synonymous with the Canal du Midi. Mostly planted in the 1830s, they were designed to provide shade from the ferocious southern sun, but a devastating fungus called *ceratocystis fimbriata platani* (commonly known as canker stain) has sadly meant that many of the original trees have had to be felled, and replaced with a hardier species that's resistant to the fungus.

*"Then it's a picnic lunch on the canal banks –
or, if I'm lucky, the menu du jour at a local cafe."*

Riquet, who died a few months before the canal's inauguration in 1681. Along with the Canal de Garonne, it formed part of the epic Canal des Deux Mers, which permitted uninterrupted passage across southern France from the Atlantic all the way to the Mediterranean. In many ways, the Canal du Midi heralded the start of the Industrial Revolution in France; it's been a World Heritage Site since 1996.

I'm walking the first 105km (65 miles) of the canal between Toulouse and the medieval city of Carcassonne, a journey of between five and seven days across the historic region of Languedoc. Rather like a boat trip on the canal itself, it's a walk that encapsulates the essence of the south of France: hilltop castles, drowsy southern villages, glossy green vineyards, fields filled with fragrant lavender and sunflowers. It's also mercifully flat; although the canal traces a gentle downhill gradient as it rolls towards the Mediterranean coastline, it's almost indiscernible as you tramp the towpaths. Much of the route is paved, but even where it isn't, there's an easy-to-follow trail – and thanks to the canal's constant presence, it's impossible to get lost.

In its heyday in the 18th century, the canal would have carried huge amounts of traffic; everything from wood to wine barrels once relied on the Canal du Midi for transit. But its commercial

importance dwindled after the arrival of the railway, and today it's the preserve of pleasure-boaters. Walking it is equally tranquil: apart from a few cyclists, a fellow walker or two and the narrowboats that beetle past, I have the canal mostly to myself. I watch herons stalking along the banks, and kingfishers flitting and darting across the water's surface. I eat my picnic lunch (baguette and cheese, *bien sûr*) under the canopy of a plane tree that was probably planted sometime in the 1830s. In the afternoon, I stop for coffee and a pastry at a waterside cafe, chatting to a couple of boaters about their adventures before heading off to the nearby town of Donneville to pick up supplies and find somewhere to pitch my tent for the night.

The days fall into a pattern: a breakfast of coffee, fruit and croissants, followed by a few hours of walking before the heat of the day becomes too ferocious. Then it's a picnic lunch on the canal banks – or, if I'm lucky, the menu du jour at a local cafe, washed down by a *pichet* (jug) of local Languedoc wine. In the village of Villefranche-de-Lauragais, I shop for supplies at the morning market, picking up pungent cheeses, oversized tomatoes, fresh olives and sweet, plump strawberries to snack on along the trail. In Castelnaudary, I sample the Languedoc's signature dish: cassoulet, a hearty, slow-cooked stew of duck,

Clockwise from top left: a French breakfast; refueling with duck cassoulet; the towpath. Previous page: cruising the Canal Du Midi

sausage and white beans. Then it's back onto the towpaths, counting off the locks as I travel ever southwards.

There are 328 structures dotted along the course of the Canal du Midi, including more than 60 *écluses*, or locks, 40 aqueducts, countless feeder canals and France's first subterranean water tunnel. No matter how many I pass, I always stop to watch when I see a boat passing through an *écluse*. They are more than a practical solution to a topographical problem: each is its own small work of mechanical art, a reminder of the great age of European industry – and, arguably, of a more elegant engineering age.

Six days of walking slip by, and before I know it, I find myself on the outskirts of Carcassonne. Ahead of me, framed against the hazy horizon, the town's medieval fortress squats on the hilltop, its turrets topped like witches' hats. From here, the canal rolls on for another 153km (95 miles), mingling with the saltwater lagoons around Agde before finally emptying out into the dazzling Mediterranean blue. But for me, it's journey's end.

I follow the towpath into town, watching as another handsome old *péniche* chugs past, its diesel motor throbbing like a vintage motor-car. I salute the skipper, and he waves back cheerily, guiding his boat beneath an old arched bridge and disappearing downstream. I can't help wishing I could climb aboard. **OB**

ORIENTATION

Start // Toulouse
Finish // Carcassonne
Distance // 110km (68 miles)
Duration // Five to seven days
Getting there // Fast, frequent TGV trains serve Toulouse from Paris' Gare Montparnasse and Montpellier.
When to go // April to May or September and October.
What to wear // Light, breathable clothing and sturdy, waterproof footwear or trail shoes.
What to pack // Map, waterproof jacket, corkscrew.
Where to stay and eat // Hotels, *chambres d'hôtes* (B&Bs) and campsites are plentiful, as are cafes and restaurants. Donneville, Renneville, Castelnaudary, Bram and Carcassonne make useful bases.
More info // www.hautegaronnetourisme.com; www.toulouse-visit.com; www.tourism-carcassonne.co.uk

*Opposite: the windmills of Kinderdijk,
a Unesco World Heritage site*

MORE LIKE THIS
AWESOME CANAL TOWPATHS

CANAL DE BOURGOGNE, FRANCE

Conceived a century after the Canal du Midi, the Canal de Bourgogne connects two of Burgundy's great rivers: the Yonne (in the north) and the Saône (in the south). Work began in 1777, but engineering difficulties and debate over the optimal route meant that it wasn't finished until 1832 – and by then, the railway had effectively put the canal out of business. It's 242km (150 miles) end-to-end, a trek of 10 or 11 days, but the flat terrain and well-marked paths means it's a long walk that's achievable even for novice hikers. Since this is the heart of France's most famous wine region, there's also plenty of opportunity to stop off and sample a few local vintages – with the added benefit that, since you're walking, there's no need for a designated driver. *Santé*!

Start // Migennes
Finish // Saint-Jean-de-Losne
Distance // 242km (150 miles)
More info // www.burgundy-waterways.com

KINDERDIJK, THE NETHERLANDS

The Netherlands has more miles of canals than anywhere else on earth, so if it's towpath walks that float your boat, you're really spoilt for choice. One of the best areas to explore (in terms of quintessentially Dutch scenery, at least) is the area around Kinderdijk, where rows of windmills rise up along the banks, and artificial polders have reclaimed many acres of low-lying land from the water. There are miles and miles of paths to explore; the easy Kinderdijkpad loop runs right past the windmills, while the longer Polderhoppen & Vogel-spotten route ventures out into the green countryside around Alblasserwaard. For an even longer route, you could follow cycle-paths all the way from Rotterdam. Alternatively, it makes a good day-trip, thanks to the regular water-taxi which runs directly from downtown Rotterdam.

Start/Finish // Kinderdijk
Distance // 7.5km (4.5 miles) short loop or 17km (10.5 miles) for the longer trail
More info // Download the Kinderdijk Unesco Official app for route maps

THE OLD BARGERMAN'S PATH, DENMARK

Denmark has a huge network of rivers, canals and waterways to explore. This *trækstien* (towpath) connecting the once-important industrial towns of Silkeborg and Randers is arguably the loveliest. During the 19th century, the only way to transport goods was along the Gudenå, Denmark's longest river, which snakes through central Jutland. The waterway was still being used by barges right up to the beginning of WWI – although these days, the only vessels you're likely to see are kayaks and canoes. The trail is about 70km (43 miles), and can be split into four or five easy sections, staying at the same inns once used by the river bargemen. Along the way, you'll also pass Tange Sø, Denmark's largest artificial lake, also home to the country's biggest hydroelectric power station.

Start // Silkeborg
Finish // Randers
Distance // 70km (43 miles)
More info // www.visitdenmark.it

FOUR DAYS ON THE ALPINE PASS ROUTE

Explore the glorious vistas of Switzerland, a country that's almost a byword for mountains and hiking, and feel the gravitational pull of some of the world's most famous peaks.

On the Alpine slopes above Engelberg, the marmots are whistling while they work, but it's a scream that catches my attention. I look up and there, plunging from a gondola towards me, is a woman, her ankles tied to a bungee cord, her scream bouncing between the mountains. Around me, cowbells chime like applause.

As the scream fades away, I walk on. This woman may have fallen for the Alps – literally – in an instant, but I have days rolling on ahead of me.

I'm here to walk across Switzerland, or at least a sizeable chunk of it. I'm hiking on the Alpine Pass Route (APR), a puzzle of trails that cross the entire country – Lake Geneva to Liechtenstein. Broken into 15 stages, it's more than 320km (199 miles) in length and crosses 17 passes, condensing Switzerland into one single glorious journey on foot.

I'm tackling four stages of the APR, covering its finest and most dramatic section, walking through and past some of the most

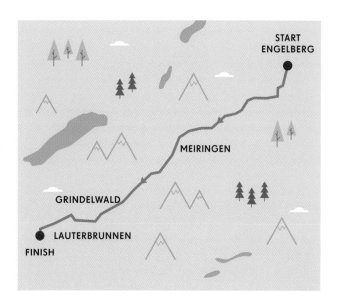

famous names in the Swiss Alps: the resort towns of Engelberg, Grindelwald and Lauterbrunnen, and mountains such as Titlis, Eiger and Jungfrau.

I've started in Engelberg, climbing first into clouds and then suddenly above clouds as I near 2207m (7241ft) Jochpass. Though it's late summer, fresh snow covers the slopes, and an archipelago of peaks rises from the clouds now beneath me.

The APR has no official status as a hiking route across Switzerland, leaving the way open to individual interpretation. Past Jochpass, paths fray and fray again, and I gravitate towards those that lead higher into the mountains, heading past lakes so still they look painted on to the landscape. At times I'm far from any traditional APR lines, but so long as my feet are pointing west, it doesn't matter because in the town of Meiringen all paths come together again.

It's here, in the town that was the scene of Sherlock Holmes' fictional death, that I'm about to enter one of the most dramatic mountain areas in Europe, rising up past the Wetterhorn, tiptoeing across the waist of the Eiger and plunging into the narrow abyss of the Lauterbrunnen Valley.

Mountains jostle the path as I climb out of Meiringen where, around 400m (1300ft) above the town, the trail detours on to a ledge overhanging Reichenbach Falls. It was from this very ledge that Holmes plunged to his end, duelling with Professor Moriarty.

For five hours, I'll hike relentlessly uphill to Grosse Scheidegg pass, squeezing through a narrow, forested gorge. On one side of the valley, Alpine meadows rise gently up the slopes. On the other side of the valley, the Wetterhorn bristles with rock spires and glaciers fractured with icefalls.

By the time I cross Grosse Scheidegg, grey cloud drapes from the mountains like damp laundry. My greatest hope when starting this hike had been to stand on this pass and eyeball the Eiger – that mightiest of Alpine peaks – but in these conditions even Grindelwald, 1100m (3600ft) below me, is obliterated. As I descend, so do my spirits.

However, there's alchemy in the sky when I wake in Grindelwald the next morning to find the sharp lines of the Eiger sawing at a blue sky. The timing is impeccable because today I have a date with this mountain.

The APR beelines straight out of Grindelwald to Kleine Scheidegg pass, but I've planned a bigger and better day. I will walk 25km (16 miles) and climb around 1500m (4900ft) to take me up to and along the Eiger's famed North Face. It will be one of the finest hiking days I can remember.

From Grindelwald a trail coils tightly through the Eiger's forested lower slopes, rising above the bent and tortured nose of the Lower Grindelwald Glacier. Wild strawberries grow beside the trail, providing grazing fodder. Within an hour, Grindelwald is like an ant farm below and the North Face is near.

The trail crunches across slopes of scree that has crumbled from this mighty rock wall. I peer down on to Grindelwald, across to

EIGER NORTH FACE

It's debatable which climb of the Eiger's North Face is more famous – the first ascent in 1938, or Clint Eastwood's in the 1975 film *The Eiger Sanction* – but we're going with the former. Before that successful climb, most attempts to scale the North Face had ended in death, but finally four members of a German–Austrian team (two independent teams who joined up on the mountain) completed the puzzle of the mighty wall, surviving an avalanche to reach the summit on 24 July 1938.

Clockwise from top: the Bernese Alps, seen from Jungfrau; happy on the trail; an Alpine marmot. Previous page: meadows and mountains

"Fresh snow covers the slopes and an archipelago of peaks rises from the clouds now beneath me."

the Wetterhorn and up – most bizarrely – to a line of holes drilled through the North Face that are windows for the Jungfrau Railway, which travels inside the mountain.

The fact that this wall of rock is one of the touchstones of mountaineering is acknowledged along the trail. Near its end, just a few yards from the path, is the point where the first successful climb of the North Face commenced, as marked by a sign outlining the course of that route. A short distance on, just before the trail reaches its highest point, the clay handprints of famous Eiger climbers are bolted to the rock face.

All that remains of my walk now is a final descent into Lauterbrunnen, but it's no ordinary finish. It will take me 1500m (4900ft) down into one of the most dramatic valleys in the Alps, past the revered Mönch and Jungfrau mountains. Glaciers drape from the so-called 'Young Woman' like a string of pearls, and as I walk, seracs continually shear away, the ice smashing itself apart as it avalanches down the rock faces.

A short distance ahead are the cliffs that enclose Lauterbrunnen, a town huddled in a valley so narrow it's like a paper cut in the Alps. Some of Europe's highest waterfalls plunge over the edges of these 500m (1650ft) cliffs, but they aren't the only things that fall here. Lauterbrunnen is also one of the world's prime BASE-jumping locations, and as I approach the valley I see a handful of people in wingsuits step to the cliff edge and leap. The Swiss Alps ring with screams once again. **AB**

ORIENTATION

Start // Engelberg
Finish // Lauterbrunnen
Distance // 77km (48 miles)
Duration // Four days
Getting there // Switzerland's major airports are Zurich, Geneva and Basel. A superbly efficient public transport system makes it easy to access points all along the route.
Tours // Utracks (www.utracks.com) runs a 14-day self-guided Alpine Pass Route trip, beginning in Engelberg and ending in Saanen, covering eight of the route's 14 stages.
When to go // Snow often lingers on high passes into early summer, so its best to hike the route July to September.
Where to stay and eat // This is a civilised trail, passing towns and mountain huts, providing ample options.
More info // For a dedicated guide to the route, pick up a Cicerone's *Alpine Pass Route*, by Kev Reynolds.

Opposite from top: an ibex finds its perch on the Europaweg near Zermatt; a hiker sees the Chamonix Valley stretch before him

MORE LIKE THIS
LONG-DISTANCE ALPINE HIKES

TOUR DU MONT BLANC, FRANCE/ITALY/SWITZERLAND

Arguably Europe's most famous hike, the TMB passes through three countries as it makes a lap around the highest peak in the European Alps. This circuit of about 170km (110 miles) loops out from Chamonix, crossing into Italy and Switzerland before returning to the Alpine resort town. There are low- and high-route options in many places, and the scenery is sublime, whether it be the Toblerone skyline of the Grandes Jorasses or the grandstand views along the Aiguilles Rouges. For most hikers, it's a journey of 10–11 days (if that seems pedestrian you can always run around it in the Ultra-Trail Mont Blanc), and accommodation is plentiful, though the popularity of the trail means it's wise to book ahead during July and August. In total, expect to climb the equivalent of summiting Everest from sea level.

Start/Finish // Chamonix, France
Distance // 170km (110 miles)
More info // www.autourdumont blanc.com

HAUTE ROUTE, FRANCE/SWITZERLAND

With Mont Blanc as its starting block and the Matterhorn as its finish post, the Haute Route is like a date with the mountain gods. Created originally as a ski-touring route, it quickly also morphed into a summer hiking trail, adopting a slightly different course but sticking to its brief as the 'High Route'. It passes beneath 10 of the 12 highest mountains in the Alps, and though it never rises above 3000m (10,000ft), it's two weeks that'll see you ascend more than 15,000m (50,000ft). The 200km (125-mile) route is dotted with mountain huts, and the safest time to be on the trail is from about mid-July to September – early summer may require crampons. One of the most enticing features of the walk is that it ends in a blaze of glory, finishing along the 33km (21-mile) Europaweg into Zermatt, a trail itself widely regarded as among Europe's most spectacular.

Start // Chamonix, France
Finish // Zermatt, Switzerland
Distance // 200km (125 miles)
More info // www.hauteroutehiking.com

EAGLE WALK, AUSTRIA

One of the Alps' longest hiking trails, the Eagle Walk is a compendium of Austrian Alpine highlights. It begins along the Wilder Kaiser (Wild Emperor) mountains near St Johann in Tirol, and then spools out for more than 400km (250 miles), ending across the slopes of 3798m (12,461ft) Grossglockner, the highest mountain in Austria. The trail is partitioned into 33 stages – 24 in North Tyrol, nine in East Tyrol – and almost traverses Austria north-south. If the idea of hiking in the Austrian Alps lulls you into a fantasy of *Sound of Music*-type strolls, think again – there's more than 30,000m (98,000ft) of ascent along the Eagle Walk, which is exhausting just to write! If you only fancy a few days with the Eagle, it's easy to tap into short sections of the trail, with bus stops and train stations regularly intersecting with the route.

Start // St Johann in Tirol
Finish // Lucknerhaus
Distance // 413km (257 miles)
More info // www.tyrol.com

HIGH DRAMA IN THE CARES GORGE

This short and spectacular chasm-tracing walk is the classic way to squeeze through Spain's Picos de Europa National Park – just don't look down.

Halfway along the walk into northern Spain's Cares Gorge, I remembered how much I didn't like heights... Looking around, the world above was wonderful: walls of sheer, craggy limestone soared splendidly into a deep-blue sky where griffon vultures whirled. Down, though, was a different matter. A quick glance over the side of the (oh-so narrow) path and my head started to spin. Everything – path, trees, safety – seemed to disappear in an instant, falling to the distant river below. Instinctively I reached out for the cool, solid stone to my left, ignored the empty air to my right, forced my eyes forwards and carried on.

For the non-acrophobic, the Garganta del Cares (Cares Gorge) offers arguably the best day-walk in Spain. It has drama and daring: sometimes this limestone chasm is so skinny you feel the need to breathe in; sometimes its drop-offs are so abrupt, you can barely breathe at all. It is a marvel of geology, a masterstroke of engineering, and a test of nerve.

The gorge lies within the Picos de Europa, a striking surge of crinkled, creviced massifs topping out at over 2500m (8202ft) yet only 20km (12.5 miles) inland from the Bay of Biscay coast. The Picos was designated a national park in 1918, Spain's first, and one of Europe's earliest too (only Sweden and Switzerland have older such protected wildernesses). Originally the national park covered a much smaller area, focused on the pilgrimage site of Covadonga – it was at the Battle of Covadonga (718 CE) that a Christian uprising, spearheaded by nobleman Don Pelayo, managed to push back 63,000 invading Moors, a victory that helped lead to the eventual reconquest of Spain. However, in the 1990s the park was expanded, and now reaches across parts of three provinces:

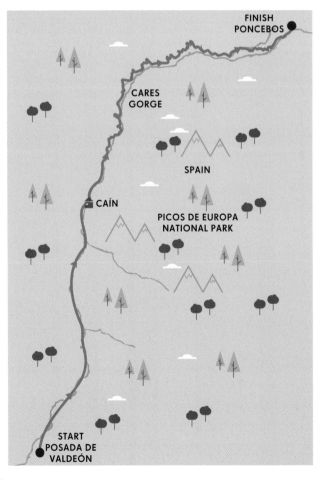

TASTE OF THE MOUNTAINS

Farmers have been moving their flocks of cows, goats and sheep up to the high pastures of the Picos for centuries; to experience the essence of the Picos, they say, you must eat its cheese. There are many varieties. Valdeón (made in Posada de Valdeón) is an intense, semi-soft blue-veined cheese, traditionally wrapped in sycamore leaves. Asturian Cabrales is similar but stronger and smellier. Gamonéu is a nutty, lightly smoked, semi-hard variety.

Cantabria, Castilla y León and Asturias. The gorge cuts through the centre of the mountains, straddling the latter two.

There never used to be a trail running length-wise through this dizzying defile. The only access was across the gorge, via a path that runs from Covadonga; it descends steeply to the river bottom, and then ascends equally steeply up the other side. This path – now known as the Reconquista Route – is said to have been the one taken by the skedaddling Moors after their historic defeat. However, in 1916, when a canal was audaciously blasted into the gorge's rock walls to feed a hydroelectric station, a somewhat hazardous maintenance footpath was also created. In the 1940s, the current route was installed to provide workers with easier access – and, subsequently, provide heady thrills for adventurous hikers.

The most spectacular, and most walked, section of the trail runs between the villages of Caín (Castilla y León) and Poncebos (Asturias). However, I set off from Posada de Valdeón, a little further south of Caín. This meant a longer walk – around 21km (13 miles) one-way. But, beginning here, where the 2000m- (6562ft)-high mountains sit further apart, I felt the increasing squeeze more keenly – like I was being drawn into an immense grey-green funnel. I got to walk without the crowds for a while, too: the main stretch can get busy on a sunny day, but on the trail from Posada

de Valdeón, I saw only fat green lizards, bees buzzing around the wildflowers and two old hombres in flat caps, out for a morning stroll. It was also on this section that I followed the Cares River past Ermita de Corona, a cluster of small stone buildings in a forest clearing where it's alleged Don Pelayo was crowned King of Asturias following his momentous victory.

With every forward step, the mountains pressed tighter, the river grew louder, the air became scented with wild herbs and lime. Caín itself is tucked deep in the valley, amid the Central Massif's highest peaks. I side-stepped the cars performing U-turns (there's no way to drive further than this), paused at a cafe festooned with geraniums and then joined the small but steady stream of other hikers plunging into the gorge's most dramatic innards.

Here, the trail felt part eagle, part mole: there were stretches that edged along ledges and hung over precipices usually fit only for birds; other sections burrowed right through the rock in dark, dripping tunnels, emerging to ever more astounding views. Rocks reared and fell away. Foliage clung on: bushes in-filled the couloirs and, in damp places, carnivorous plants thrived, catching flies on their sticky leaves.

Clockwise from top left: a Cantabrian sheep; heading into the Cares Gorge; a chapel en route; sampling Cabrales cheese. Previous page: walking a narrow ledge in the gorge

> *"It is a marvel of geology, a masterstroke of engineering, and a test of nerve."*

After a while I was too wowed to be scared. I was too astonished that Mother Nature had formed such a chasm, too impressed that humankind had found a way to tame it. Perhaps I shouldn't have been surprised, the Picos de Europa has long been a place of people. It was inhabited in Palaeolithic times and transhumance farming (the seasonal moving of livestock) has been practiced here since around 500 BCE, moulding both the area's landscape and culture. Few still work these difficult mountains now but, deep in the ravine, I noticed the traces of shepherds' trails and the ruined remains of old cave dwellings, now taken over by goats.

It was a wild, wonderful walk, worth every nail-biting step. And when I reached the finish in Poncebos, I sank into a busy bar and celebrated in the only possible way: with an Asturian *sidra*. This cider is traditionally served by an *escanciador*, an experienced bartender who holds a glass low in one hand and pours the fizzy elixir from on high with the other. More precipitous drama, equally delicious. **SB**

ORIENTATION

Start // Caín
Finish // Poncebos
Distance // 12km (7.5 miles)
Duration // Three hours
Getting there // The nearest airports to the Picos are in Santander and Asturias (near Oviedo). Public transport within the national park is limited. The Cares Gorge walk is linear; buses (summer only) and taxis link Caín and Poncebos but, as driving between the two takes two to three hours, some hikers choose to walk both ways: 24km (15 miles); six hours.
Where to stay // There is limited accommodation in Poncebos. Nearby Arenas de Cabrales has more choice; the larger hub of Cangas de Onís has better links and facilities.
Where to eat // Many restaurants offer great-value *menú del día*, usually including three courses and drinks.
More info // There is a Picos visitor centre in Cangas de Onís; www.parquenacionalpicoseuropa.es

Opposite from top: approaching the jagged headland of Ponta de São Lourenço, Madeira; taking a breather on the precipitous Caminito del Rey

MORE LIKE THIS
VERTIGINOUS TRAILS

CAMINITO DEL REY, SPAIN

The 'King's Little Pathway', which clings to the steep sides of southern Spain's Desfiladero de los Gaitanes gorge, once had a different nickname: The World's Most Dangerous Walk. Originally built in 1905 to provide access to a hydroelectric plant, the *caminito* fell into disuse; sections crumbled into ruin, leaving only rotten planks and corroded metal spurs sticking out of the rock, 100m (328ft) above the Guadalhorce River. Some foolhardy hikers attempted it anyway; some died in the process. But in 2015 the route was renovated. Walkers now pay with their wallets (there's an entry fee of €18) but not with their lives. After donning a mandatory hard hat and hiking through forest, you reach the gorge section where new wooden boardwalks, safety barriers and sections of overhanging glass floors make the walk less hazardous, but still a thrill.
Start // Ardales
Finish // El Chorro
Distance // 8km (5 miles)
More info // https://entradas.mientrada.net

AONACH EAGACH RIDGE, SCOTLAND

Running almost the entire length of gorgeous Glen Coe, Aonach Eagach is infamous among scramblers – some say it's the British mainland's narrowest ridge, and certainly isn't for the inexperienced. From a small car park on the A82, the trail climbs up the steep slopes of Am Bodach, where, the knife-edge fun really starts. There follows a rollercoaster of difficult drops, increasingly exposed rock ledges, craggy chimneys, two munros (953m/3127ft Meall Dearg and 967m/3173ft Sgorr nam Fiannaidh) and the Crazy Pinnacles, a 500m- (1640ft)-long section of serious, sustained, spine-tingling scrambling. The views every which way are spectacular. The Pap of Glencoe path leads back down; the best end point is a bar stool at the Clachaig Inn, a legendary hill-walking pub, for a nerve-settling dram or two.
Start // Allt-na-reigh
Finish // Glencoe village
Distance // 9.5km (6 miles)
More info // www.thebmc.co.uk/how-to-scramble-aonach-eagach

VEREDA DO LARANO, MADEIRA, PORTUGAL

Looking down from its narrowest sections, it's hard to believe that this old footpath between the coastal towns of Porto da Cruz and Machico is used as the final stage of the 115km (71-mile) Madeira Island Ultra Trail race – you wouldn't want to be running this slender route on tired-out legs and lose concentration... From Engenhos do Norte, Madeira's last remaining steam-powered rum distillery, the path follows the shore out of Porto da Cruz, climbs into lush plantations and weaves along flat *levadas* (irrigation channels). Then things get wild, as the path barrels along the cliff edge. On one side, it drops straight into the Atlantic swell, so keep your eyes ahead: the views stretch along a series of jagged headlands jutting into the waves, all the way to Ponta de São Lourenço, the island's easternmost point.
Start // Porto da Cruz
Finish // Machico
Distance // 16km (10 miles)
More info // www.gotrailmadeira.com

HELVELLYN'S STRIDING EDGE

Oli Reed heads into the mountainous heart of England to conquer a fearsome ridge that has been calling him since childhood.

There's something about a great mountain name. If you're anything like me, it calls to you, buries itself deep in your soul, and nibbles away at the back of your brain until it draws you, inevitably, to it.

I distinctly remember the first time I heard the name Striding Edge. Some kid in my school won top prize in one of our assembly raffles, which turned out, bafflingly, to be a guided walk across England's most famous mountain ridge, on an expedition led by our local vicar. I was jealous.

I couldn't get that name, Striding Edge, out of my head. To my eight-year-old self, stuck in a small rural town and plotting adventurous escapes, it was perfect. I pictured myself high on its windblown crest, marching triumphantly towards the summit of the third-highest mountain in the country, returning to our school the following Monday like a conquering hero. I asked my dad about it. He'd been up there, he told me, but had decided it wasn't for him. Too steep, too dangerous, too scary, he said. That made me want to go even more.

Over the next 10 years I devoured every book, map and photograph of that ridge I could get my hands on. I knew the names of all its key features: Hole-in-the-Wall, Low Spying How, High Spying How, The Dixon Memorial, the Bad Step... I interrogated everyone I knew who'd crossed its spiky backbone until, finally, I was old enough and brave enough to do it myself.

And so I arrived in Glenridding, the small and typically charming Lakeland village at the foot of Helvellyn's wooded eastern flanks, in an unreliable Fiat Cinquecento crammed to bursting point with five ill-equipped university students and a tattered old guidebook. The sympathetic looks we received from local farmers and fellow walkers, as we sweated our way out of the valley and up the steep pull to the summit of neighbouring peak Birkhouse Moor, suggested we were very close to being out of our depth.

Then suddenly, dramatically, magnificently, there it was. I've since climbed a lot more mountains in Britain and abroad, but very little has ever got hold of me quite like that first look at Striding Edge. Helvellyn's great eastern wall dominated the skyline ahead, its shadowy slopes tumbling steeply into the still waters of Red Tarn at its base. To the left, Striding Edge did exactly what I knew it would, rising, rippling and snaking upwards towards the mountain's plateaued summit. To the right, Swirral Edge, which could almost

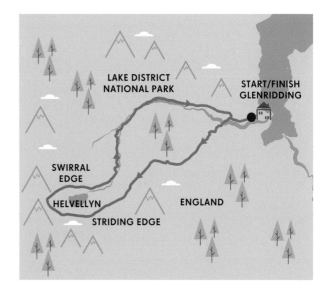

be Striding Edge's identical twin, looked just as menacing. Which was a concern, as this was pencilled in for our descent route.

We approached the start of the ridge with cautious excitement. I was considered the mountain expert in our inexperienced group, but this type or terrain, this level of exposure, this sense of impending danger, was completely new to me. Striding Edge is a long ridge, stretching for more than 1km (o.6 miles) from its start at Hole-in the-Wall to its steep, scrambly finish directly beneath Helvellyn's summit. It went by in a blur.

I remember the path starting to narrow, the rocks becoming sharper, the drops getting bigger, and the views around us making my heart thump against the inside of my ribcage. There are obstacles on the ridge that, if they were in your local park, you would skip over without a second thought. But up there it's different. The penalties for a slip or a fall are serious, and in many places almost unthinkable.

> *"I've since climbed a lot more mountains... but very little has ever got hold of me quite like that first look at Striding Edge."*

As we got closer to the business end, we were faced with a simple choice. Stick to the thin footpath that ran a few feet beneath the true crest of Striding Edge, or take the ridge by the horns and tackle it head on. Three of our party chose the first option, while two of us tiptoed onto the pointed apex of the arête and began bum-shuffling slowly along it, like two out-of-their-depth burglars suddenly realising their escape route across the roof of the house they'd just plundered was a bad idea.

I remember thinking what a good thing it was that my mum couldn't see me doing something so brilliantly precarious, but then just as soon as I'd started to really feel like a proper mountaineer, it was almost over. The ridge tapered out, leaving a short, steep, scrappy section of shattered rock wall between us and the summit.

This was probably the most nervous I'd been all day, but also the most giddy. Behind us Striding Edge swept in a beautiful crescent around the southern shore of Red Tarn, the people following in our footsteps spread out like ants across its backbone. Like much that had come before it, the wall was easier than it looked, as we tussled our way to the highest point in the Lake District's glorious Eastern Fells using a combo of hands, elbows, knees and adrenaline.

Then that was it, Striding Edge had been struck off my bucket list, but a fire had been lit. I've been back to that mountain, that ridge, many times with many different people in the 20 years since and it never gets old. For the adventurous hiker, this is as good as English mountain routes get. It's the kind of place that makes you feel like a king for the day, as though there's nobody on the planet doing anything cooler than you at that given moment. And that, for me, is what climbing mountains is all about. **OR**

HELVELLYN HIJINKS

Helvellyn offers more than just hiking. You can climb, camp, swim and even ski on its slopes, thanks to the Lake District Ski Club who run the only button lift in the National Park. And if that's not adventurous enough, back in 1926 two pilots landed a light aircraft on Helvellyn's summit, just a few steps from Striding Edge.

Clockwise from top: Herdwick sheep grazing on the fells near Helvellyn; Glenridding; putting hand to rock on Striding Edge. Previous Page: the fearsome Striding Edge from Helvellyn

ORIENTATION

Start/Finish // Glenridding, Lake District
Distance // 12.5km (7.8 miles)
Duration // Five to seven hours
Getting there // Train to Penrith then use the 508 bus route to Glenridding.
When to go // This trip is well suited to the summer months (June to August), with long daylight hours and more chance of dry rock. It is best avoided in high winds, low cloud and under snow or ice.
What to wear // This is serious mountain terrain, so wear appropriate warm and waterproof clothing and suitable walking shoes or boots.
What to pack // All your supplies for the day, as once you leave Glenridding there is nowhere else to stock up. Ensure you carry a map and compass – and know how to use them.
More info // www.lakedistrict.gov.uk

*Opposite: keeping balance on one of
the exposed ridges of Jack's Rake*

MORE LIKE THIS
ENGLAND'S LAKE DISTRICT SCRAMBLES

SHARP EDGE, BLENCATHRA

If Striding Edge is the most iconic hiking ridge in the Lake District, Sharp Edge is the most intimidating. It's shorter than its Helvellyn counterpart, but possibly packs even more drama into its exposed traverse. The classic route starts from the busy A66 road beneath Blencathra's southern face, but soon leaves the crowds behind as it loops around Scales Fell to the base of Sharp Edge. From there, a steep ascent brings you up on to the ridge scramble, which requires commitment; it's exposed so best saved for perfect weather conditions. The technicality of the route is within the capabilities of most hikers, but the drops are big and a severe test of nerve. At the end of the ridge, a thrilling scramble up Foule Crag leaves you with just a short stroll to Blencanthra's 868m (2848ft) summit.
Start/Finish // Scales layby, on the A66 road
Distance // 7km (4.5 miles)
More info // www.walkingbritain.co.uk

JACK'S RAKE, PAVEY ARK

This is one of those routes that seems as though it was carved by nature with adventurous hikers in mind. Rising from right to left in a spectacular slash across the impressive southern cliff face of Pavey Ark, Jack's Rake feels like half-ridge and half-gully, with sections of nerve-jangling exposure and others where you feel so enclosed that you're almost part of the surrounding crags. Once you've located the beginning of the Rake on the northern shore of Stickle Tarn, route-finding becomes easy as the only way to go is up. The biggest challenge of Jack's Rake is holding your nerve and always making sure you secure solid hand and footholds as you scramble upwards before it opens out on to the wonderful viewpoint of Pavey Ark's summit. Best avoided in the wet, but overall tremendous fun.
Start/Finish // Sticklebarn pub, Great Langdale
Distance // 5km (3 miles)
More info // www.ukscrambles.com

COCKLY PIKE RIDGE, ILL CRAG

There are three great things about this ridge. The first is that hardly anyone ever goes there because it requires a long walk to reach its base, meandering along silent footpaths for a couple of hours through Eskdale to the magnificent grassy expanse of Great Moss. The second is that as well as being the longest continuous Grade 1 scramble in England, it's also for the most part very straightforward and low on technicality. And the third is that when you top out of it, you're just a short walk from the summit of Scafell Pike, England's highest mountain. This is a hugely enjoyable route set in among the most impressive mountain scenery in England. The scrambling is so varied that you could probably do this route 10 times and never go the same route twice, and you'll probably have it all to yourself.
Start/Finish // Brotherilkeld parking layby
Distance // 17km (10.5 miles)
More info // www.walklakes.co.uk

ACROSS THE MUDFLATS OF THE WADDEN SEA

Race the incoming tide as you slog through the mud of the Wadden Sea on a filthy hike between the mainland and the Netherlands' offshore island of Ameland.

One moment I was walking across a wide slick of mud. Skidding and slipping a bit maybe, but still essentially on top of the wet gloop under my cheap high-top sneakers. And then, suddenly, I was thigh-deep in the mud. One foot had punched through the grey gritty surface, into what felt like deep, wet cement. And as I tried to pull that leg free, the other foot plunged down into the ooze below. A bubble of pure stink erupted around me: rotten fish, ozone, old cheese, school laboratory chemicals.

The Wadden Sea, shared between the Netherlands, Germany and Denmark, has the largest unbroken system of inter-tidal mud and sand banks in the world. Its 11,434 sq km (4415 sq miles) of shallows, dunes, beaches and tidal waters were declared a Unesco World Heritage site in 2009, putting the Wadden Sea National Park on a par with the Grand Canyon and the Great Barrier Reef. The larger of the 14 Dutch Frisian Islands are populated by rugged farming and seafaring communities used to the savage winter storms. For adventurous walkers, crossing the drying mudflats between the islands and mainland in the few hours of low-tide provides a chance for some extreme hiking in a country famously lacking mountains, wilderness and other outdoor challenges.

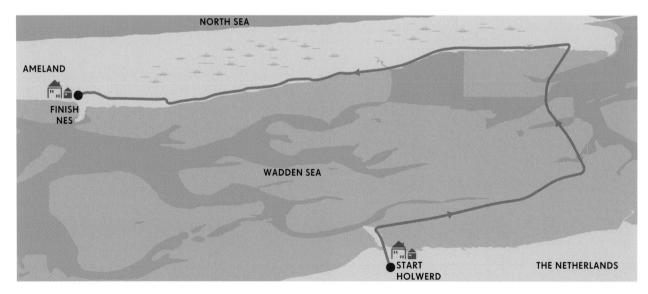

NORTH SEA

AMELAND

FINISH
NES

WADDEN SEA

START
HOLWERD

THE NETHERLANDS

On a summer morning, as the tide fell, I had joined nearly a hundred wadlopers (mudflat walkers) as they stepped from the solid ground of the dunes for the 10km (6.2-mile) crossing that separated the island of Ameland from the mainland. We were led by Ypke Bouma and his team of professional guides, each of whom had undergone three years of training to lead trips, and who walked this surreal and dangerous sand-scape in all seasons, studying the movements of its ever-changing channels, and learning the safe routes.

At first it had seemed easy. The damp sand was firm underfoot, etched with the gentle ripples left by the retreating tide. It was like strolling on a very big beach. We were relaxed, stopping to take photographs, scanning for birds with binoculars or chatting with the guides. After an hour of walking I looked around to see scattered clumps of walkers, their bright-coloured day-packs, shorts and windbreakers providing the only colour in the vast monochrome expanse of grey sand and grey sky. On the horizon, there was a tiny spire rising from a scribble of dry land, marking our destination. It didn't seem so very far to walk.

Then we got to the mud. Pulling myself free I struggled to keep moving forward, propelling in a hard-work gait I thought of as 'sludging' (a mix of sliding and trudging). Looking around me I could see other walkers were also wading through the thick clag. Our

> *"Our speed was reduced to comical slow motion. Everyone was coated in thick gunge, some from head to toe."*

speed was reduced to comical slow motion. Everyone was coated in thick gunge, some from head to toe. Walkers plunged their arms down into the slob to find shoes sucked from their feet One woman was bogged up to her waist, stuck fast until pulled out by a couple of other sludgers, the mud making a huge belching sound as it released her. A gang of teenage boys were diving and belly-flopping onto the slicked surface and mud-tobogganing like playful otters.

It was surreal to be wading across the dried-out seabed, knowing that in a few hours' time the incoming waters would be far higher than our heads and that seals and porpoises would soon be swimming where we were walking. Our crossing felt like a seafaring voyage, dependent on shipping forecasts, tide tables and marine charts. The guides guaranteed our safety as, Moses-like, they led us through the parted seas. Sietse Bouma, a marine biologist as well as a guide, tried to reassure, 'We know this land in all its changes, so we never get lost', while I looked around the confusing two-dimensional world where sky, shifting land, incoming sea and distant horizons were all just different shades of grey. The guides had already walked the 10km (6.2 miles) in the other direction on the previous low tide, through the dark of the night, 'for the fun of it,' as they told me. Their enthusiasm and knowledge were catching, helping me to refocus my attention to notice small details. As I walked across a sand bank

AMELAND HORSE LIFEBOAT

Over the centuries the islanders of Ameland saved hundreds of seafarers from the treacherous tides of the North and Wadden Seas with their horse-drawn lifeboat. Hearing the siren, islanders would race their farm horses to the lifeboat station in Hollum, hitch them to the trailer and speed across the sands and deep into the sea to launch the boat on its rescue mission. Only decommissioned in 1988, it is still used in demonstrations several times a year. See www.vvvameland.com.

Clockwise from top: a red knot feeding in the mud; setting out on a guided hike; the squelchy perils of mudflat walking. Previous Page: crossing the Wadden Sea at low tide

far out in the middle of the sea – a glorious stretch without mud – a breeze blew up a shimmering veil of minute sand crystals around my ankles. Further on, a tiny, plump-fingered, rosé-coloured common starfish lay marooned in a pool of water shaded by a frond of seaweed, like a castaway on a watery desert island.

I was immersed, literally at times, in an ecology with a biodiversity as rich and varied as a temperate forest. Over a hundred species of fish, I learnt, ride the rise and fall of the tides to feed, use the shallows as nurseries and shelter from bigger predators. Avocet, curlew, shelduck, dunlin, spoonbill and tens of other bird species moult, winter, feed and breed across the Wadden Sea and its shores. Meanwhile, for more than 10 million individual birds, the mudflats are a critical hub for the east–west and north–south migratory routes that join Eurasia to the Atlantic and the Subarctic to Africa.

The comings and goings of the sea had cut deep channels into the seabed. At one point we climbed down into a wide trench to wade to the other side, the water getting deeper until I was – wincingly – crotch deep in cold water. Hikers hoisted up jacket hems and shirts and backpacks to keep them dry. Strangers held hands to keep their balance as they struggled across.

There were more channels to cross, and more mud, and more sand. But now the land was visibly getting closer. And then it was underfoot as we stumbled up onto the shore, our feet weighed down by blocks of mud as if plodding along in old-fashioned divers' boots. We had raced – slowly – the tide and had won. **JW**

ORIENTATION

Start // Holwerd
Finish // Nes, Ameland
Distance // 21km (13 miles)
Duration // Five to seven hours
Getting there // Trains from Amsterdam's Zuid station to Leeuwarden (www.ns.nl), then regular buses to Holwerd. Catch the ferry back from Ameland (www.wpd.nl).
When to go // May to August offer the best opportunities.
What to wear // High-top, lace-up sneakers. Shorts are practical, but take warm layers and rain gear.
What to pack // Spare set of clothes, shoes, sun cream, snacks and water.
Tours // The Wadloop Centrum runs mud walks of different challenges including night walks (www.wadlopen.com).
Things to know // Mudflat walking is dangerous in bad weather and tours can be cancelled at short notice.
More info // www.holland.com

MORE LIKE THIS
MUD AND SAND WALKS

LINDISFARNE, ENGLAND

Nearly 1300 years after the 635 CE founding of the monastic settlement on Lindisfarne, or Holy Island, a causeway road was built to – sort of – span the tidal waters between the offshore community and the Northumberland mainland. But for walkers, the traditional route – crossing some 4.8km (3 miles) of tidal flats and running parallel to the causeway – is still marked by poles. Both causeway and walking route are impassable for several hours around high tide, and hikers must walk in daylight hours, in good weather, and as the tide is falling to allow time to reach the far side, though there is a refuge box – a platform on stilts – at the halfway mark as a last resort for those who get it wrong. Apart from its monastic history (the incredible 8th-century illuminated Lindisfarne Gospel was likely made on the island), Lindisfarne also has a spectacular castle and is part of a 3540-hectare (8748-acre) nature reserve covering the mud flats where over 300 bird species have been recorded.
Start // Beal
Finish // Lindisfarne village
Distance // 5km (3 miles)
More info // www.holy-island.uk

DENMARK'S WEST COAST TRAIL

The North Sea is your constant companion on this uplifting 80km (50-mile) hike along Denmark's strikingly lovely northwest coast. Walking and camping here, you'll feel the elemental force and poetry of this region of wide-open skies, billowing clouds, rolling dunes and terrain defined by the ever-changing wind, sea and sand. Starting in Agger, the trail is marked by red wooden posts and follows the old lifeboat route as it inches its way north, taking in vast beaches of blonde sand and fizzing surf, lighthouses and former fishing villages, and delving into the remote moors and pine forests of Thy National Park. Going slow maximises your chances of spotting wildlife. Listen for the delicate trills, warbles and honks of migratory geese and coastal birds such as golden plovers, wood sandpipers and cranes at the Hanstholm Wildlife Reserve, and spot breeding kittiwakes at Bulbjerg, the only limestone cliff in northern Jutland.
Start // Agger
Finish // Bulbjerg
Distance // 80km (50 miles)
More info // www.visitdenmark.com; www.visitthy.com

SES SALINES, IBIZA, SPAIN

This three-hour coastal ramble at Ibiza's southern tip presents the island's coastscapes at their ravishing best. The Unesco World Heritage Ses Salines Natural Park preserves a unique ecosystem of wetlands, salt flats, beaches, dunes and pine forests. Starting at 16th-century watchtower Sal Rossa, built to ward off marauding pirates, the trail meanders south to the salt flats, which attract migratory flamingos in winter, alongside other birds such as black-winged stilts, herons, ospreys and peregrine falcons. From here the hike dips south to the wildly beautiful nudist beach of Es Cavallet and more popular Platja Ses Salines, where flour-white sands ease gently into a glass-blue sea. From the conical watchtower at Ses Portes, there are fine views across the Es Freus strait to Formentera. The walk ends at the pebbly beach of Cap des Falcó, where astonishing sunsets and views of the mythical rock island of Es Vedrà captivate.
Start // Sal Rossa
Finish // Cap des Falcó
Distance // 16km (10 miles)
More info // www.santjosep.net

Clockwise from top: poles marking
the way to Holy Island; white dunes
edging the North Sea in Denmark; a
beach in Ses Salines Natural Park

FROM THE RIVER'S SOURCE ON THE LECHWEG

Follow the free course of a wild Austrian river from its first stirrings to a last big show near one of the world's most storied castles.

D oes the source of a stream offer any clue as to what adventures lie ahead? Will the current swiftly be swallowed up by more forceful rivals, or does it flow on proudly under its own name all the way to the sea?

The river that begins in the sodden patch of grass where I'm treading, 1840m (6037ft) high in the Austrian Alps, competes in the middle league of European waterways: it runs a respectable 256km (159 miles) before handing over to a true champion, the Danube. But within its mountain stretch, the River Lech has been left largely to its own devices, and it's this wildness that's part of the appeal of the hiking path that runs in parallel.

The Lechweg (Lech Way) is waymarked in white stencil on rocks and tree trunks: two sinuous pen-strokes making up a vaguely Gothic-style capital L. With the path taking 125km (78 miles) to descend 1000m (3281ft), it averages out gently. But the founders of the route were aware that sticking faithfully to the riverbank can feel a bit samey after a while, and when the Lech reaches flatter valley floors, and hikers begin to grow complacent, they may suddenly find the path darting up the mountain flanks.

It's a trail whose first stage I had unknowingly followed a dozen times even before it was officially launched in 2012. My family has been coming to the village of Lech (named after the river) for over seven decades, and as I set out for my first day on the Lechweg, my mental map includes its own, unofficial place names, such as the Elvis Memorial Walkway, honouring the Jack Russell terrier of some family friends, daringly rescued by my dad when he fell into some rapids.

The path that follows the first infant gurgles of the Lech darts to and fro over rocks, through wild and open mountain meadows of a

kind that won't be repeated further down the trail. Within two hours I reach the first of the forests that will recur at every stage, alternating with pastures of a lushness that's startling given that they can be covered by snow for up to half the year. While the Lechweg has greater spectacle to come, I already know I will miss this fleeting stretch where the river can still be crossed in a bound or two.

There's a certain dedication to following the Lechweg, in coming to the Alps but then waving aside each offer of a path that leads to the mountains. I get into a pattern similar to watching a subtitled film: chin up to see the stern heads of rock framing the view, then down, perhaps for the flowers by the path. Most are

yellow and purple, but there's also the occasional spray of pink Alpenrose, or gentians in a transcendent shade of blue.

Lech am Arlberg, with its satellite village of Zug, is the first settlement encountered on the path, and not until the Lechweg reaches Füssen right at the end will there be such a variety of restaurants, shops and hotels. Its first settlers got the land that nobody else wanted, and six tough centuries later, their descendants found that travellers from far away were prepared to pay good money to slide around in the snow. When I stop in the village of Holzgau two stages later and 300m (984ft) lower, I admire the famous frescoes on many of its houses – from a time when farmers higher up would not have had the wealth or leisure to paint Baroque frills around their windows.

After Lech village, the gorge-funnelled river and the steeply perched path both aim towards the Biberkopf. On the steep, forested slopes of this pyramid-shaped mountain, it's as if the Lechweg crosses a spiritual boundary between the high realm and the low. After 8km (5 miles) with no sign of habitation, my first sight on reaching the hamlet of Prenten is a field of alpacas. From here on, the valley floor takes on a green-baize smoothness, staked out at short intervals by church steeples, sharply pointed or topped with onion domes. The villages clustered around them each seem to have their own woodcarver's shop, and the rowan trees by the path are thick with orange berries, often distilled into schnapps.

> ## "It's as if the Lechweg crosses a spiritual boundary between the high realm and the low."

Here in the Lechtal (Lech Valley) the mountains that birthed and nurtured the river feel remote but still watchful. Downstream from Stanzach is the Lechzopf (Lech braid), where the pale turquoise waters snake and intertwine freely across wide shingle beds. I venture out onto one gravel bank, where someone has had fun building a mock dam out of driftwood.

A river can only stay unconstrained for so long, and already on the penultimate stage, the trail takes a wide and hill-climbing detour to avoid the Lech's route through the built-up surroundings of Reutte. On the last day, the path spends a whole five hours away from its namesake. After crossing the Austrian–German border, it zigzags down to the Alpsee, a perfectly serene mountain lake that reflects two castles at its far end: Hohenschwangau and the turreted extravagance of Neuschwanstein.

Ever publicity-shy, the path ducks to the left before it gets within range of horse-drawn carriage tours and shops full of the finest Bavarian kitsch. The final reunion comes at the Lechfall, an artificial five-tier cascade set in a gorge just before the castle town of Füssen. I lean on the bridge that spans the churning waters, and gaze downstream. The Lech has most of its course still to run, but already the mountains are fading into memory. **RG**

STEINBOCK

Near the start of the Lechweg stands a bronze statue of an Alpine ibex, sporting splendidly curved horns. The monument commemorates the wild goat, called steinbock in German, which was nearly driven to extinction by the mid-19th century, hanging on only in Italy's Gran Paradiso region. Reintroduced locally in the 1950s, it now thrives on high, rocky slopes.

Clockwise from top: the River Lech keeps almost constant companion along the trail; rowan berries; crossing Austria's longest pedestrian suspension bridge near Holzgau. Previous page: the headwaters of the Lech

ORIENTATION

Start // Formarinalpe, Austria
Finish // Lechfall, Füssen, Germany
Distance // 125km (78 miles)
Duration // Seven to nine days
Getting there // Regular buses from the centre of Lech village serve the early stages of the walk, and with a change of bus in Reutte, it's possible to cover the whole length of the route by public transport.
When to go // Mid-June to early October, though some facilities close in September.
Where to stay // You'll find the widest choice of hotels in Lech and Füssen at the start and end of the route, but villages in between will usually have at least two or three options each, searchable on the Lechweg website. In Holzgau, Hotel Neue Post offers Lechweg packages, as well as baggage forwarding (www.holzgau-wel.com).
More info // www.lechweg.com

*Opposite from top: Hafren Forest –
birthplace of the River Severn; the
Loire River reflecting the grandeur of
the Château de Chambord; Katz Castle
on the banks of the Rhine*

MORE LIKE THIS
RIVERSIDE WALKS

SEVERN WAY, WALES/ENGLAND

The River Severn (or Afon Hafren if you're speaking Welsh) is the longest in Britain, although it's often overlooked compared to the Thames. The Severn Way follows its course from its first stirrings in desolate moorland in the heights of the Cambrian Mountains, until the river opens out into the Severn Estuary, whereupon the path heads back inland again and upstream along the River Avon. After an initial descent through the serried pines of Hafren Forest, the scenery stays hilly until you reach the English border.

When it's not passing willows or apple orchards, the route acts as an historical guide: Wroxeter Roman City, Worcester's medieval cathedral, half-timbered Tudor houses in Shrewsbury, and Ironbridge Gorge – cradle of the Industrial Revolution. Along the river's lower reaches, try to time your walk for an appearance of the Severn bore: a wave up to 2m (6.5ft) high, which surfers can ride upstream for miles.
Start // Pumlumon Fawr
Finish // Bristol
Distance // 338km (210 miles)
More info // www.ldwa.org.uk

GR3 SENTIER DE LA LOIRE, FRANCE

The first of France's official GR (Grande Randonnée) walking paths to be marked out, this is a Francophile pilgrimage of the highest order. The Loire is the longest river to flow entirely within France, and before Paris entrenched its role as capital, the Loire Valley was the country's centre of gravity, as royal courts wandered between a host of chateaux. These turreted visions right out of a Charles Perrault fairy tale remain the first-billed attractions of the route, but gastronomy is a running theme at every stage, from Bleu d'Auvergne cheese in the highlands to fine salt from the marshes of Guérande where the Loire reaches the sea, with the vine-covered hillsides of Sancerre at the halfway mark.
Start // Mont Gerbier-de-Jonc
Finish // La Baule
Distance // 1243km (772 miles)
More info // www.ffrandonnee.fr

RHINE CASTLES TRAIL, GERMANY

Covering a sixth of the Rhine's length, the Rheinburgenweg (Rhine Castles Trail) takes in neither the river's Swiss source nor its Dutch conclusion, but concentrates on what is probably its most famous stretch. The Middle Rhine snakes between steep banks, with vineyards and old-world towns, such as Boppard and Bacharach tucked into the folds. The Rheinburgenweg follows the left bank of the river, with the more challenging Rheinsteig running in parallel on the far side. It's a landscape that inspired Romantic-era poets such as Heinrich Heine and Lord Byron, watched at every stage by castles built over the centuries, from the times of the original robber barons. Look out for small but sturdy Pfalzgrafenstein, set like a battleship in the middle of the river.
Start // Rolandsbogen, north of Rolandseck
Finish // Bingen
Distance // 196km (122 miles)
More info // www.rheinburgenweg.com

GODLY WAYS: IL SENTIERO DEGLI DEI

Follow the Path of the Gods along Italy's awesome Amalfi Coast, a cliff-hugging hike via siren-haunted isles, ancient vineyards and glittering sea views.

The limestone crags of the Monti Lattari poke into a deep-blue sky. Sure-footed goats graze on herby pastures, far from bothered by the verdurous, vertiginous valleys on all sides of them. And, over by the side of the kerb, a film crew zooms in on a testosterone-red Ferrari that's noisily negotiating the tarmac curves.

Well, this is the Amalfi Coast, after all. Glamour central. A place of 1950s beauties in cats'-eye shades, and tanned Adonises all loose trousers and louche charm. An Italian sports car fits right in. But, actually, automobiles of any type are a relatively recent feature here. Until 1815, when Ferdinand II of Bourbon ordered the construction of the Nastro Azzurro (Blue Ribbon), there was no road access to the remote hamlets and tiny fishing villages clinging around these cliffs. Before that, the only way to get between them was to walk. The irony is that, now that human highways have conquered the headlands, what do many of us visitors choose to do? We go old-school and use our feet.

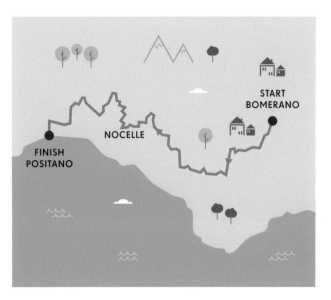

FINISH
POSITANO

NOCELLE

START
BOMERANO

"There's a small, vertigo-inclined part of me that feels an urge to leap for the islands... perhaps the sirens do still sing?"

People have long been drawn to the wildly wonderful Amalfi Coast. Greeks, Romans, Normans, Saracens, Arab-Sicilians and more have left their traces. But for millennia, visitors and settlers alike were reliant on boats or a steep network of footpaths and mule tracks to get around; their grape, olive and lemon harvests had to be hand-carried up staircases hewn from the stone. The Sentiero degli Dei – Path of the Gods – is the most famed of these old farmers' trails, running for around 8km (5 miles) between the hamlets of Bomerano and Nocelle, then onwards to the seaside resort of Positano. And when you don't have to carry a huge basket of fruit on your head, it's the most spectacular of strolls.

Having taken the slow road over the mountains, I arrive in Bomerano. This tiny village sits in Agerola, a district famed for its *fior di latte*, a fresh, sourish mozzarella made from the milk of the local cows. With a short but undulating task ahead, I pop into the little salumeria by the church to pick up some fresh focaccia and balls of the smooth white cheese, in case I happen to get peckish.

Leaving the piazza, I weave through the narrow streets to find the trailhead sign: *Benvenuti sul Sentiero degli Dei*. Immediately ahead the coast unfurls; in both directions great grey dolomitic rock surges up from the dazzling sea. It's rugged and raw, yet somehow has been semi-tamed: farming terraces cut into the sheer slopes, farmhouses perch, paths wriggle. It's an incredible combination of Mother Nature and human tenacity. A case in

point: right here is the Grotta del Biscotto, where strange, rust-like geological formations sit alongside the ruins of ancient dwellings embedded in the walls.

I turn to the west, sun on my back, and let Amalfi work its magic. The trail is mostly downhill in this direction – a descent from Bomerano (at around 580m/1903ft) to sea-level Positano – but concentration is required. Some parts are narrow, dropping off to the waves. Some require scrambling. Virtually all is rough and uneven. But the rewards are unending. A peregrine falcon hovers above, trained on some unsuspecting prey; when the raptor finally makes its dive I hear the swoosh of its lightning-quick wings. There are deep-green gullies cloaked in holm oaks, pungent thyme and sweet wild roses. There are teetering vineyards, some cultivating gnarled *ped'e palomma*, Campania's oldest grape variety. And there are farmhouses balanced on improbable precipices, surely reliant on the trail's titular gods for their continued survival.

In the distance, the chi-chi island of Capri provides the dot of the Amalfi Coast's exclamation mark. Nearer though, the glittering blue is broken by a smaller scatter of offshore rocks – the Sirenusas. According to Greek myth, this archipelago was once inhabited by sirens, dangerous bird-women whose beautiful music lured sailors to their deaths. I strain to listen, and do hear a melody. I'm fairly sure it's just the birds, but there's a small, vertigo-inclined part of me that feels an urge to leap for

WHEN LIFE GIVES YOU LEMONS

The Amalfi lemon (*Sfusato Amalfitano*) has Protected Geographical Indication status and is known for its flavoursome rind, lack of bitterness and sweet aroma. When scurvy-beating lemons became compulsory for sailors in the late 18th century, Amalfi farmers hacked out cliff terraces to cope with demand. Now, with a decline in the skilled farmers who maintain the groves, the landscape's integrity is at risk.

From left: looking towards Positano and Capri from the Path of the Gods; fishers discuss the day's catch; famed Amalfi lemons. Previous page: colourful homes on the Positano hillside

the islands, to dive off this cliff and plummet down into the sea. Perhaps the sirens do still sing?

Far below, the white pumice-stone houses of Praiano are stacked on the slopes. There are trails that detour down there, but I continue over the rock crags, relishing occasional forest shade but largely at the mercy of the Mediterranean sun. There are plenty of other walkers – families, route-marchers, red-faced tourists in inappropriate footwear. We're all equally bewitched by the view.

I pause in Nocelle for my picnic, gazing out to sea just as the coastguards once did. At around 400m (1312ft), the village was an ideal vantage point for spotting pirate ships. Today it passes its time in sleepy fashion; there's little more here than a family trattoria and a muss of broom bushes, vineyards, and lemon groves growing the Amalfi citruses craved by chefs worldwide.

Nocelle is technically the end of the Sentiero degli Dei, and you can catch a bus from here to Positano. But, feeling some loyalty to the hardy forebears who had no choice, I walk down instead, a thigh-jellying descent of 1700 steps to reach the Mediterranean.

Standing in the harbour, I turn to look back at the houses of Positano, themselves rippling wave-like down the cliffs in a palette of lemon-yellow, pale peach and bold terracotta. I shift my gaze further up to pick out the path whence I came. And I raise my eyes higher still, to where the mountaintops meet the sky, and where the gods surely must be smiling down on this walk. **SB**

ORIENTATION

Start // Bomerano
Finish // Positano (or Nocelle)
Distance // 8km (5 miles)
Duration // Three hours
Getting there // Buses run from Amalfi to Agerola; journey time is around two hours. Buses from Positano back to Amalfi take one hour. Private transfers are possible but expensive for individuals.
What to wear // T-shirt, shorts and sensible shoes. A warm layer and waterproof, just in case. A sun hat is essential.
When to go // April to June and September to October are quieter and cooler than peak summer months.
What to take // A head for heights. Sunscreen and water.
Need to know // The route is waymarked by white-and-red '02' signs. A guide is not necessary but can be arranged.

MORE LIKE THIS
ITALIAN COASTAL WALKS

CINQUE TERRE HIGH TRAIL, LIGURIA

The oh-so-picturesque medieval fishing villages of the Cinque Terre ('Five Lands') tumble down the cliffs of the Ligurian Riviera, seemingly detached from the rest of the world. A network of centuries-old coastal paths links them, the most popular of which is the (12km) 7.5-mile Sentiero Azzurro (Blue Trail). However, a tougher but less-trodden option is the High Path No 1, which takes a loftier route above Monterosso al Mare, Vernazza, Corniglia, Manarola and Riomaggiore, offering sea-glittery views throughout. Going from south to north, the trail starts in the harbour town of Porto Venere and follows the coastal range, running via fragrant pine, vineyards and tiny hamlets to Levanto. A highlight is reaching the Sella di Punta Mesco, from where you can look out over all five villages at once.

Start // Porto Venere
Finish // Levanto
Distance // 40km (25 miles)
More info // www.incinqueterre.com

TRAIL OF THE FOUR BEACHES, PUGLIA

The Sentiero delle Quattro Spiagge (Trail of the Four Beaches) traces the edges of the wild Gargano Peninsula, a promontory of limestone cliffs, secret grottoes, aged forests, and almond and olive groves protected within a national park in Italy's lesser-visited heel. From the pretty little seaside resort of Mattinata the path leads northwards via bird-rich valleys, high cliffs fuzzed by pungent pine, a 450m (1476ft) lookout, and a succession of beautiful coves where it's virtually impossible not to leap into the crystal-clear waters. You'll definitely want to pause at the Baia dei Mergoli, a bay that is sweetly scented by citrus groves and hugged by sheer white cliffs; a precarious-looking rock arch sits just offshore, daring you to swim through...

Start // Mattinata
Finish // Vignanotica Bay
Distance // 21km (13 miles)

STROMBOLI CLIMB, AEOLIAN ISLANDS, SICILY

Stromboli is like a big black beast breathing fire and fury in the middle of the Tyrrhenian Sea. Indeed, this super-active 924m (3031ft) volcano-island has been erupting almost continuously for around 2000 years. Miraculously, you're still permitted to climb it, as long as you join a guided group. Trips up its ashen flanks usually leave late afternoon or early evening to ensure that you arrive at the summit in time to see a spectacular sunset sinking into the sea. It also means you're in time to appreciate the full effects of Stromboli's impressive red-hot magma-spewing pyrotechnics against the darkening sky. The descent is then completed by head-torch, lunar glow, star twinkle and the lights of the Italian mainland dancing across the waves.

Start/Finish // Stromboli town
Distance // 8km (5 miles)
More info // www.magmatrek.it

From top: Riomaggiore, one of the Cinque Terre; curious coastal rocks in Puglia

THE DINGLE WAY

A demanding walk around a spectacular Atlantic peninsula in the south of Ireland, rich in early Christian remains, chieftain's castles, polar explorers, and pubs pulsing with music.

It was late afternoon when I arrived at the South Pole. That morning I'd crossed from coast to coast over the Slieve Mish Mountains at the point where the Dingle Peninsula joins the 'mainland' of County Kerry. The narrow neck of high ground and the way the peninsula ran far out into the sea gave me the feeling of being on an Atlantic island, remote from the rest of Ireland. My route had followed a variety of small roads, unpaved boreens (lanes) and rugged tracks. The September weather had been as varied as the route, with gusting winds, showers of rain and sudden calms. As I started the descent towards the beach at Inch the sky cleared and shafts of sunlight lit up the long crescent

of white sand and turned the waters of Dingle Bay electric blue. They might have been Caribbean colours but in the mercurial Irish weather the azures and turquoises had the fleeting come-and-go quality of the more unsettled Kerry climate. As I walked on to the pub a curtain of rain was already coming in over the hills.

The South Pole Inn, at Annascaul, is where local man Tom Crean settled after working with Scott and Shackleton on three Antarctic expeditions. Sitting at the bar I supped a pint of stout while looking at the framed black-and-white photographs of snow fields, ships caught in ice, and polar landscapes. Shackleton had relied on Crean for the open-boat rescue trip from Elephant Island to South

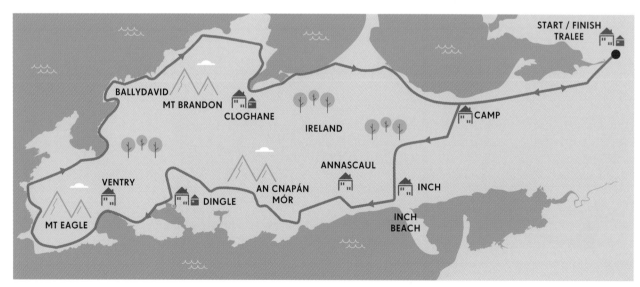

Georgia after the wreck of the *Endurance* in pack ice, describing him as resourceful, strong and always cheerful.

Crean's virtues, especially the being cheerful bit, are what you want when walking the 180km (112 miles) of the Dingle Way. You need a bit of focus, too. This was my third attempt to walk the whole route. Previously I'd got sidetracked into following pilgrim routes across the mountains rather than sticking to the way around the coast. Another time, pubs alive with traditional music kept me in Dingle for days, happier playing harmonica than walking out in the rain. This time I had left Tralee, the way's start point, determined to do better.

The next day's stage, from Annascaul to Dingle town, rollercoastered – if slowly, at walking pace – back and forth between high ground and the coast. So, there was Minard's 16th-century sea-level castle, then a traverse high across the flank of An Cnapán Mór, before a final straight track down into town. There was a night of bars, music and dancing, but early morning sun lured me back onto the trail, and soon I was kicking my way across the sands fringing Ventry Bay before heading around Mt Eagle. I found and crawled into a hermit's cell, like a stone beehive, to marvel at the preternatural silence they gave in this weather-busy landscape. Cliff walking above Ballydavid, I stopped to watch red-beaked, black-feathered choughs tumbling on the updraughts, and to look down on a large seal lounging in the swell like a contentedly plump man in a spa pool. The seal might have been peaceful, but the history of this coast told of tumultuous times: Viking raids – they'd left the Norse name Smerwick attached to one harbour I'd passed – and lost Armada galleons. More recent sea-going exploits were made by locals rowing traditional canvas-skinned currachs. Such a skin boat was a key component in Dingle's most enduring legend: St Brendan's voyage to America, a trip allegedly made in a leather boat from Brandon Creek.

St Brendan is celebrated in the names of many natural features on the Dingle Peninsula, including the most impressive landmark of

ST BRENDAN'S VOYAGE

Based on medieval texts describing 'The Voyage of St Brendan', some believe that the 6th-century Dingle abbot sailed a currach-like leather-skinned boat between Ireland and America. In the 1970s, historian and adventurer Tim Severin and crew navigated a replica boat from Brandon Creek to Newfoundland via the Hebrides and Iceland. Severin noted the icebergs, volcanoes and whales that recalled the 'crystal towers', 'mountains hurling rocks' and 'sea monsters', ascribed to St Brendan's story.

Clockwise from top: waterfall on the way to Conor Pass; traditional music in Dingle; the ruins of Minard Castle. Previous page: sheep looking out to the Blasket Islands from the Dingle Peninsula

"I found and crawled into a hermit's cell... to marvel at the preternatural silence they gave in this weather-busy landscape."

them all. Mt Brandon – Brendan's Mountain – Ireland's ninth-highest peak, had been on my horizon for the past few days of walking. Here the spine of high ground running the length of the peninsula rises higher, climbing up the Brandon Range to just under 1000m (3281ft). It made the Dingle Way, which so far had been a fairly low-level, sometimes muddy, but mainly easy walk, a serious challenge.

After a pint in An Bóthar Pub, ('If you can't see the top of Brandon it's already raining up there. If you can see it then it's going to rain soon,' I was advised from behind the bar), I set off on a rough track that soon became a steep, rocky path. For a while I climbed fast enough to stay in the last rays of light, even as the sun fell towards the western horizon and America, while the shadows, and then the actual darkness, rose up the hillside behind me. It was too late in the autumn day to cross the Brandon Range that night but I'd wanted the experience of being up high to watch the sunset and the sunrise, and had planned for a night sleeping out.

From high up on the mountain's side I looked out over the Atlantic. The sky lit up with streaks of red and gold, then slowly dimmed into violets and mauves and finally, still slowly, darkened into deep blue-black. Ahead of me there remained the north coast of the peninsula to walk, with its dunes, small harbours, and the hill tracks that would take me back to Tralee. But it was all downhill from this point and I was confident that this time I'd finally complete the whole of the Dingle Way without getting sidetracked. **JW**

ORIENTATION

Start/Finish // Tralee, County Kerry
Distance // 180km (112 miles)
Duration // Seven to ten days
Getting there // Trains from Dublin or Cork to Tralee.
When to go // Early autumn (September to October) and late spring (April to May) are ideal. In winter much infrastructure is closed. Summer tourist traffic can make road walking frustrating.
What to wear // Good walking boots and rain gear is essential. For crossing Mt Brandon a compass, proper map and high-ground hiking kit is recommended.
Where to eat // Dingle is where to blow-out in restaurants and pubs. Otherwise, grab meals in village cafes.
Things to know // If you play a walk-friendly musical instrument, there'll be chances to play in traditional Irish music sessions along the way.
More info // www.dingleway.com

MORE LIKE THIS
IRISH TRAILS

WICKLOW WAY

Established in 1980 as Ireland's first long-distance way-marked trail, the Wicklow Way is a walk of two very different halves. The southern section means hiking on (mostly) small peaceful lanes through farmland, while the northern path runs through the Wicklow Mountains. This section crosses Ireland's largest continuous upland area and, with its bogs, rough tracks and exposed vastness, can make navigation and comfortable walking challenging in poor weather.

Rewards include views of – or perhaps a side trip to – Lugnaquilla, Ireland's highest peak outside Kerry, as well as waterfalls, hidden valleys and high passes. The well-preserved early Christian monastic settlement at Glendalough, with its 'stone rocket' round tower, is on the route. Deer are a common sight, while far rarer but worth looking out for is the flash-by flight of a hunting merlin, Ireland's smallest falcon.

Start // Clonegal Village, County Carlow
Finish // Marlay Park, Dublin
Distance // 127 km (79 miles)
More info // www.wicklowway.com

GREAT WESTERN GREENWAY

The first, and longest, of a new generation of traffic-free shared walking and cycling routes, the Greenway follows the line of the old Westport Railway that once carried local produce and many 19th-century tourists to Achill Island in the far west of Ireland. Though decommissioned in the 1930s, many of the original platforms, station cottages and bridges remain, and the route follows the landscape's lowest, flattest contours, giving easy walking. The southeast section, from Westport, gives views over Clew Bay with its hundreds of islands, and, further out to sea, the bulk of Clare Island: the stronghold of the 16th-century 'Pirate Queen', Grace O'Malley. Beyond Mulranny the gravel track skirts high ground in the shadow of the Nephin Beg Range to the northeast. Permanent artworks draw on the history of the route, like the piles of bronze suitcases recalling when passengers threw their luggage from the train near their homes to be picked up when they walked back.

Start // Westport
Finish // Achill Island
Distance // 42km (26 miles)
More info // www.greenway.ie

GRAND CANAL WAY

The Grand Canal Way is a little-used, and mostly off-road, towpath route across the centre of Ireland, running between the Dublin and the Shannon River. It may have taken nearly 50 years to build the canal, but after it finally opened in 1804 it was operational for 150 years. Goods carried included the ingredients for the Guinness Brewery and barrels of their finished product, while passenger boats pulled by galloping horses provided speedy transport across the country. Now only used as a leisure waterway, the 43 locks, aqueducts, waterside towns and branch lines form a tranquil linear park. The canal also provides a wildlife corridor for otters, bats, kingfishers, dragonflies and other wildlife. The vast and bleak Bog of Allen might have caused the canal builders problems, but thanks to them, walkers are left with a well-made raised towpath that makes the crossing of Ireland on foot from the east coast to the Shannon River possible in all weathers.

Start // Third Lock, Inchicore, Dublin
Finish // Shannon Harbour
Distance // 126km (78 miles)
More info // www.sportireland.ie

Clockwise from top: the Grand Canal passing through central Dublin; echoes of the former Westport Railway; the heather-lined Wicklow Way

IN THE SHADOW OF THE ALETSCH GLACIER

With views of the Aletsch Glacier and snow-encrusted summits to make your heart sing, this is hands-down one of Switzerland's most ravishing day hikes.

t is not only me who is dumbstruck by the view. As I peer across the seemingly infinite frozen swoop of the Aletsch Glacier and up to the dark horns of 4000m- (13,123ft)-high mountains, a posse of inquisitive Valais blacknose sheep joins me. With dreadlocks flopping in their eyes, I'm surprised they can see anything at all, yet they prance around with the agility of mountain goats, totally at ease in this wilderness of rock and ice. One comes over and licks my hand by way of a *wilkommen* – they seem pretty friendly as sheep go.

The scene feels ridiculously Swiss: the cute-as-can-be sheep, the colossal glacier raging its way past peaks as high as the sky. Part *Heidi*, part box-office blockbuster. If this were anywhere else, it would probably be off-bounds or accessible to only the most intrepid of climbers. But, this being Switzerland, where nature is harnessed in the most delightful and sustainable way, you can reach it on a moderately challenging day hike. One of the most sensational you will find anywhere in the Alps, in fact, as I am now discovering.

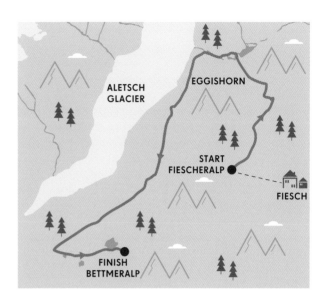

Even the tiniest hamlet, barely a speck on the map, has a cable car in Switzerland, where the obsession for altitude and the outdoors knows no limits. My high-elevation hike predictably began with a ride in one from Fiesch, a village in the Goms region of the Rhône Valley, where blackened timber chalets are dwarfed by the grand scale of their backdrop, with spruce forests sweeping up to some of the country's highest mountains. As tantalising as the views are from below, it isn't until I have taken the cable car up to Fiescheralp at 2212m (7257ft) that I get a proper sense of what is to come.

As I hit the trail heading north towards Eggishorn, silver-grey, doe-eyed cows clang their bells, creating a fitting soundtrack for the grandstand views that begin to open up around me: the crown-like peaks of the Aletsch Arena, the more distant (yet ever distinctive) pyramid of the Matternhorn and, further away still and over the border in France, the mighty Mont Blanc etched on the horizon.

A sharp early summer light makes the Bernese Alps feel as though they have been made fresh this morning. The first Alpenrosen (snowroses) are making the high pastures blush pink. Bilberries are coming into flower. The sky is so blue it looks Photoshopped. Mountains 4000m (13,123ft) high are topped with the lightest dusting of snow – like frosting on a cake.

> "Even the tiniest hamlet, barely a speck on the map, has a cable car in Switzerland."

I lunge for my camera as I reach a viewpoint overlooking the Fiescher Glacier, a moraine-streaked swirl of eternal ice, which at 16km (10 miles) long is the second-longest glacier in the Alps. The glacier snakes down from the eastern flank of Grosses Fiescherhorn, a razor-edge peak at 4049m (13,284ft). Dark mountains thrust up like shark fins above it. I nod a *grüezi* (hello) to the couple of other walkers up here on this fine day, as wholly captivated by the vista as I am.

Buoyed by the panorama, I wind around the slopes above Fieschertal and up through a grassy, rock-strewn gully. At first slow and steady, the ascent gradually steepens as I round switchbacks to a wooden cross erected on a rock platform. The handy white-red-white waymarkings that signal a mountain trail in Switzerland keep me on track as I head westward across rocky ledges to the remote valley of Märjela. As if on cue, a rustic mountain hut slides into view, the Gletscherstube. But my dreams of rösti and cold beer are blown out of the water when I find it isn't open until July, more than a month away.

Still, the shores of nearby Märjelensee are as a phenomenal a picnic spot as any. This milky turquoise splash of a lake is buttressed by immense mountains and the rim of the Aletsch Glacier. The view has few rivals in Europe: horn-shaped peaks glower down, among them the 4193m (13,757ft) Aletschhorn, a

HIGH SUSPENSE

If you fancy ramping up the adventure further, swing across to the 124m- (407ft)-long Aletschji–Grünsee suspension bridge, which takes a gigantic leap across the wild, 80m-(262ft)-deep Massa Gorge. Dangling between forested crags that rise above a milk-blue glacial river, the bridge is the climax of the 11km (7-mile), four-hour hike between Riederalp and Belalp, commanding gasp-eliciting views of the tongue of the Aletsch Glacier. Surefootedness and a head for heights are prerequisites. The trail is accessible from June to October.

Clockwise from top: the winding Aletsch Glacier; crossing the Aletschji-Grünsee suspension bridge; easy access to the trail. Previous page: the Aletsch Glacier – the largest glacier in the Swiss Alps

pearly white fang of a mountain. Looking north there is the holy trinity of the Bernese Alps: Eiger, Mönch and Jungfrau.

As I press on along a rocky ridge, I am blown away by the majesty of the Aletsch Glacier, which now remains my constant companion, as the path shadows the deeply crevassed ice, which streams down around the Aletschhorn like a three-lane superhighway. Though it has suffered the same retreating fate as many of the world's glaciers in the face of global warming, this 23km (14-mile) river of ice is still Europe's longest and, as such, the showpiece of the Unesco World Heritage Jungfrau-Aletsch-Bietschhorn region. It's so ludicrously beautiful it almost seems unreal. And indeed Tolkien found much fictional inspiration in these dark, snarling mountains, which feel more than a little like Middle Earth.

The Aletschwald softens the picture somewhat: a pretty sweep of Swiss stone pine forest, where I startle a chamois into flight and set the marmots off whistling with my approaching footsteps. I pass jewel-coloured tarns as I continue along a ridge and on to the grassy slopes of Moosfluh, where a strategically placed bench offers staggering glacier views.

I soon reach the glass-blue lake of Blausee, where the mountains pause to admire their reflection. From here it is just a stone's throw to my chalet for the night in Bettmeralp. But I'm in no rush to leave. So instead I throw down my backpack, take out the last of the cheese and watch the day fade into a pastel sunset, summits glowing the softest gold-pink as valley and glacier fall slowly into shadow. **KW**

ORIENTATION

Start // Fiescheralp
Finish // Bettmeralp
Distance // 17km (10.5 miles)
Duration // Five to six hours
Getting there // Regional trains link Fiesch to Brig, with high-speed onward connections to major Swiss cities, including the capital Bern and Zurich (www.sbb.ch).
When to go // June to September.
Where to stay and eat // Stop for a snack or break up the walk into two days with an overnight stay at the Gletscherstube (www.gletscherstube.ch), open from early July to mid-October.
What to pack // Bring a fleece, waterproofs and sturdy walking boots, plus a hat and sunscreen. Take ample water and snacks; if the hut is closed there is little in the way of sustenance en route.
More info // www.aletscharena.ch

*Opposite: ice climbing on
Svínafellsjökull glacier*

MORE LIKE THIS
GLACIER HIKES

SVÍNAFELLSJÖKULL, ICELAND

Spilling between dark, gnarly mountains
like crushed meringue, Svínafellsjökull
is the showstopper in Iceland's high
drama Vatnajökull National Park. The
spectacularly crevassed and contorted
glacier is an outlet of the mighty
Vatnajökull, Europe's largest and most
voluminous ice cap, which spreads across
8300 sq km (3205 sq miles). The blues and
greens of the ice are surreal, whether seen
on a dark winter's day or in the dazzle of
summer. A guide is essential for heading
out onto the ice – as is the right gear
(crampons, axe and helmet) – whether
you want to embark on a half-day hike or
try your hand at ice climbing. The glacier's
beauty has not gone unnoticed: it featured
in *Game of Thrones* season seven as the
region 'north of the Wall'.
**Start/Finish // Most guided glacier
hikes begin at the car park and visitor
centre off Route 998 (itself just off the
Ring Rd that encircles the country).
More info // www.extremeiceland.
is; www.guidetoiceland.is; www.
funiceland.is**

GROSSGLOCKNER PASTERZE GLACIER, AUSTRIA

The Pasterze Glacier is the icing on the
bell-shaped cake of Grossglockner,
Austria's highest peak at 3798m (12,461ft).
Slithering down from the snow-capped
mountains that are the country's highest,
this 8.5km (5-mile) swirl of fissured ice is
rapidly retreating, so see it while you can.
After a dramatic, hairpin-bend-riddled drive
on the Grossglockner High Alpine Rd up
to the starting point, Kaiser-Franz-Josefs-
Höhe, you can hook onto a family-friendly
guided walk across the ice. Slightly more
challenging, however, is trekking the
Glacier Trail with a park ranger, which
gets you up close and personal with this
astonishing landscape of rock and ice.
**Start/Finish // Visitor centre at Kaiser-
Franz-Josefs-Höhe
More info // www.nationalpark-
hohetauern.at; advance booking is
essential**

BØDALSBREEN, NORWAY

Glaciers, blue ice and imperious mountains
shape the Jostedalsbreen National Park
the way skyscrapers shape Manhatten.
This utterly wild corner of Norway's western
fjordland is a delight and its centrepiece
is the Jostedalsbreen ice cap, the largest
in Europe covering a whopping 487 sq km
(188 sq miles). The ice cap dips its frozen
fingers into the deeply riven surrounding
valleys, one of which is the Bødalen Valley, a
God-like canvas of pastures, forests, raging
waterfalls and craggy peaks. An hour-long
stomp through it brings you to Bødalsbreen,
a dramatically fissured, moraine-streaked
glacier located 585m (1919ft) above sea
level. Some of the best photo-ops are from
the azure-blue lake at its foot. It's no longer
possible to actually walk on the ice because
of dangerous crevasses.
**Start/Finish // Bødalsseter,
Jostedalsbreen National Park
More info // www.fjordnorway.com;
www.visitnorway.com**

A WALK THROUGH TIME: THE THAMES PATH

Urban, easy, with plenty of concrete. Nevertheless, a day spent walking the Thames through central London shows off constructed beauty spanning more than a thousand years.

I hear you: surely I'm not saying that 8.5km (5.3 miles) of paved riverside path in the middle of Europe's biggest city is one of the epic hikes of Europe? Surely?

But yes, that's exactly what I'm saying.

For a hike to be truly epic – a real world-class, mind-blowing zinger – what does it need?

Most people would put scenery at the top of the list. You'll want to be astounded by dramatic views, to round corners and stop with a gasp at the new vista that's suddenly opened up before you. You'll know you're somewhere truly staggering when you get that feeling of panic that you can't take it all in – the view overwhelms you. Or that feeling when the view becomes unreal, because it looks like you've entered a film set.

But walk from Tower Bridge to Lambeth Bridge and you will see some of the finest scenery on earth. You'll start at the oldest palace, fortress and prison in Europe, the Tower of London; then walk across the most famous bridge in the world (sorry, San Francisco), Tower Bridge. The views are instantly spectacular – as you get over the water, the river gives you the space you need for long views – one of the reasons this particular route through London is so visually rewarding.

The skyline from here may not be natural, but the pinnacles and spires are every bit as sublime as those above Chamonix or Jackson Hole. There's the Shard, the Gherkin, the Cheesegrater, the Walkie-Talkie – each a gleaming testament to the human capacity to create beauty from glass, steel and concrete...and to Londoners' capacity to give anything a ridiculous nickname.

As you reach the South Bank and stroll along the broad walkway past City Hall, the incongruity of the skyscrapers next to the squat

11th-century Tower and the Victorian Gothic marvel of Tower Bridge becomes apparent. It brings a smile to your face.

But views aren't everything. What about local life? Is this hike epic from a cultural point of view? You betcha. The people watching is as good as the view. The Thames Path is spacious here, especially after the crush on Tower Bridge, so it's easier to excuse the selfie-sticks jammed in your face, the families stopping in your path to pose or point, the teenagers cycling too fast and too close. Enjoy the show. A band is playing in The Scoop, an open amphitheatre. Buskers, floating Yodas and giant bubbles compete for the attentions – and cash – of kids walking past. Mixed in with

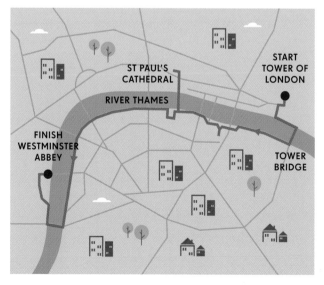

the joggers, hand-holding couples, lunching bankers and dog-walkers, you'll see more nationalities here than almost anywhere else on earth. This is, after all, the most visited city on the planet.

Hopefully by now you're feeling hungry. Passing under London Bridge, your nose will start to lead you. Borough Market, under the railway arches, is a 1000-year-old food market where wholesalers supplying restaurants and pubs crowd next to stalls catering for office workers and tourists. Your eyes will be drawn to French pastries, Welsh cheeses and North Sea fish; but your nose will win, tempted by Indian dosa, Dutch pancakes and English bacon. Grab a taste from as many stalls as you can, make your choice, then sit under the spire of Southwark Cathedral to eat. If good food and drink make a hike epic, there would be no competition.

But what about a bit of history, art and culture to add to the all-round epic-ness? Easy. This next stretch of the Thames is historic, even by London standards. Whether you choose to stop for a show at Shakespeare's Globe, whisper across the dome of St Paul's, or contemplate the works of Picasso, Rothko and Warhol at Tate Modern, your main problem is getting this tiny hike done in just one day when there's so much to stop you in your tracks.

But as you walk further and become accustomed to the changing views, the mishmash of architecture and the human

"You'll see more nationalities here than almost anywhere else on earth."

wildlife on show, two subtleties of this particular hike become apparent. The first is the presence of the river. At the start of the walk it is no more than a handy gap between you and the view, a handrail to stop you getting lost. But spend a few hours in its company and you see the tide change, watch eddies swirl behind the piers of the bridges as the current flows swift. You notice the traffic on the river, not just the roads – pleasure cruises full of tourists, police boats speeding up and down, barges carrying goodness-knows-what. Gulls wheel above, screeching. As the tide goes out, the bridges seem to grow taller, and the riverbanks reveal themselves. A bulldog chases a stick, a couple of amateur archaeologists pick their way along the water's edge. All the while, the river flows by. The Thames isn't big by global standards, but it is the heart of this city today, as it has been for 2000 years.

The second thing you'll notice is that this hike isn't just about landscape. The soundscape is just as varied and interesting. Sure, there's traffic sometimes. But most of the time, there are the sounds of water, boats and gulls to remind you that you're in a port. You hear snatches of conversations in Cockney and Catalan, Arabic and Urdu. Sounds dip in and out. Eaters and drinkers add hubbub, punctuated by raucous laughs. Music undercuts it all.

It may not be natural beauty, but if you want to spend a day marvelling at what others have created, then a stroll along the banks of the Thames is, well...epic. **PP**

ROYAL PERKS

While Tower Bridge to Lambeth Bridge hits the most sights, the section from Hampton Court Bridge to Richmond Bridge is almost as spectacular, but shows a different side to the city. It starts at King Henry VIII's Hampton Court Palace and meanders past stately homes and country parks built as weekend retreats in centuries past. Or the keen can walk the whole 296km (184 miles) from the source of the Thames to the sea.

Opposite, clockwise from top: looking west along the Thames past Tower Bridge; the route starts at the Tower of London; stopping for supplies at Borough Market. Previous page: St Paul's Cathedral

ORIENTATION

Start // Tower Hill Underground station, London
Finish // Westminster Underground station, London
Distance // 8.54km (5.3 miles)
Duration // Allow at least a full day to visit some of the attractions. This is a route that is worth revisiting.
Getting there // London has four international airports. The nearest stations are Tower Hill and Tower Gateway.
Attractions // Choose just two or three from this list to visit, and try to pre-book online: Tower of London; Tower Bridge Exhibition; HMS *Belfast*; Borough Market; The Clink Prison Museum; Shakespeare's Globe; Tate Modern; St Paul's Cathedral; concerts, theatre and cinema at the South Bank Centre; London Eye; Westminster Abbey.
More info // Detailed route descriptions and maps can be found at https://tfl.gov.uk/modes/walking/thames-path.

MORE LIKE THIS
URBAN HISTORY WALKS

BERLIN WALL TRAIL, BERLIN

Where once there was concrete 3.6m (12ft) high, patrol guards and a 'death strip' for daredevils attempting escape, now there are but scant remains of the Berlin Wall, which divided the former East and West Germany from 1961 to the epoch-defining day when it fell in 1989. Tracing its former path, the history-loaded Berlin Wall Trail (Mauerweg), also doable by bike, provides a fascinating insight into the era, as it takes in wall remnants and memorials along the old patrol route. You'll begin in the city's beating heart, observing icons of the GDR such as Checkpoint Charlie, skyscraping Potsdamer Platz and the East Side Gallery, the longest stretch of the wall at 1.3km (0.8 miles) and now the world's largest open-air mural collection. From here you're thrust into surprisingly peaceful countryside, following the Teltow Canal, then heading through fields and woodlands to Wannsee lake. On the return leg to Berlin, the trail threads through the Spandau Forest and along the banks of the Havel River.
Start/Finish // Hermsdorf
Distance // 160km (99 miles)
More info // www.berlin.de

VIA APPIA ANTICA, ROME

Built and named after the politically powerful consul Appius Claudius Caecus, who laid the first 90km (56-mile) section in 312 BCE, ancient Rome's *regina viarum* (queen of roads) was extended in 190 BCE to reach Brindisi on the Adriatic Sea. The road that once connected an empire still remains; its cobbles grooved with chariot wheels and polished smooth by millennia of shoe leather. The first leg of the hike in Rome is a feast of ancient history. It begins at the 5th-century Porta San Sebastiano, the largest of the gates in the Aurelian Wall, then makes its way to Parco Appia Antica, essentially a giant open-air museum, flanked by fields and pine trees, which turns up the archaeological heat with its classical remains, mausoleums, graves and tombstones. Unmissables include the 2nd-century Villa dei Quintili, with its well-preserved baths complex, and the cavernous Catacombe di San Callisto, where dozens of popes and martyrs lie buried.
Start // Porta San Sebastiano
Finish // Parco Appia Antica
Distance // 16km (10 miles)
More info // www.parcoappiaantica.it

BELÉM, LISBON

The Rio Tejo is broad, the views expansive and the lure of the Atlantic irresistible in Belém on Lisbon's western cusp. A saunter through this nautical-flavoured neighbourhood catapults you back to Portugal's golden Age of Discovery – the 15th and 16th centuries – when explorers like Vasco da Gama set sail for lands rich in gold and spices. Start on Praça do Império, backdropped by the Mosteiro dos Jerónimos. This whimsical fantasy of a monastery, commissioned by Manuel I to trumpet Vasco da Gama's discovery of a sea route to India in 1498, reveals a riot of ornate detail in its honey-stone cloisters. Other notable stops include the mosaic map on the riverfront promenade, charting the routes of Portuguese mariners, and the 52m (171ft) *Padrão dos Descobrimentos* (Monument of the Discoveries), caught like a caravel in mid-swell. The walk culminates at Torre de Belém, an icon of the age and a prime example of Manueline style.
Start // Praça do Império
Finish // Torre de Belém
Distance // 2.5km (1.6 miles)
More info // www.visitlisboa.com

Clockwise from top: 'World's People' by Schamil Gimajew, the East Side Gallery, Berlin; Monument of the Discoveries, Lisbon; the cobbled Via Appia Antica, Rome

PORTUGUESE COASTAL WAY

*Inhale the sea breeze on a lesser-trodden, Atlantic-side alternative
to the Camino de Santiago, via the Portuguese coast.*

It was the most perfect day on the northern Portuguese coast: blazing blue, hot without fierceness, the wind stirring up the Atlantic swell and salt-spritzing the air. Ahead, the trail wriggled into the distance, skirting the shore, weaving between sand dunes and sail-less windmills. I hefted my pack onto my shoulders, adjusted my hat and did the only thing left to do: I started to walk.

The definition of pilgrimage? 'A journey to a place associated with someone or something well known or respected'. But why bother? When medieval devotees set off for Santiago de Compostela – as I was doing now – they were on a religious mission; they walked from all corners of the continent to prostrate themselves before the remains of St James, whose bones were allegedly found in the Galician countryside in the early 9th century. Within 300 years, that spot had become one of Europe's most important pilgrimage sites.

And so it is again today. Numbers of pilgrims following various Caminos to Santiago – the Ways of St James – are booming. In 1988 just 3501 *peregrinos* (pilgrims) made the journey. In 1998, it was 30,126; 125,141 in 2008; 327,378 in 2018. Religion still draws some. I met two Swedish ladies in their 70s who were on their eighth hike to Santiago: 'It will make it faster for us to get into heaven,' they told me. But many Camino walkers are not Catholic, or of any faith. Yet still they come.

Because a pilgrimage isn't just a walk. It is to travel with a sense of purpose, with a defined goal, and in so doing, strip everything else away. It is an escape from everyday life to look from a different perspective. In a world of escalating noise and complication, the simplicity and motility of a pilgrimage can offer salvation no matter what your beliefs.

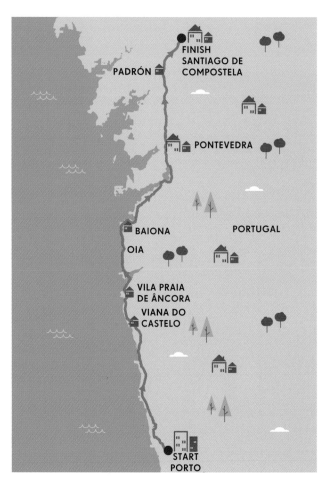

FINISH
SANTIAGO DE
COMPOSTELA

PADRÓN

PONTEVEDRA

BAIONA

OIA

PORTUGAL

VILA PRAIA
DE ÂNCORA

VIANA DO
CASTELO

START
PORTO

I felt this almost immediately. I was following some of the Portuguese Coastal Way, which runs from Porto to Santiago, hugging the Atlantic for most of its length before joining the inland Portuguese Camino for the last few days, when it hops the border into Spain. The coastal route was only designated an official Camino in 2016 and remains far less used than either the inland journey, or the classic Camino Francés across northern Spain.

All this meant that, to begin with, I had the trail mostly to myself. My companions were gulls and waders, piles of pebbles and flour-soft beaches, empty lanes and the odd beachcomber foraging for seaweed. In the town of Viana do Castelo I joined the locals at a port-side restaurant and ate the freshest of fish. In Vila Praia de Âncora, I wandered into the church to find it packed with tinselled floats, waiting to be paraded at a fiesta. But I saw no other pilgrims.

Soon I was in Spain, where the coastal way passes Oia's 12th-century monastery and Baiona's Monterreal Castle (now a swish hotel). From the battlements I watched as the Vigo estuary and outlaying Cíes Islands were bathed in a powder-pink glow and I felt my stresses disappearing as the sun did.

That calmness intensified with every step towards Santiago. I felt it as I crunched along golden sands, wove around tiny fishing coves and blushed at nudist beaches. I felt it as I used my limited Spanish to order beer and empanadas, as I dipped my weary feet into the cool blue-green sea.

At the handsome old town of Pontevedra, where the coastal Camino meets the inland route, the pilgrim dial was cranked up. Here, in the early morning, it was as if a church bell had called the faithful to arms: streams of walkers with backpacks and blisters appeared from all corners, all following the scallop-shell signs – the symbol of St James that marks the Camino. At first I was affronted: what had happened to my peaceful trail? But then I

THE ROAD MORE TRAVELLED

Most pilgrims bound for Santiago – 56% of them in 2019 – walk the Camino Francés, the classic route that begins in St-Jean-Pied-de-Port in France, crosses the Pyrenees and cuts across northern Spain. It takes 30 to 35 days to cover the 780km (485-mile) route. It's busy year-round, and during peak season (June to September) hostel space fills quickly. Camaraderie is a large part of the experience; if you want a quieter Francés, and don't mind rain, walk in winter.

Clockwise from top: Vila Praia de Âncora; pilgrims marching on; salt-rubbed grilled sardines; 15th-century statues adorning of the portal of the cathedral in Viana do Castelo. Previous page: sweeping Atlantic Ocean views accompany the route

"The simplicity... of a pilgrimage can offer salvation no matter what your beliefs."

rather liked it, joining this international cast, united by a common goal. I chatted with a German wearing Camino-themed socks, swapped life histories with a girl from Brazil, chatted politics with two Democratic Americans. I swapped emails with Gregory, a bank manager from Poland, who'd just turned 40 and, for some reason, had felt compelled to complete a Camino: 'Some things can't be explained,' he said. And even if they could, the explanation might be different for every *peregrino*. Each makes a pilgrimage for their own reasons; each takes something different away.

By the time I readied to leave the hot-pepper town of Padrón – to which the body of St James was allegedly ushered by angels in the first century – I was ready to keep walking forever. I dallied with an espresso at Cafe Don Pepe, which was festooned with mementos left by past pilgrims. As I left, the titular owner hailed me with the heartiest 'Bon Camino!' Santiago was now only a day away.

The final leg wound via busy roads and churches, quiet lanes and pungent vines. Not the world's most beautiful walk but enhanced by the history of all the feet that had trodden here before. Finally, standing before Santiago de Compostela cathedral's magnificent Portico da Gloria, I felt...what? A little sad, a little sore, rejuvenated, invigorated. Later, I wondered how Polish Gregory had found the experience, so I sent him a message. 'There were less emotions than I expected,' he wrote, from back home in Wrocław. 'But now I feel fantastic. People say I am radiating peace.' **SB**

ORIENTATION

Start // Porto
Finish // Santiago de Compostela
Distance // 280km (174 miles)
Duration // 11 to 12 days
Getting there // The official start is at Porto Cathedral. Many pilgrims start from Matosinhos (accessible via Metro) to avoid walking through the city outskirts.
What to pack // Traditionally pilgrims carry a scallop shell (the symbol of St James). Obtain a credential (pilgrim passport) before setting off – hotels, churches and cafes will stamp this; pilgrims that prove they've walked at least the last 100km (62 miles) earn a *compostela* (certificate of pilgrimage).
Where to stay // Guesthouses, hotels and *albergues* (cheap pilgrim hostels; credential required) are plentiful.
More info // For official Camino information, consult the Confraternity of St James (www.csj.org.uk); www.caminhoportuguesdacosta.com.

Opposite, clockwise from top left: pilgrim's end in Santiago de Compostela; Romanesque turrets and domes of the church in Toro, Zamora province; Interlake, one of the lakeside towns on the Jakobsweg

MORE LIKE THIS
ALTERNATIVE CAMINOS

CAMINO INGLÉS, SPAIN

A good choice for the time-poor, the English Way is one of the shortest options for hiking to Santiago and still earning your *compostela* certificate (which requires you to cover at least 100km/62 miles on foot). The Inglés was traditionally used by sea-voyaging pilgrims who would sail from places such as England, Wales and Ireland and begin their walk to Santiago from Spain's northern coast. Today most pilgrims start in the old ship-building port of Ferrol (home to especially lively Easter celebrations) before setting off into the green Galician countryside. There are some steep ascents but also fine walking via quiet farmland and marshes, riversides and estuaries, medieval bridges, interesting towns (notably Pontedeume and Betanzos) and glorious woodlands, including a stretch through the magical Bosque Encantado (Enchanted Forest).
Start // Ferrol
Finish // Santiago de Compostela
Distance // 120km (75 miles)
More info // www.csj.org.uk

JAKOBSWEG, SWITZERLAND

This Camino feeder route, which runs east–west right across Switzerland, historically conveyed overlanding pilgrims from Germany, Scandinavia and beyond towards Santiago de Compostela. Starting at the German border, on the shores of Lake Constance, it wends west to Geneva, on the border with France; from Geneva, committed pilgrims can pick up the Via Gebennensis to Le Puy-en-Velay, then the Chemin du Puy to reach the Pyrenees and cross into Spain. The main Jakobsweg route skirts the edges of the Alps, cutting through the country's rural heartland before surmounting the Brünig Pass to reach Interlaken and Thun, Fribourg and Lausanne. It's a fabulous unfurling of cow-grazed pasture, snow-capped summits, pretty hillside villages and dazzling lakes all connected – as you'd expect from wonderfully efficient Switzerland – by clear, well-waymarked trails.
Start // Konstanz
Finish // Geneva
Distance // 350km (218 miles)
More info // www.viajacobi4.ch; www.jakobsweg.ch

CAMINO DE LA PLATA, SPAIN

Time-rich pilgrims wanting to avoid other people might consider the lengthy, little-used Via de la Plata (also known as the Camino Mozárabe) – only around 3% of the pilgrims that reach Santiago use this particular Way of St James. Following an old Roman road, the route was used by Christians from the south and other parts of the Mediterranean, before and during Spain's Moorish occupation. It begins in the flamboyant river-port city of Seville and runs through the regions of Andalucía, Extremadura and Castilla y Léon before entering Galicia. This means a huge diversity of terrain, from olive groves and vineyards, to parched plains, rolling farmland, eucalyptus forests and oak woods. There's plenty of historical interest too, from medieval Cácares and Mérida's ancient remains to sublime Salamanca and the Romanesque churches of Zamora.
Start // Seville
Finish // Santiago de Compostela
Distance // 1000km (621 miles)
More info // www.viaplata.org; www.csj.org.uk

ENCHANTED FOREST: THE WESTWEG

Get your fill of Germany's bewitching Black Forest on this challenging multiday trek to dark woods, deep valleys, mountains of myth and lakes of lore.

Early morning and the Black Forest is shaking off its dewy slumber. There's a wonderful stillness at this hour and an almost visible sensation of everything coming back to life. Ferns are lazily uncoiling their fronds, tall firs and pines are stretching towards the light, the day's first rays of sun are raking through the treetops. It's silent but for the tentative hammering of a woodpecker and the occasional crack of a branch underfoot. I'm totally alone. I take a deep breath and inhale the freshness of a golden autumn day. The mist draping the valley is lifting and I can make out a cluster of dark-timber farmhouses and a slender church steeple in the valley below. The pleats and folds of the forest rise above it like multi-layered curtains.

Of all the hikes that dip into Germany's remaining pockets of true wilderness, the Westweg is one of the most celebrated. Running the rolling length of the *Schwarzwald* from top to bottom, the trek is a serious undertaking, involving two solid weeks of moderately challenging, high-altitude hiking. But boy are the blisters worth it. The waymarked trail heads to off-the-radar viewpoints and cascading waterfalls, half-timbered hamlets, post-glacial lakes and mountaintops that peer across to the not-so-distant Alps – and, *natürlich*, deep into those necks of the woods that are inaccessible to cars. This is a hike through a forest straight from the pages of a Grimm bedtime story, steeped in legends of lake nymphs, witches and paths easily strayed from.

The Westweg takes in the best of the Black Forest's crochet of tightly woven valleys and sharply rising hills, allowing moments of quiet contemplation in among the spruces, where moss grows thick like the plushest of carpets. Some might find the loneliness disconcerting, but I've always found solace in its darkest depths.

John Muir once said that 'the clearest way into the universe is through a forest wilderness' and he had a point. In the protective embrace of the trees, it is easy to unplug from the world and get that bit closer to nature. As my hike begins, I feel a near-meditative sense of calm. Everything becomes more intuitive: the gentle stirring of trees, the profile of a startled deer, the play of light as day turns to dusk, the rhythm of my own stride.

Pforzheim is the gateway town to the trail, but I do not linger. I'm too eager to strike out into the heart of the forest. And so I walk through the upland moors of the Enz Valley, where medieval Schloss Neuenbürg stands high on a hill, and on to the plateau

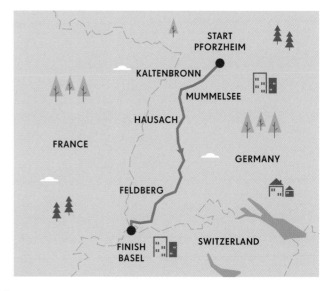

of the Dobel, with views to the Rhine Valley. Soon after I stumble upon the huge blockish boulders of the Volzemer Steine, partially hidden by forest undergrowth. From here, a boardwalk trail cuts across the protected highland moor of Kaltenbronn, one of the largest in Germany, so as not to disturb the fragile wetland ecosystem. It then descends to the steep-carved Murg Valley to Forbach, a pretty village of gabled houses with an impressive covered wooden bridge straddling the River Murg. The surrounding landscape has a green and quiet beauty, with traditional hay barns, or *heuhütten*, tucked in between forest and meadow.

The spa town of Baden-Baden spreads out before me from the lookout tower of Friedrichsturm atop Badener Höhe, some 1000m (3280ft) above sea level. The view takes in the full swoop of the northern Black Forest, the Rhine Valley and the Vosges Mountains over the border in France.

The going gets tougher and the scenery increasingly dramatic and mountainous as I reach the trail's biggest natural draw and centrepiece: the Black Forest National Park. Created in 2014, this 100 sq km (39 sq mile) pocket of forest is the Schwarzwald at its wildest and untamed best. These heights are often buried under snow in winter, and flecked with purple heather in summer. But now, in the cool, sharp days of autumn, they are dappled tawny-gold, with mushrooms and toadstools popping up on the side of the track. I join the day-trippers to admire the reflecting waters of Mummelsee, a lake where legend has it that an underwater king

> *"This is a hike... straight from the pages of a Grimm bedtime story, steeped in legends of lake nymphs and witches."*

WANDERN STAR

The concept of *Wandern* (walking for pleasure) was born here in 1864, with the founding of the *Schwarzwaldverein*. Germany's oldest hiking and mountaineering club still maintains and waymarks 23,000km (14,300 miles) of footpaths in the Black Forest. The Romans might have appreciated them when they reached its fringes 2000 years ago. So dark and forbidding did they find their surroundings that they named the impenetrable forest 'Silva Nigra' – a black, murky forest.

Clockwise from top: strolling on the Westweg; Triberg waterfalls; the town of Forbach; Black Forest mushrooms. Previous page: track through the trees

and nymphs dwell. A stiff climb leads from here up to the 1163m (3816ft) peak of Hornisgrinde. A little further south is the lesser-visited, forest-rimmed Glaswaldsee, a wonderfully peaceful lake in which to rest my aching feet a while. The glow of sunset renders the forested hills into relief as I arrive at the tower of Brandenkopf, with the Alps just a smudge on the horizon.

Just as the forest and hills roll on, so too do the days. Hiking has become second nature and each stage of the Westweg brings unexpected surprises. After a couple of quiet days rambling through dense forest, where occasionally the canopy cracks open to reveal the valleys below, I reach the gentle hills of Kinzigtal, where the half-timbered village of Hausach hunkers below a ruined medieval castle. Nearby is Titisee, a shimmering green-blue lake in the southern Black Forest, now devoid of its summer crowds. The same is true of the bald hump of Feldberg, further south, which is the highest peak in these parts at 1493m (4898ft). The mountain itself is not particularly attractive, but the views are superb – reaching all the way to Mont Blanc in the furthest reaches of the Alps on clear days.

The landscape softens in one of the hike's last legs through the Markgräflerland, whose orchards and vineyards are now turning gold. The smell of new wine hangs in the air and pumpkins in all shapes and sizes are sold in carts outside farmhouses. My walk is drawing to a close and I know that I'll miss this forest. But for now, Basel awaits. **KW**

ORIENTATION

Start // Pforzheim
Finish // Basel
Distance // 285km (177 miles)
Duration // Two weeks
Getting there // The closest airports are Karlsruhe-Baden, 61km (38 miles) west, and Stuttgart, 45km (28 miles), east. The train journey into Pforzheim takes about 1½ hours.
When to go // April to October is best. The trail is rarely crowded, even in summer when the weather is more stable.
Where to stay // Take your pick from the rustic shelters, hotels and campgrounds en route; www.westweg.info.
What to take // Come prepared for all eventualities with waterproofs, layers, sturdy boots, hiking poles, supplies, insect repellent and a decent backpack.
More info // Find maps at www.top-trails-of-germany.de. Cicerone publishes *Trekking the Westweg* guide.

MORE LIKE THIS
FOREST HIKES

BALTIC FOREST HIKING TRAIL, LATVIA/ESTONIA

Twisting and turning through enchanting, thrillingly remote forests bordering the Baltic Sea, this long-distance trail is quite an undertaking, for which you'll need to set aside stamina, willpower and around three months of your time. But the rewards are many, not least the quiet beauty of being alone in valleys, highlands, national parks and deep woods where brown bears roam. Forming part of the E11 route, the trail is expected to be fully waymarked by summer 2021. Moments to remember in Latvia include the glacier-carved Abava River Valley Nature Park and the tranquil fishing villages and spa towns of Ķemeri National Park. Estonia brings highlights, too, in the form of Lahemaa National Park's, bays, lakes, bogs and pine-stippled hinterland, and Lake Peipsi straddling the Estonian–Russian border. If you can't hike it all, tackle one of its 50 sections, each around 20km (12.5 miles).

Start // Rīga, Latvia
Finish // Tallinn, Estonia
Distance // 2100km (1305 miles)
More info // www.era-ewv-ferp.org; www.baltictrails.eu

WYE VALLEY WALK, ENGLAND/WALES

Delving into some of Britain's most ancient and beautiful woodlands, this long-distance hike shadows the River Wye from castle-topped Chepstow in the south to its source at the wind-buffeted peak of Plynlimon (752m/2467ft). Demanding a decent level of fitness, the 12-day hike swings from gentle riverside walking to rocky scrambles as it meanders through gorges, meadows and orchards and past soaring limestone cliffs on the English–Welsh border. It occasionally dips into the mysterious depths of the Forest of Dean, Britain's oldest oak forest, which allegedly fired Tolkien's imagination. Highs are many, among them romantically ruined Tintern Abbey, Symonds Yat viewpoint (look out for peregrine falcons), the literary town of Hay-on-Wye and medieval Hereford Cathedral with its Mappa Mundi. On the final days, the trail gets tougher and the Wye turns to rapids as you enter the wild, lonely Cambrian Mountains, before a final clamber up to the summit of Plynlimon.

Start // Chepstow
Finish // Plynlimon
Distance // 219km (136 miles)
More info // www.wyevalleywalk.org

MALA UHOLKA, UKRAINE

This short but spectacular hike takes you deep into Europe's largest virgin beech forest in the Ukranian Carpathians. Beginning at the Carpathian Biosphere Reserve visitor centre in Mala Uholka, this woody wonderland comes under the wider umbrella of the Unesco World Heritage Primeval Beech Forest of the Carpathians. This gentle ramble takes you through pale-green, sun-dappled woods, frilled with moss and lichens, which look ripe for a children's bedtime story. This is still very much an untouched wilderness – so much so that predators like bears, wolves and lynx still roam at large, though you're unlikely to see them. The landscape here has been dramatically shaped by limestone, with karst wonders to admire such as Druzhba Cave and Karstovyi Mist rock arch. The forest is perhaps at its loveliest when wearing its autumn mantle of russet and gold. Reach the starting point by taking a bus from the town of Tyachiv.

Start/Finish // Carpathian Biosphere Reserve in Mala Uholka
Distance // 5km (3 miles)
More info // www.traveltoukraine.org

Clockwise from top: a boardwalk through the boggy terrain of Estonia's Lahemaa National Park; the joy of forest hiking; the Tolkienesque Forest of Dean

THE TOUR DE MONTE ROSA

Hike around the Alps' second-highest mountain straddling the Switzerland–Italy border to discover that sometimes second can be best.

Y ou have to feel for poor old Monte Rosa. Sprawled across the Italian–Swiss border, the Alps' second-highest mountain sits in the shadow of greatness.

The 4634m (15,203ft) peak stands shoulder to shoulder with the Matterhorn, arguably the most recognisable and alluring peak on the planet, while 80km (50 miles) to the west rises Mont Blanc, 174m (571ft) taller and drawing all the mountain attention like an Alpine starlet.

For hikers, the Tour du Mont Blanc (TMB), circuiting the Alps' highest peak, is a siren call, but relatively few venture onto the counterpart Tour de Monte Rosa (TMR). And yet this is a rare case where the real prize comes in being second.

I've hiked around both mountains, and given the choice to do so again, I would pick Monte Rosa, and not simply because hours can pass around this massif without sight of another hiker. The TMR ascends far higher than the TMB, and it's more challenging, with a queue of high climbs and descents as well

as the thrill of a long stretch atop a glacier beneath the crooked nose of the Matterhorn.

The TMR typically begins and ends in popular Zermatt, but I'm setting out from the Swiss village of Grächen, near the massif's northern point. Instead of beginning with the Matterhorn in sight, I'm hoping that, if the weather gods play nice, I will, like a child saving the sweetest treat for last, be delaying my first views of that mighty mountain until I near the end of the hike.

From the top of a chairlift above Grächen, it's a precipitous start, with the slopes plunging more than 1000m (3281ft) away beneath my feet into the Saas Valley. Rhododendrons grow stunted and tiny on the slopes, and the purple flowers of crocuses hang like street lamps. Within two hours, I'm skimming beneath Balfrin Glacier. As I lunch beside a stream pouring from the glacier, butterflies land on my hands, my feet, my shirt and my hat. It's as though I've become part of the mountain already.

I stay this night in the town of Saas-Fee, where the new day brings an added sense of excitement. Like the TMB, the TMR is an international hike, crossing and recrossing borders. This day, atop 2845m (9334ft) Monte Moro Pass, where a tall golden Madonna stands like a border guard, I will step out of Switzerland and stride into Italy. The pass also provides my first glimpse of the summit of Monte Rosa, briefly peeping above cloud.

The vertiginous nature of the Tour de Monte Rosa is exemplified by the descent from Monte Moro Pass to Macugnaga, the Italian town so near to the border that it still looks Swiss, right down to its window boxes of geraniums. It's a knee-crunching 1500m (4921ft) plunge into Macugnaga, set inside a valley so narrow and deep that I won't be able see the valley floor until I'm well down the slopes. It's a pattern that continues for the next few days, ascending up to 1500m (4921ft) at a time and then descending into valleys as narrow as paper cuts.

By the time I stand atop the Cime Bianche pass, the TMR's penultimate pass, a few days later, high above a pair of vibrant blue lakes at the massif's southern edge, I will have crossed five passes since leaving Saas-Fee, racking up climbs of around 5500m (18,045ft). But now only one pass remains, and it's unquestionably the most dramatic and spectacular of all.

From Cime Bianche, the walk descends into the Cervinia ski fields, where I should be craning my neck to soak in a view of the Matterhorn, the mountain I've wanted to see for the past six days and my entire hiking life, directly overhead. But clouds have stolen it. In summer, the Cervinia ski fields are as bleak as the surface of the moon. Nothing grows here except desolation, and as the trail rises above 3000m (9843ft) for the first time, the altitude begins to bite. I climb slower, but I breathe faster. The ascent tops out at the 3296m (10,814ft) Theodul Pass, the TMR's highest point. Balanced across a rock ridge beside the pass is Rifugio Teodulo, a hut split by the Swiss–Italian border. When I stand in its lounge, I'm in Italy, but when I head to the bar I'm back in Switzerland.

WALK OF CLIMB

In the centre of Zermatt, a series of plaques is embedded into the cobblestones. This is the Walk of Climb, with each plaque honouring one of the seven climbers in the expedition party on the first ascent of the Matterhorn in 1865. Their glory might now be bronzed, but the climb was tragic, with four of the seven killed during the descent. One of them was 18-year-old Lord Francis Douglas, whose death led Queen Victoria to propose a ban on Englishmen climbing the mountain.

Clockwise from top: a golden Madonna greets hikers on Monte Moro Pass; a typical day on the Tour de Monte Rosa; spying the Matterhorn. Previous page: a high Alpine valley

"As I descend, a familiar mountain shape begins to emerge. The fog is lifting and suddenly the Matterhorn towers into view."

I spend the rest of the afternoon beside the refuge's wall-length windows, which peer out onto the Matterhorn... Or at least they would on a fine day. For hours, cloud intermittently rises and sinks on the mountain, revealing all but its famously dislocated summit.

By morning things are even bleaker. I can barely see a metre outside the windows as a thick fog grips the mountains. I delay my start, waiting for two hours before setting out for the start of the TMR's final march north, but the cloud remains locked in place. Grinding down the slopes behind the refuge is the Theodul Glacier. If the word 'glacier' conjures challenging images of seracs and icefalls, think again. This glacier doubles as the Alps' highest ski field, and as I hike down its smooth runs in my crampons, I step around a few small crevasses but otherwise there are no dangers here. As I descend, a familiar mountain shape begins to emerge. The fog is lifting and suddenly the Matterhorn towers into view, where it will stay for two hours before beginning to cocoon itself in cloud again.

Across the glacier, I remove the crampons and look around me. The high peaks of Monte Rosa rise to one side, and the Matterhorn stands sharp and tall on the other. The TMB has some grand Alpine views, but none that compare with this glacial moment on the TMR. I walk on, happy that I've settled for second. **AB**

ORIENTATION

Start/Finish // Grächen
Distance // 167.5km (104 miles)
Duration // Nine to ten days
Getting there // Trains run from Zurich and other major Swiss centres to St Niklaus or Visp, from where PostBus services climb to Grächen.
When to go // July to September.
Where to stay // The TMR dips into several towns, such as Zermatt, Saas-Fee and Macugnaga, with refuges sprinkled elsewhere along the trail. The refuges also offer meals.
What to pack // Carry a pair of hiking crampons for the crossing of the Theodul Glacier. Prepare for cold conditions by carrying plenty of layers and wet weather gear.
Tours // UTracks (www.utracks.com) and KE Adventure Travel (www.keadventure.com) run guided hikes of the TMR.
More info // Zermatt Tourism (www.zermatt.ch) is a good starting point for TMR information.

Opposite from top: all eyes on second prize: the climb to Glittertind summit; en route to Ben Macdui

MORE LIKE THIS
SECOND-HIGHEST PEAKS

BEN MACDUI, SCOTLAND

By virtue of being just 36m (118ft) lower than Ben Nevis, 1309m (4295ft) Ben Macdui maintains a satisfying anonymity. Unlike many second peaks, Ben Macdui doesn't sit beside its larger sibling, but is away instead in the wild Cairngorms, almost 100km (62 miles) northeast of Ben Nevis. The open, arctic-like nature of the terrain means the peak, which Queen Victoria climbed in 1859 (though, granted, a pony did most of the work), can be approached from several directions. The most popular route begins from the Cairngorm Mountain ski centre's upper car park at Coire Cas, rising to the UK's highest lake, tiny Lochan Buidhe, and on to the summit, which has sweeping views across the Cairngorms. Legend has it that Ben Macdui is inhabited by Am Fear Liath Mòr, Scotland's answer to the Yeti, so you might have company on the walk.
Start/Finish // Cairngorm
Mountain ski centre
Distance // 17km (10.5 miles)
More info // https://visitcairngorms.com

GLITTERTIND, NORWAY

Jotunheimen National Park is the standard bearer for Norwegian mountains, containing the vast bulk of the country's highest peaks. Second loftiest among them is Glittertind, which at 2464m (8084ft) stands just five metres lower than Norway's (and northern Europe's) highest mountain, Galdhøpiggen. For a time there was even debate about which was really taller – Glittertind is capped by a glacier, meaning its true height fluctuates and it was considered at times to be higher than Galdhøpiggen, though ice melt in recent times has settled the argument in favour of Galdhøpiggen. It's the presence of this glacier that gives Glittertind its sense of high-mountain terrain at relatively low altitude, with both approaches – from Glitterheim or Spiterstulen – taking you onto the glacier to reach the summit and a grand view. The going on the ice is fairly simple, with just a few small crevasses, but you still need to be prepared for ice travel with crampons and an ice axe.
Start/Finish // Glitterheim
Distance // 12km (7.5 miles)
More info // www.jotunheimen.com

BEENKERAGH, IRELAND

Ireland's second-highest mountain might stand at just a smidge over 1000m (3281ft), but don't be fooled by the numbers. The 1008m (3307ft) Beenkeragh is a serious hike-and-scramble that brings with it the additional opportunity to climb Carrauntoohil, Ireland's highest peak, right next door. The ascent is along the narrow Hag's Tooth Ridge, which is as toothy as the name suggests. The views down into the Eagle's Nest corrie and Lough Cummeenoughter, the country's highest lake, are spectacular. The fun has just begun when you reach Beenkeragh's summit, for the peak is connected to 1038m (3406ft) Carrauntoohil by the Beenkeragh Ridge, a narrow and exposed ridge that makes for one of Ireland's most exciting bits of walking. The loop, also taking in the country's third-highest mountain is known as the Coomloughra Horseshoe.
Start/Finish // Hydro Rd car park,
near Glencar
Distance // 12km (7.5 miles)
More info // www.mountaintrails.ie

A DIP IN THE GORGES DE L'ARDÈCHE

Trek through this vast canyon to experience France's wilder side – and enjoy some of its best fresh water swimming.

'Bonjour! A fine afternoon for a swim, non?' booms a voice. The sound takes me by surprise, as I've spent most of the day hiking through the Gorges de l'Ardèche solo and pretty much in silence. But the voice isn't what's really taken me aback: it's the fact that, save for a pair of sunglasses and a battered straw hat, the voice's owner is stark naked.

Somewhat flummoxed, I tramp down onto the beach, agreeing that it is indeed a perfect day for a swim while battling to keep my eyes from straying to places they shouldn't.

'I'm Alain,' the man explains, shaking my hand, oblivious to the fact that I'm fully clothed and he – well, isn't. 'You have hiked from Pont d'Arc? You must be exhausted! Here, let's get you something to drink.'

He retrieves a beer from a cool-box, handing it to me with a jovial grin. The beer is blissfully cold after a day of hiking, and I sip it gratefully as Alain chats away. This is Plage des Templiers, he explains, one of the only beaches in the Ardèche where naturists like him and his wife Marjorie can sunbathe *au naturel.* 'Say hello, Marjorie!' he shouts. A naked woman sits up from her sunbathing and gives me an enthusiastic wave.

Running for 26km (16 miles) between the villages of Vallon-Pont-d'Arc and Saint-Martin-d'Ardèche, the Gorges de l'Ardèche have

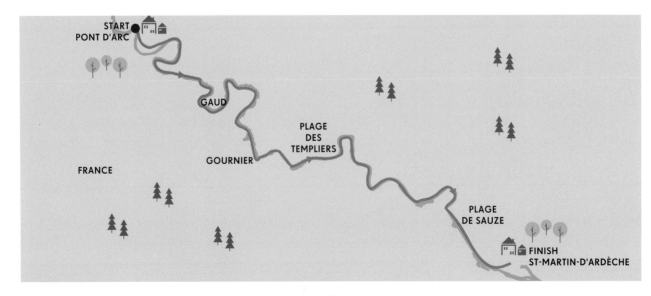

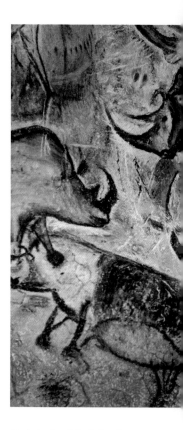

CHAUVET CAVE PAINTINGS

Discovered in 1994, the Grotte Chauvet-Pont d'Arc contains a collection of spectacular prehistoric paintings. Dating from 37,000 to 30,000 years ago, the paintings depict more than 13 animal species, including reindeer, bison, lions, panthers, bears and even rhinoceroses. There are also stencilled human hand prints, and – hauntingly – the preserved footprints of a child. The original caves are closed to the public, but a pixel-perfect replica can be visited nearby (www.archeologie. culture.fr/chauvet).

Clockwise from left: shades of green and teal in the Gorges de l'Ardèche; rhinoceroses stencilled in a replica of the Chauvet Cave paintings; cruising the gorge. Previous page: taking a dip in the Ardèche

been called France's answer to the Grand Canyon, with limestone cliffs reaching up to 300m (984ft) high. Most people explore them by canoe, but I'm taking two days to hike through on foot, with an overnight bivouac halfway. I'm also looking forward to the gorge's many swimming spots: the numerous pools, hollows, basins and swimming holes carved out by the river over countless millennia, now perfect for cooling off after hours of hot hiking.

I set off early from the gorge's northern end at Pont d'Arc, where a natural rock bridge photogenically spans the chasm. At midday, the river here will be thronged with swimmers, but at 8am, I'm the only one here. I strip off for my first dip of the day, diving into the clear water as the sun crests over the clifftops. Then, I hike up the road, leaving touristy Pont d'Arc behind, and take the trail into the canyon.

Before long, I've left all signs of civilisation behind. The sun soon heats up the valley, and I'm sweating hard as I follow the trail under the canyon walls. Green oaks and fragrant wild shrubs known as *garrigue* carpet the valley's lower slopes; higher still, the walls are sheer and bare, rising towards a sky of unbroken blue.

Soon, I have to ford the river. At this time of year, in late summer, the water is just over my knees, but after snowmelt or a sudden storm, the water can rise frighteningly fast: hikers are required to check-in with park staff to confirm the weather forecast before setting out. Even now, the current is still strong; I wade across carefully, holding my pack overhead to keep it dry, looking down into water so clear I can see the pebbles at the bottom. Further along the valley, I cross a second ford. Two canoeists drift past, and generously help ferry my pack across before paddling downstream.

Humans have inhabited the gorge since ancient times. Many prehistoric paintings have been discovered in the valley's caves, most famously the Grotte Chauvet, documented by director Werner Herzog in his 2010 film *Cave of Forgotten Dreams*. It's not hard to see why prehistoric people chose this spot: with shelter, fresh water and a plentiful supply of fish and game, it must have seemed like paradise to our ancient ancestors. Maybe, like us, they just enjoyed the views, too.

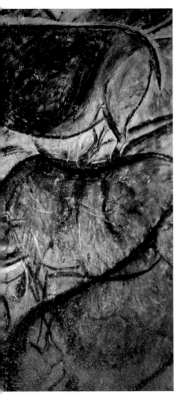

"Canoeists float past as I'm swimming, and we holler greetings to each other, our calls ringing back from the canyon walls."

I reach my bivouac at Gournier in late afternoon. The camp is basic, with rudimentary facilities and space for only a few tents, but it feels gloriously off the beaten track. I pitch my tent, then head down to the water for another swim, followed by an evening barbecue with my fellow campers. Night falls, and the Milky Way materialises above the gorge. I fall asleep watching shooting stars streak through the sky, soothed by the clatter of the river as it rushes past.

I set off early on my second day. The walking's harder: there are steep, rocky sections, and in some places metal ladders have been put in place to traverse the steepest sections. Sometimes, the trail veers up into the cliffs, snaking along ridges high above the river before heading back down to the water's edge. It's hot, hard, perspiring work, and I take every chance I can for a dunk to cool down. Canoeists float past as I'm swimming, and we holler greetings to each other, our calls ringing back from the canyon walls.

I arrive in Saint-Martin-d'Ardèche as the sun is setting. I'm tired and dirty, my legs ache, and I'm desperate for a beer. After my night roughing it in the gorge, I've treated myself to a hotel – but there's one thing I need to do before I settle in. I head down to the Plage de Sauze, strip down to my shorts and plunge in, feeling the cold waters of the Ardèche glide over my skin.

I lie back in the water, watching swifts race through the sky, and the cliffs turning the colour of candy floss. I've never enjoyed a swim as much. **OB**

ORIENTATION

Start // Pont d'Arc
Finish // Saint-Martin-d'Ardèche
Distance // 24km (15 miles)
Duration // Two days
Getting there // Trains run to Orange, Avignon and Alès, where you can hire a car or catch local buses to the Ardèche.
When to go // May, June or September to avoid crowds.
What to pack // Map, tent, sleeping bag, mosquito repellent, food and water for your night in the gorge.
Where to stay // There are two bivouac sites at Gournier and Gaud. Places can be reserved at the tourist offices in Saint-Martin-Ardèche (04 75 54 54 20; contact@rhone-gorges-ardeche.com) or Pont d'Arc (04 28 91 24 10).
Things to know // It's essential to book campsites and check the forecast with tourist offices before setting out.
More info // www.ardeche-guide.com; www.pontdarc-ardeche.fr; www.rhone-gorges-ardeche.com

Opposite from top: taking a soothing dip at the end of the the Reykjadalur valley trail; Crystal Lagoon, one of many swimming spots on a circuit of Comino Island

MORE LIKE THIS
WET WALKS

PURCARACCIA CANYON, CORSICA, FRANCE

Hidden high up in the rugged, needle-like mountains of Bavella in central Corsica, Purcaraccia Canyon is home to a system of tumbling waterfalls and plunge pools filled with emerald-green water. Hollowed out over millions of years from the granite rock, the smooth, hollow-shaped bowls seem like they've been placed there specifically for bathing on a hot summer's day – like Mother Nature's own water park. There's a bit of a hike to get there, but it's worth the effort. And if you're up for something more adrenaline-fuelled, local guides offer canyoning trips that involve sliding, gliding, abseiling and plunging through the waterfalls and pools. Wetsuits and hard-hats are provided, but you'll have to muster up the necessary moxie yourself.
Start/Finish // Bocca di Larone
Distance // 4km (2.5 miles)
More info // www.visit-corsica.com

REYKJADALUR, ICELAND

When it comes to outdoor dips, Iceland is the jackpot; thanks to its abundant geothermal activity, there are thousands of hot-water bathing spots to explore, from such well-known sites as the Blue Lagoon near Reykjavík to much lesser-frequented ones like Reykjadalur (Hot River Valley). Located a 45-minute drive from the capital, this valley walk is a delightful way to experience Iceland's geothermal power. From the trailhead carpark, it's a 3km (2-mile) hike through fields of sulphur-belching plains into the steaming heart of the valley, where dozens of hot springs feed a bath-warm stream. Stick to the marked paths, lest you melt your shoes.
Start/Finish // Parking Reykjadalur (just off the Ring Rd near Hveragerði)
Distance // 6km (3.8 miles)
More info // www.gotoiceland.is

CIRCUIT OF COMINO ISLAND, MALTA

Located between Malta and Gozo, this rocky limestone island is a magnet for wild swimmers and snorkellers. It's tiny – only 3.5 sq km (1.5 sq miles) – car-free and practically uninhabited, save for a single hotel. The island's main drawcard is the sheltered bay known as the Blue Lagoon, filled with dazzlingly clear, sapphire-coloured waters – you'll probably have seen it on a postcard long before you get to visit. Unsurprisingly, the lagoon attracts hordes of yachts and snorkelling boats in high summer – but there are several more out-of-the-way swimming spots to discover if you don't mind a bit of walking, including the quiet bays of Santa Marija and San Niklaw. And if you visit outside July and August, there's a chance you'll find even the waters of the famous Blue Lagoon relatively tranquil.
Start/Finish // Blue Lagoon Ferry Terminal
Distance // 7.2km (4.5 miles)
More info // www.outdooractive.com

CAUSEWAY COAST WAY

The rock formations of Northern Ireland's Giant's Causeway are spectacular, but there are other geological wonders to be discovered on this multi-day coastal walk.

Over the aeons it seems that large pieces of the Earth's crust have wandered around the planet like gap-year travellers, crashing into each other, joining together, breaking up and heading off again to arrive in unexpected places, in unlikely combinations. Northern Ireland's Antrim coastline has had a particularly restless and party-happy geological history. The result is a stone-scape of stunning diversity.

As I hiked westwards on the Causeway Coast Way, the marked walking route that runs for 50km (31 miles) between Ballycastle and Portstewart, my feet were striding over rocks from many different geological eras. Some had, over millions of years, travelled up

from the equator. Others had once been part of a mountain chain higher than the Himalayas. More still had hung out at the bottom of ancient oceans. And some – the most incredible – had burst up from the Earth's interior in volcanic explosions. It is a dynamic landscape, as if the rocks are only lounging around at the top of Ireland for a bit before deciding where to go next.

On this coast, where the sea pounds and slices into the land, strata and muddles of rock have been exposed like one of those anatomy diagrams that reveal the bones and muscles under the skin. From the track above the cliffs near Ballycastle I looked seaward to Rathlin Island out in the Atlantic. For early Neolithic

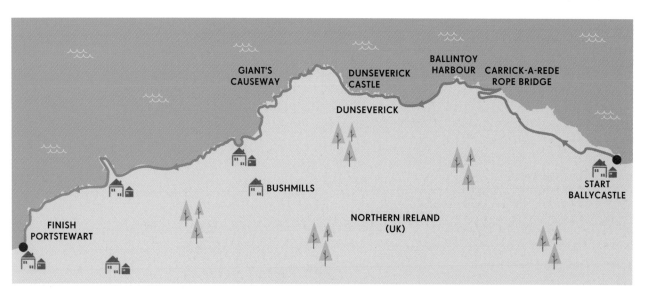

settlers, the island, and other parts of the Antrim Coast, provided a supply of porcellanite, a dense rock which could be knapped into blades sharper and harder than flint. It was so highly prized that Irish axe heads were traded in places as far away as southern England. Here on the mainland the stone shaping and rock-piling of Ireland's earliest people laid the foundations for what would over time become ring forts, boulder-built court tombs, early houses and eventually the castles, quays and lime kilns whose remains still dot this coastline.

There's also plenty of zoology on the route, with crowds of fulmars, kittiwakes and guillemots nesting on the rock ledges worn into the cliff faces below me. And botology – oops, botany, I mean – with the thrift plants, campions and frog orchids flourishing on soil rich with minerals leached from the rocks. There was, too, the anthropology of the people who had lived and worked on this coast for millennia.

It was a steep walk down the sinuous loops of a narrow lane to reach Ballintoy Harbour. Throughout the 18th and 19th centuries, ironstone, coal, limestone and hard dolerite rock that were used to pave city streets were extracted and sent off from small harbours along this coastline. In the case of Ballintoy it was chalk, dug from the cliffs above my head, that was shipped away in small coasters from the neat limestone quays. It's the same little port that in more recent times served as the location of Lordsport in *Game of Thrones*.

Walking westwards along White Park Bay I was at sea level, shuffling through a mile of silky yellow sand to reach Portbradden. It was difficult to comprehend that a continuing process of erosion and compression were, even now, changing and cracking even the hardest of rock here. But the clues were all around me: in the boulders and cobbles thrown above the tideline by winter storms; in the lumps of Ulster White Limestone, a hard chalk from the Cretaceous period, containing fossils of early sea-urchins, belemnites, and skeletons of squid; in the tunnel I walked through, eroded by sea and wind to form a needle's eye through a narrow headland; in the soft, powdery crushed seashells and mineral crystals under my feet that might, in an unimaginably distant future, be compacted into new limestones and sandstones, to be found somewhere else entirely on the planet.

Back in the here and now, it was a 'pet day', to use a local phrase – a short, calm and clear spell in a period of wet and windy weather. A perfect time for walking. The sea was Mediterranean azure in the sunlight. A peregrine falcon arrowed out of the sky and stooped down through a flock of gulls. I stopped to explore the medieval ruins of Dunseverick Castle, noting where the 1700s cliff erosion had tumbled its north walls into the sea. I was pleasantly surprised to find that, once away from the honey-pot attractions, this busy tourist area was empty of people for mile after mile.

From the high cliffs west of Benbane Head I got my first sight of the Giant's Causeway, looking down on tiny figures scrambling over the tiers of rocky pillars. I made my way down to the shoreline to step out across the 40,000 interlocking basalt columns – most are pentagonal or hexagonal in section though there are also octagons

BUSHMILLS DISTILLERY

Whiskey has been made at Bushmills – a few miles inland from the Giant's Causeway – for four centuries. The water used in the process still comes from nearby sources. Having absorbed traces of calcium and magnesium on its rise through limestone and basalt rock, this water is softened from flowing across peatlands. Added to malted barley, the result is the mash that becomes whiskey. A visit to the distillery allows you to – literally – drink in the geology of the land you've been walking across.

Clockwise from top: the walk passes through the small village of Portbradden; the ruins of medieval Dunluce Castle; the hexagonal basalt columns formed 60 million years ago. Previous page: the Giant's Causeway

"It is a dynamic landscape, as if the rocks are only lounging around... for a bit before deciding where to go next."

and heptagons. Created 60 million years ago when volcanic lava was extruded from the depths, geologists say it was the rapid cooling and contraction of the liquid rock that created the myriad honeycomb shapes. For Neolithic and other early settlers, the Giant's Causeway must have seemed other-worldly, as if sculpted by supernatural forces. Indeed, Irish mythology tells how the rocks were built by the giant Finn McCool as a sub-sea stairway to reach Scotland – where a similar formation of basalt pillars rises out of the sea at Fingal's Cave – so he could fight his rival giant, Benandonner.

In the late 17th century the rocks were 'discovered' by scientists, after a paper presented to the Royal Society by Sir Richard Bulkeley, and during the 18th century neptunists and vulcanists argued over whether the coast's rock formations had precipitated out of the ocean or been created by volcanic action. The wider world soon heard about the strange landscape, and a growing tourist industry underwrote opulent hotels, a 19th-century electric tramway, and increased trade for the nearby Bushmills whiskey distillery. In the 1960s, the causeway and then coastline were taken into the stewardship of the National Trust. In 1973 ultimate fame arrived when Led Zeppelin thought the rock-scape weird enough for the cover of their *Houses of the Holy* album.

That's the thing about rocks – they inspire myth, art and science just to make sense of them. Above all, they should be experienced first-hand. Walk Northern Ireland's Antrim coast and a narrative of planetary violence stretching an unimaginable timespan ends in a geological punchline: the Giant's Causeway itself. **JW**

ORIENTATION

Start // Ballycastle
Finish // Portstewart
Distance // 51km (32 miles)
Duration // Two to three days
Getting there // There are trains from Belfast to Ballymena, and then buses onwards to Ballycastle.
When to go // April to May and September to October provide the best combo of good weather and fewer people.
What to wear // Supportive footwear and waterproofs. Take your swimming kit if you're a keen sea swimmer.
Tours // Sean Mullan (www.walktalkireland.com) hosts guided walks along the Antrim coast.
Things to know // Between Ballycastle and Ballintoy the route is on busy roads, and can be skipped by taking Ulsterbus 252. Ulsterbus 402 (June to September) aids access to the rest of the walk route (www.translink.co.uk).
More info // www.causewaycoastway.com

*Opposite: sunrise behind Durdle Door,
on the Jurassic Coast*

MORE LIKE THIS
GEOLOGY WALKS

MULLAGHMORE LOOP, IRELAND

For a landscape laid down 350 million years ago in the Lower Carboniferous period, the limestone karst of the Burren has a remarkably dynamic past. The rock, compressed from the remains of the dead corals and sea creatures of an ancient tropical sea, has been gouged by glaciers, eroded by Atlantic storms, shuffled like cards by tectonic shifts, and hollowed out by seeping rain water. To best appreciate this landscape, walk the looped route to the 180m (591ft) summit of Mullaghmore in Burren National Park. The hill may not seem high, but the landscape is challenging in poor weather and feels other-worldly, particularly on the stretches of grykes and clints (cracks and slabs) where the hollows shelter scaled-down jungles of flowers, mosses and lichens. The odd ecology of the Burren mixes alpine and Mediterranean plants never normally found together, and there are some 23 species of orchid to be found.

Start/Finish // Gortlecka Crossroads, Burren National Park
Distance // 7.5km (4.5 miles)
More info // www.burrennationalpark.ie

JURASSIC COAST PATH, ENGLAND

The Jurassic Coast, a 150km (93-mile) stretch of Britain's South West Coast Path, is a 185-million-year-old geological theme park, sliced and diced by the sea to show the inside workings of our planet's crust. Start in the west, striding over the billions of microscopic Cretaceous-age seashells, that make up the chalk of the Hooken Cliffs, before entering the Undercliff Walk, a jungly wilderness of land slippage, rock falls and boulders. The beach below the cliff at Charmouth is a fossil-hunter's pick 'n' mix sweet-shop, and source of many early palaeontology finds including Mary Anning's early 19th-century discovery of a whole ichthyosaur skeleton. At Chesil Beach be warned that it's illegal to remove even one of the quartz and chalcedony pebbles. From here, the eastern path takes to the clifftops again giving views of the natural stone arch at Durdle Door before ending at the three chalk formations of Old Harry Rocks at the end of the Isle of Purbeck.

Start // Exmouth, Devon
Finish // Old Harry Rocks, Dorset
Distance // 150km (93 miles)
More info // www.jurassiccoast.org

HAUTE PROVENCE GEOPARK, FRANCE

Recognised by Unesco in 2000, the Haute Provence Geopark covers 2000 sq km (772 sq miles) of forested, alpine meadows and stark peaked mountainous land. Base yourself in Digne-les-Bains for an easy walk to the Dalle aux Ammonites, a slab featuring 1500 ammonite fossils; or for a longer hike, head to the ichthyosaur skeleton pressed into the stone at La Robine-sur-Galabre. Given the vastness of the geopark and the scattered nature of its geology, one of the most encompassing if challenging walks is the 150km (93-mile) Andy Goldsworthy Refuge d'Art hike. Though conceived as a long walk around contemporary art sites in the area, it embraces the geology of the region and takes in high mountain passes, cliffs, forested valleys, scree slopes and boulder fields. A highlight of the route is the road through the deep, narrow river gorge cut through the limestone at the Clue de Pérouré.

Start/Finish // Digne-les-Bains
Distance // 150km (93 miles)
**More info // www.refugedart.fr;
www.geoparchauteprovence.com**

STEPS AND LADDERS:
THE KAISERJÄGER

*Extremes of beauty and barbarity intermingle in the Italian Alps, where
WWI relics and 'iron roads' sit amid the most magnificent mountains.*

M y feet had already been itching for the peaks of northern Italy. But now this. A sentence glimpsed in a vintage guidebook (John Ball's *Guide to the Eastern Alps* published in 1868): 'A traveller who has visited all the other mountain regions of Europe, and remains ignorant of the scenery of the Dolomite Alps, has yet to make acquaintance with Nature in one of her loveliest and most fascinating aspects.' Sold.

The Dolomites are part of the Alpine chain that sweeps across the continent, but feel like a land apart. The remains of an ancient coral reef, encompassing 18 summits over 3000m (9843ft), the Unesco-listed Dolomites are *bellissima* indeed, with their sheer slopes and gnarly crags, rock spires and pinnacles, long, deep valleys and rippling plateaux. They're an outdoor playground, rugged and ravishing in equal measure. But they also have a darker side.

During WWI, this redoubtable range became a fiercely fought-over front line. For four years, Italian and Austro-Hungarian troops did battle here, in unimaginable conditions, fighting at altitude,

FORCELLA SALARES

FANES-SENNES-BRAIES NATURAL PARK

LAGAZUOI PICCOLO

START / FINISH PASSO DI VALPAROLA

RIFUGIO LAGAZUOI

ITALY

PASSO FALZAREGO

through freezing winters, on precipitous, precarious slopes. They dug in trenches, bored tunnels and built encampments; they also constructed via ferrata ('iron roads'), networks of fixed lines, ladders, steps and bridges to help them negotiate the dangerous terrain. Many of these relics remain today.

So when I arrived in the valley of Alta Badia, it was to be both wowed by the Dolomites' natural drama – the delicate grey rock, the forested foothills, the flower-jewelled meadows, the magical sunset glow they call the *enrosadira* – and moved by remainders of one of Europe's darkest hours.

With time I might have attempted the whole Alta Via 1, a long-distance trail that moseys around the mountains, in parts following WWI tracks. But for a more succinct history-hit I focused on the Kaiserjäger Trail, named for the Austro-Hungarian alpine divisions once stationed on Mt Lagazuoi; the supply route they constructed to transport their food and munitions has been repaired and is now a high-'n'-wild hiking path, with a bit of easy via ferrata thrown in.

I was staying in the pretty mountain village of San Cassiano – all red-checked tablecloths, sunny terraces and geranium window boxes – but soon swapped this alpine cheeriness for wilder territory. Hairpinning up, up, up the valley, the bus deposited me at Passo di Valparola, a 2168m- (7113ft)-high pass where the temperature was 10°C (50°F) cooler, and mischievous clouds were toying with the great grey peaks. Here, against the moody backdrop, squatted Tre Sassi fort, built by the Austro-Hungarians before the Great War and repeatedly bombed by the Italians from 1915. Its ruins now house the Museo della Grande Guerra (Great War Museum), which contains more than 2000 relics – grenades, helmets, mess tins, an old guitar – collected from the surrounding mountains.

That's exactly where I was headed. Soon, I was hiking up a desolate slope, wending between rocks and through the remains of Austrian battlements; the concrete arch of an old door provided a perfect frame for the snow-dusted peaks across the valley: the beauty through the beastly. I continued, along preserved trenches, climbing steeper and steeper on skiddy gravel, bitten by the wind – it was cold even in June. How did those bygone soldiers survive the winters? I shivered, at the thought, and at an ominous entrance to a who-knows-how-deep tunnel. The pitch-black was so quickly absolute I ventured only a few steps inside. The soldiers, of course, had no choice. They burrowed kilometres of tunnels into this mountain, often simply guesstimating which was the right way, and excavating until they saw sunlight. Around 1km (0.6 miles) of this underground warren has been restored, and can be followed by hikers who hopefully have torches and no fear of confined spaces...

I continued upward, to reach the Kaiserjäger's most spine-tingling stretch. After a half-hike, half-haul up a set of steps, I reached a section where the path had fallen away. I inched along, grasping a wire rope, dangling over an abyss. I made it over, then across a ravine-spanning suspension bridge and up a dizzying trail to reach the ridge-top, an eerie netherworld where a snow-splotched plateau spread below and the summits had been swallowed by cloud.

👢 NERVES OF IRON

Via ferrata once enabled soldiers to fight amid the Dolomites. Now, these 'iron roads' allow hikers to feel like mountaineers, and access otherwise climber-only realms. They vary in difficulty. Some trekking routes have short sections of ladders or cables; many via ferrata are more technical and require helmets and harnesses. A popular choice is the Via Ferrata Pisciadù, built by the Tridentina brigade, which involves a vertical climb of 600m (1968ft) and crossing a gorge via a hanging bridge.

Clockwise from top: back to civilisation; a war-era tunnel; high in the range. Previous page: the mighty Dolomites

> *"Peaks loomed on all sides, snow melt churned and angular rocks made the going sharp underfoot."*

More restored relics lay here. The Austro-Hungarians had a chain of lookout posts forming a defensive line across the saddle and up Mt Lagazuoi, which can still be seen; the Italians, for their part, had a stronghold halfway along the mountain's face. The Austrians repeatedly attempted to drive the Italians away, even pummelling them with *Rollbomben* (cast-iron balls filled with explosives), but the impasse continued. I contemplated all this inside the convivial Rifugio Lagazuoi; I gave silent thanks that this place was now for tourists and apple strudel rather than a theatre of war.

A cable car drops down from the hut to Falzarego, but I walked on, following cairns across the lonely plateau. Peaks loomed on all sides, snow melt churned and angular rocks made the going sharp underfoot. But slowly, gradually, I descended from this landscape of icy inhospitableness into a lusher, kinder place. The world seemed warmer, both in temperature and welcome. I could hear the bell-clunk of goats. I was glad to have taken a walk back in time. And I was glad to re-emerge in the peaceful present. **SB**

ORIENTATION

Start/Finish // Passo di Valparola
Distance // 9km (5.5 miles)
Duration // Four hours
Getting there // The Alta Badia valley is a two-hour drive from both Venice and Innsbruck. Bus companies connect these airports (as well as Munich, Verona and Treviso) to towns in the valley, such as La Villa and Corvara. Local buses serve trailheads.
When to go // There's a range of hotels and guesthouses in the valleys. Most atmospheric are Alpine *rifugi* (mountain huts), usually teetering in high-up locations, offering simple dorms and hearty food; these must be booked in advance.
More info // www.dolomiti.org; www.lagazuoi.it

The Kaiserjäger

*Opposite: making the descent from
Montenvers to the Mer de Glace*

MORE LIKE THIS
VIA FERRATA

TENNENGEBIRGE, AUSTRIA

Get an early start for this moderately challenging day hike on a *Klettersteig* (fixed-cable way) that dives head-first into the dramatic karst landscapes of the Tennengebirge Alps in Salzburgerland. The four- to five-hour trek begins on a high above Werfen: take a minibus and cable car up to Eisriesenwelt, the world's largest accessible ice caves. The via ferrata starts nearby, negotiating breathtakingly sheer cliffs that plunge 1000m (3281ft) down to the Salzach Valley. You'll need a good head for heights to brave the rungs that spider up the vertical rock face, eventually emerging onto a lonely, majestically wild karst plateau. From here, make your way across the other-worldly rockscape. Listen out for the screech of golden eagles as you ascend cross-topped Hochkogel (2281m/7484ft), where dress-circle views of the Berchtesgaden Alps over the border in Germany await. From here, make a zigzagging descent back to Werfen.
Start/Finish // Dr-Friedrich-Ödl-Haus, Werfen
Distance // 12km (7.5 miles)
More info // www.werfen.at; www. bergsteigen.com

LEUKERBAD, SWITZERLAND

As close as you'll come to flirting with hardcore rock climbing with the safety of a harness, karabiner and helmet, this beast of a via ferrata is Switzerland's longest and most demanding, taking in a phenomenally wild, off-the-radar stretch of the Bernese Alps. Starting at the 2322m (7618ft) Gemmi Pass above Leukerbad, the big eight-hour tour is exposed all the way, with near-vertical rock faces plunging into the void as you make your way along steel cables and up knee-tremblingly sheer ladders. Graded K5-6 (extremely difficult), you'll need to be physically fit, surefooted and experienced to even consider it. But if you do, your reward is top-of-the-beanstalk views from the 2942m (9652ft) peak of Daubenhorn, before a beautiful descent via a white-blue-white marked route across the crevasse-free Daubenhorn Glacier and back to the Gemmi Pass. Choose a fine-weather day and watch out for falling rocks.
Start/Finish // Gemmi Pass, Leukerbad
Distance // 9km (5.6 miles)
More info // www.gemmi.ch; www. viaferrata-leukerbad.ch

BALCONS DE LA MER DE GLACE, FRANCE

If you're up for a serious challenge and have the skill, stamina, kit and fitness to match, the Mer de Glace (Sea of Ice) is out of this world. A combination of via ferrata, scramble and glacier traverse, this physically tough and staggeringly scenic route begins at the Montenvers mountain station. Feel your pulse quicken and the earth drop away as you descend ladders gripping the near-vertical rock face to the moraine-streaked Mer de Glace, France's largest glacier, which snakes down the northern flank of Mont Blanc. The trail then picks its way up and down ladders and over the deeply crevassed glacier, inching its way gradually up to the Refuge du Couvercle, where a hearty meal and dorm bed have never been more welcome. From here you can descend back to Montenvers. Unless you are an experienced mountaineer, a guide is highly advisable.
Start // Montenvers
Finish // Refuge du Couvercle
Distance // 11km (7 miles)
More info // www.chamonix.com; www. guides-mont-blanc.com

WHISKY TASTING ON THE SPEYSIDE WAY

Follow the River Spey through gentle woods, over barren moors, in the footsteps of moonshiners and excisemen, to where Scotland's most famous whisky is crafted.

Standing in the smart-but-uninspiring harbour town of Buckie, I wonder why a long-distance hike along the Spey, a river renowned across the globe for the prolific, high-calibre whisky that is made along its banks, should begin here, where there is no River Spey and no whisky distillery. However, Buckie and its vicinity add an agreeable sandy coastal element to what is otherwise a route of river – first estuary, then waterside woods, then hillsides and settlements that have long depended upon the Spey for the water that fuelled the region's lucrative whisky production. But for perhaps the first time in a lifetime of seeking out scenic trails to tramp, terrain is not my primary consideration.

I am here for what the Gaelic Scots called *uisge beatha* – the 'water of life' or whisky, to plonk a relatively modern (18th-century) label on a drink distilled in the Scottish countryside for almost a millennium. Lots of walks meander along pretty rivers but only one leads you between some of the world's finest single malt whisky distilleries as it does so. This is it.

You see, walking between distilleries is not just a great idea because I say so, or because there will be no drams wreaking havoc with your driving. Scotch whisky has Protected Designation of Origin (PDO) status, partly because a drink never did depict a country's topography quite like whisky does Scotland's: it is an interactive roadmap for the palate, where the colours, aromas and flavours of the land, from snowy uplands through peaty, heathery moors to briny ocean, converge in a glass. In short, it is only by walking through the landscape surrounding the distilleries that you gain time to really appreciate everything that goes into crafting their drams. What you experience on a walk is what you'll taste.

I consider myself properly on my whisky way once the trail turns inland at the Spey estuary. Here, the might of this 172km (107-mile) river is palpable, the river mouth yawning wide enough to have its own islets. The water seems exceptionally clear for this far downstream. It is said the Spey has the lowest dissolved mineral content of any Scottish river system and that this lends its water, and thus the region's whisky, a particularly pure taste. I quickly cover this first section of the trail, mostly on forestry tracks with intermittent vistas of sleepy riverside crop fields, passing Fochabers and reaching Craigellachie at the close of day one.

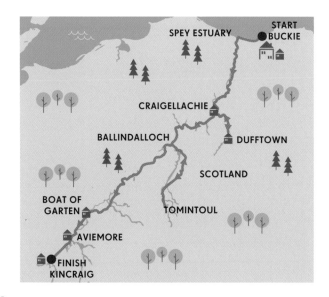

"A drink never did depict a country's topography quite like whisky does Scotland's."

WAY AHEAD

A 22.5km (14-mile) extension to the Speyside Way, from Kincraig to Newtonmore, is in the offing. Bringing the trail up to this point will offer hikers a greater sense of River Spey completion: Newtonmore is the first major settlement downstream from the river's source. This will make the route, with additional spurs to Dufftown and Tomintoul included, almost 170km (106 miles) long altogether.

Clockwise from top left: working in the cooperage; the River Spey; whisky appreciation; hikers making their way along the Spey. Previous page: view over a glen to Aberlour

Here the whisky attractions commence in earnest, although the only spirit action when I arrive at twilight is at the Quaich Bar of the Craigellachie Hotel: its 900-strong collection of single malts Scotland's biggest and best. I sample several, sticking to Speyside brands for cultural reasons. And while it is difficult to pin common characteristics on a regional whisky taste, those I try are free of the peat permeating other Scotch whiskies: lighter, zestier, with occasional butterscotch notes emerging instead. In fetching Craigellachie, you can always find an excuse for another dram, but next morning will not thank you for over-indulging. The following day I am glad of a simpler schedule to nurse my pounding head. I tour the Speyside Cooperage, Britain's only place where you can witness the age-old skill of whisky barrel making, and do the 16km

(10-mile) out-and-back woodsy stroll along a former railway line to Dufftown, worldwide capital of single malt whisky. Home to seven distilleries, the small town has a potent fug of malt hanging over it.

Craigellachie sports two distilleries including The Macallan, crafters of the planet's priciest bottle of whisky (a 1926, 60-year-aged single malt) and with a state-of-the-art visitor centre. But for me, the upstream distilleries beckon. I head out along some abandoned railway paths via Aberlour and the scenery ratchets up in drama, revealing spectacular swathes of forested gorge. My route switches banks (to my relief, as I had been growing alarmed yesterday at how the triple bill of distilleries in Rothes had been rendered inaccessible to me by little more than a bridgeless river's breadth) before arriving at the Ballindalloch Estate. The distillery here, contrasting starkly with Speyside's more venerable offerings, began life in 2011, but offers something others do not. Here, every stage of the whisky-making process, from growing the barley to feeding the spent malt back to cattle is done locally: a rarity today, but much more in keeping with how whisky was made historically.

After Ballindalloch I know the path will become momentarily wilder in the moors above Grantown-on-Spey, before a long

section of easier walking, first to captivating Boat of Garten, and then to Aviemore, Scotland's premier ski town, where the mountains feel thrillingly close, and finally to journey's end at Kincraig on lonely Loch Insh.

But I never liked things easy, and I am lured by what is purportedly the path's toughest portion: the spur from Ballindalloch to Tomintoul. Less walked than the river-hugging main route, it is certainly not necessary to complete the Speyside Way. But with the Glenlivet and Tomintoul distilleries at stake, plus the route's remotest upland country, I am not about to decline. Both distilleries are on the Glenlivet Estate, which spreads 230 sq km (89 sq miles) over the verdant mountain valleys of the Livet and Avon rivers. I climb to Tomintoul, highest village in the Scottish Highlands, and see that distillery first. Their whisky tingles with the tang of the encompassing upland grasslands. Glenlivet I save until last. The single malt produced here was King George IV's favourite tipple, and is today the second-most popular on Earth. After the tour, I follow signs out to discover the estate's three smugglers' trails, remembering the likes of the distillery's founder George Smith and legendary moonshiner Robbie MacPherson. Up on these muddy paths, half-lost between woodland and moorland, you best appreciate why it is that Speyside became such a flourishing whisky region. Yes, water quality. Yes, the proximity of lots of barley farms. But also the remoteness. You would have been very far from the excisemen, here. **LW**

ORIENTATION

Start // Buckie
Finish // Kincraig
Distance // 115km (71.5 miles) Buckie–Kincraig, plus 8km (5 miles) one-way for the Craigellachie–Dufftown spur and 24km (15 miles) one-way for the Ballindalloch–Tomintoul spur (consider getting a taxi back to the main trail).
Duration // Six to ten days allowing time for distillery visits.
Getting there // There are regular trains to Aberdeen from London and Edinburgh. From there, catch the train to Keith, then bus 10 to Fochabers, and bus 35/38 to Buckie.
Tours // Macs Adventure (www.macsadventure.com) run 6-day self-guided whisky-themed hikes along the Way.
Things to know // The Craigellachie–Dufftown spur is not part of the official trail; the Ballindalloch–Tomintoul spur is. Both spurs can be walked out-and-back or made into loops from the main trail using other paths.
More info // www.speysideway.org

MORE LIKE THIS
TASTING TRAILS

THE TRAPPIST BEER TRAIL, BELGIUM

There are only 12 true Trappist breweries in the world: that is, breweries making beer within the walls of a Trappist monastery, either by or under supervision of the monks and with proceeds from the booze sales going mostly to charity. Three of these are in Wallonia, the French-speaking southern part of Belgium, and this is the hike that connects them. Mostly on tracks and lanes through flat, gentle countryside and winsome woodlands, the route takes in resplendent Abbaye Notre-Dame d'Orval, dating from 1132 and faithfully producing Orval, the first Trappist beer to become internationally known; Abbaye Notre-Dame de Saint-Rémy in Rochefort, making the Rochefort 6, 8 and 10 beers; and Abbaye Notre-Dame de Scourmont in Chimay, making beer and cheese. There's a nearby beer and cheese museum and inn to sustain the hungry hiker.
Start // Orval
Finish // Chimay
Distance // 290km (180 miles)
More info // www.wallonia.be; www. grsentiers.org (to order trail leaflet)

CHEMIN DU VIGNOBLE, SWITZERLAND

The dazzling Rhône Valley dominates life in the Swiss canton of Valais, flanked by the country's highest peaks and with Switzerland's premier vineyards carpeting the sheer slopes between mountainside and river. The vineyards are some of Europe's steepest, reaching full glory in a blaze of golden-green from Leuk to Martigny. This several-days' saunter weaves through tracts of grapevine varietals including Chasselas, Johannisberg, Gamay and Pinot Noir, via such charming grape-growing villages and towns as Saillon, Sion and Sierre. Expect Swiss wine surprises, such as rare grape variety Amigne, an ancient grape documented by the likes of Virgil and Horace over two thousand ago; the sweet and potent Flétri, or late-harvested wines, for which Valais is well known; and glacier wine, which is matured at lofty altitudes close to glaciers. There are of course plenty of vineyard tours and tastings, plus a wine museum en route.
Start // Leuk
Finish // Martigny
Distance // 74km (46 miles)
More info // www.schweizmobil.ch

LEDBURY CIDER TRAIL, ENGLAND

This 32km (20-mile) route meanders along country lanes that penetrate the beating, scrumpy heart of England's cider country. It's an offshoot of the much more extensive Herefordshire & Wye Valley Cider Route for drivers. Herefordshire produces more than 50% of the UK's cider, and this route begins in one of the county's standout timber-framed towns, Ledbury. From here the orchard-lined loop takes intrepid tasters to Westons, one of the country's leading cider-makers, plus other highly regarded producers such as Gregg's Pit (open by appointment) and Lyne Down. With cider and perry tour tastings and ample appley refreshment in pubs along the way, this cider circular can be extended on the Herefordshire Trail or the Wye Valley Path, both of which connect with this route.
Start/Finish // Ledbury
Distance // 32km (20 miles)
More info // www.visitherefordshire. co.uk

Clockwise from top: the Abbaye Notre-Dame d'Orval; a crop of Herefordshire cider apples; above the vines on Switzerland's Chemin du Vignoble

MALLORCA'S DRY STONE ROUTE

Taking in sea cliffs, honey-stone villages, isolated coves and the limestone spires of the Tramuntana range, this multiday ramble is a tantalising taste of pre-tourism Mallorca.

Long brushed aside as being a cheap package-break destination in the Med, Mallorca wasn't always a choice among serious hikers for a multiday expedition; they would have rolled eyes in disbelief. No more: the biggest and most dramatic of the Balearic Islands is finally being fêted for the phenomenal beauty of its coastline and mountains. And striking out on the Ruta de Pedra en Sec (Dry Stone Route) – or GR221 – gets you to the bits others rarely see. Broken up into eight stages and mostly patched together from old mule tracks, the trail is named after the dry-stone walls that interweave the island's heights, hemming in silver-green olive groves, citrus-laden orchards, terraced vineyards and pine forest.

In staggering contrast to the built-up resorts, the trail, still partly unsigned, leads deep into the island's little-explored hinterland and high into the ragged wilderness and ravines of the Serra de Tramuntana, Mallorca's backbone. Tracing a rough line through the north of the island, this Unesco-listed landscape is ensnared by limestone peaks scarred by the elements. Here, ochre-stone villages cling to hilltops, cliffs drop abruptly to the deep blue sea, and terraces march up from the coast. The clang of out-of-tune monastery bells echoes through remote valleys, where nimble-footed goats share the trail.

I begin the Ruta on one of those clear spring days that make you feel glad to be alive. Leaving behind the seaside town of Port d'Andratx, the trail eases me in gently with a four-hour trudge to Sa Trapa, which dips in and out of sun-dappled pinewoods and coastal scrub heavy with the scent of wild rosemary in purple bloom. At Sant Elm, the offshore nature reserve island of Sa Dragonera looms tantalisingly into view. But more arresting still is the grandstand view of sapphire sea from Sa Trapa and its ruined Trappist monastery.

Cairns and the odd paint splash guide the way on the second leg of the hike from Sa Trapa to Estellencs. I sometimes lose the rocky trail but soon pick it up again, all the while marvelling at the dividing blues of horizon and sea. Onwards and upwards I go to the knobbly summit of Moleta de s'Esclop (926m/3038ft), where the view of the Tramuntana is out of this world, with fissured peaks rippling into the distance like waves on breaking point. A gravel trail leads down to Estellencs, a laid-back hamlet with honey-hued buildings scattered on the hills below 1025m (3363ft) Puig Galatzó.

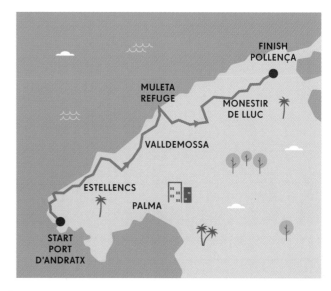

Day three ramps up the drama on a six-hour trek between Estellencs and Banyalbufar. As I follow quiet trails that occasionally reveal a glimmer of sea, the only sound is that of foot on rock and a distant braying donkey. Looking as if it will topple off the cliff with the merest puff of wind, the Torre des Verger, a 16th-century *talayot*, or watchtower, makes a fine picnic spot before the onward hike to Banyalbufar. The village is tightly laced with pot-plant-lined lanes and combed with dry-stone farming terraces – *ses marjades* – that form a series of steep steps down to the sea. I'd like to linger but I want to make Esporles before nightfall.

The morning sun warms the stone houses of the village, cradled in the foothills of the Tramuntana. It's day four and the path takes me through thick macchia, orchards and shady olive groves. Cresting rises and cutting through woodland, I pretty much have the trail to myself. Not so in Valldemossa, where crowds mill around the Carthusian monastery where composer Frédéric Chopin and his lover, George Sand, sojourned in 1838. After a quick culture fix, it's back on the Camí de s'Arxiduc, a rocky path shimmying high along the coast to Deià. Perched like an eyrie above the blue sea, this is surely one of Mallorca's most romantic hill towns. It's a romance that wasn't lost on poet Robert Graves, who now lies buried under the cypress tree in the churchyard.

From Deià, the onward coastal trail reveals mood-lifting views of the sea and rock formations like holey Sa Foradada, which resembles an elephant from afar. The tentative drone of cicadas tells me that evening is approaching on the dry-stone Camí de Castelló, twisting up through pine and olive groves to the Muleta refuge above Port de Sóller. That night, the starry sky is more brilliant than ever and moonbeams dance on the sea.

Well rested, I brace myself for a nine-hour hut-to-hut hike delving deep into the mountainous backcountry on day six.

TIME AND TIDE

So you fancy tagging on an extra day or two in Mallorca's north? Wise choice. The coastline northeast of Pollença, the island's most dramatic, is reached by a helter-skelter of a road, which you can cycle if you're as fit as a fiddle. En route are lookouts with views of a sea of deepest blue and the cliffs rearing above it like shark fins. Spend some chill time on Platja de Formentor's ribbon of pine-fringed sand or head on to lighthouse-topped Cap de Formentor for a cracking sunset.

Clockwise from top: the rocky path to Deià; a Mallorcan home; Deià; donkeys nibble at a dry-stone wall. Previous page: the village of Sóller

"Perched like an eyrie above the blue sea, Deià is surely one of Mallorca's most romantic hill towns"

After a coffee on the plaza in the lovely hill town of Sóller, the trail ambles on through lemon and orange orchards, now billowing with white blossom, climbing steadily to the sweet hamlet of Biniaraix, tucked among gardens and the Tramuntana's grey stone flanks. A stone path wends up the Barranc de Biniaraix ravine and on to the Puig de l'Ofre (1093m/3586ft), where the puckered, pale-grey peaks stand out against the azure water of the Cúber reservoir. It has been a long day and my legs are thankful when I finally reach the remote mountain hut of Tossals Verds.

As the hike edges east on day seven, it enters high, rocky terrain, making for a scramble up to the fortress-like summit of Coll des Prat (838m/2749ft), from where it's possible to ascend 1365m (4478ft) Puig de Massanella, Mallorca's second-highest peak, for captivating views over the eroded karst wilderness of the Tramuntana to the sea beyond. Pilgrims and day-trippers mill around the Monestir de Lluc, where I pause to glimpse the late-Renaissance basilica, before heading on to my bed for the night at the tranquil Refugi Son Amer.

The pockmarked heights of the Tramuntana are interspersed with pine forest on the final stretch from the refuge to the hill town of Pollença. It's late afternoon when I arrive and the shuttered houses glow like warm honey. Above the town sits a pilgrimage chapel, reached by a flight of 365 steps – the Calvari. But it's a climb that will have to wait for tomorrow. **KW**

ORIENTATION

Start // Port d'Andratx
Finish // Pollença
Distance // 167km (103 miles)
Duration // Eight days
Getting there // The trailhead, Port d'Andratx, is a 30-minute drive from Palma de Mallorca. Bus 102 runs regularly from Palma to Port d'Andratx.
When to go // Sweltering summer weather can make the hike more arduous, so it's better to dodge the heat and crowds and go in spring or autumn instead.
What to pack // Temperatures are usually mild, so bring light clothes, sturdy boots, sunscreen and insect repellent.
More info // Consell de Mallorca (www.conselldemallorca. net) has detailed trail information, tips on guides/maps and a booking service for *refugi* (refuges).

Opposite: a mule trail traces the
sublime coastline of the Pelion
Peninsula, Greece

MORE LIKE THIS
MULE TRAILS

VIA DEL SALE, ITALY

Where the Alps bow to meet the Ligurian Sea on the Italian–French border, the Via del Sale (Salt Path) snakes an ancient route of trails once used by traders to transport salt by pack mule. Beginning in the village of Limone Piemonte in the craggy Maritime Alps, the hike unravels along dry stone-walled medieval paths, taking in formidable 19th-century military fortifications that once defended Piedmont from invasion, high mountain passes and hairpin-bend-riddled roads. By night, *rifugi* (shelters) offer respite and sustenance. With enough ascent and descent to feel like a proper challenge, the walk in its entirety leads all the way to the pastel-painted seaside town of Ventimiglia. En route you'll dip into some proper remote wilderness in the Bosco delle Navette, forested with beech and conifer, and the Alpi Liguri Natural Regional Park, with its pastures, thickly wooded peaks, lakes and waterfalls. So remote, in fact, that wolves and wildcats still roam these heights.

Start // Limone Piemonte
Finish // Ventimiglia
Distance // 112km (70 miles)
More info // www.altaviadelsale.com

GRIES PASS, SWITZERLAND

For Switzerland at its thrillingly wild best, strike out on this Alpine day hike to the Gries Pass, a 2469m (8100ft) mountain pass straddling the Swiss–Italian border, which links the Upper Goms in Valais to Formazza in Piedmont. Beginning in Ulrichen, a pretty church-topped village of dark-timber chalets in the Rhône Valley, the trek makes its way along historic mule trails pounded by traders and travellers since Roman times. Hike in silent wonder through the wooded Ägenetal valley, gradually climbing to reach the head of the valley, with views of the highest wind park in Europe at 2500m (8202ft). The trail then threads above the turquoise, glacier-fed Griessee, before lurching on through bare, rugged, snow-streaked peaks to the Gries Pass, where views of the Valle di Morasco open up. The hike climaxes at the 2478m (8130ft) Nufenen Pass, which peers deep into the Valais and Bernese Alps and is accessed by a helter-skelter of a road.

Start // Ulrichen
Finish // Nufenen Pass
Distance // 21km (13 miles)
More info // www.valais.ch

PELION PENINSULA, GREECE

Tick off sun-bleached hill towns like rosary beads as you stomp along old mule trails (*kalderimis*) in quiet exhilaration on Greece's lushly green and rugged Pelion Peninsula. Once the main means of getting around before tarmac arrived, these paths take you well and truly off the beaten track in the peninsula's hinterland, through orchards, wild olive groves and forests plumed with chestnut, oak, fir and beech, past ancient ruins, churches and monasteries, and down to the bright-blue Aegean Sea. In Greek mythology, this region was the home of the centaurs, hybrid beasts that frolicked in its woods and drank deep of its clear spring waters. Bookended by the pretty mountain villages of Portaria and Milies, this hike acquaints you with a little-known corner of Greece, taking in gorges, beaches, fishing villages and one phenomenal sea view after the next.

Start // Portaria
Finish // Milies
Distance // 63km (39 miles)
More info // www.visitgreece.gr

A LOOP OF ANDORRA:
THE CORONALLACS TRAIL

This five-day hut-to-hut hike follows a circuit around the Andorran Pyrenees, showing exactly what makes this mountain principality such a special proposition.

'm not expecting the bearded vulture. I've just hauled myself up the Pic del Clot del Cavall – one of the countless craggy, green-shouldered peaks that throng the Andorran map – and I'm taking a moment to gather breath. Long swig of water. Loud, happy exhalation. Possibly a whoop. And then it appears over the ridge, as silent as the sunshine and as big as a barn door. Dark primary feathers outstretched, the giant bird tilts into the valley, thrillingly close to where I'm standing, then soars out towards Spain. Oh, for wings to unfurl.

Andorra is a small country. Study a map of Europe and it appears as a speck, a curious enclave in the Pyrenean borderlands between France and Spain. But small isn't a word that comes to mind when you're here with the wind in your hair, tackling the country's undulating five-day Coronallacs Trail. The route, which calls in at a different staffed mountain hut every night, involves between six and 10 hours of walking a day and requires close to 7000m (22,966ft) of ascent. An idle saunter, it isn't.

It is, however, a stonkingly good trek. The trail's five stages trace a spectacular, cartographic dot-to-dot around this Catalan-speaking principality, forming a 93km (58-mile) loop that begins and ends at Escaldes-Engordany, on the outskirts of capital city Andorra La Vella. The country draws most of its visitors over the coldest months, when ski tourists arrive. But I'm here in early July, and although the tallest peaks remain resolutely snow-patched, the high-altitude temperatures are pushing 30°C (86°F). Sun cream? Plenty. Water? Plenty. Trepidation? A little. And so provisioned, I set off.

The first day eases me in with a long ascent through shady woods. Burbling streams and fluting birdsong set the tone for the initial couple of hours, before the trees clear and a range of sawtoothed mountains appears to the south. This is the stuff I've come for. By the afternoon I'm crossing high grassland, where lizards dart across rocks, and wild thyme and micro-orchids squeeze out of cracks. The heat is dry and piney. When, six hours after I begin walking, the first refuge arrives – the ultra-modern L'Illa, already busy with dog-tired hikers and surrounded by fierce cols – an ice-cold can of San Miguel disappears almost before I've bought it.

All four refuges on the trail are professionally run, and act as welcome oases. They also happen to be the only four staffed refuges (or mountain huts) in the country, which gives the trail a nice sense of completism. Just as enjoyably, they're also very different from each other. L'Illa has an almost space-age vibe, while the others – in order: Juclà, Borda de Sorteny and Comapedrosa – are respectively hippyish, homely and hidden in a high-altitude bowl of mountain scenery. At all four, the dorm beds are comfortable, the conversation's easy and the communal meals are generously portioned. Supplies are helicoptered into the refuges a couple of times a season to ensure they don't run bare. Just as well, too.

These refuges act as restorative punctuation marks that break up the flowing kilometres of the trail itself. Day two is a stunner, summiting high passes, running alongside freezing streams and serving up savage lake-and-mountain panoramas (the name Coronallacs, incidentally, translates as 'Crown of Lakes'). Save for a few bumfluff wisps of white cloud, the sky is a hot blue all day. At one point the trail crosses an off-duty ski piste, made stranger still by the presence of countless whistling marmots, their furry heads sporadically bobbing into view above the grass.

That evening, over a hefty serving of cheesy pasta and a carafe of all-too-drinkable wine, the chatter at my table flip-flops between English, Spanish, French and Catalan. Some of those staying in the refuge are midway through challenging, multi-week Pyrenean traverses. Others are just up here for the night. 'We need the mountains,' a heavily bearded local tells me, smiling, 'for Andorrans, our gym is the Pyrenees.'

Early the next morning I stride out, zigzagging through pink rhododendron bushes as the scenery opens up again. Swifts scythe overhead. Waterfalls tumble from grey crags. By now I've found my rhythm, only broken by the occasions when the trail signage, generally reliable throughout, goes AWOL. It's hard to

MARMOTS

You'll likely hear the high-pitched whistle of marmots along the trail. More readily heard than seen, these chunky ground squirrels live in burrows, only emerging during the warmer months. High mountains such as the Pyrenees are their natural environment, although there's more to their presence here than meets the eye – they were extinct in this region for several millennia before being reintroduced in the 1940s, to give livestock-killing birds of prey an alternative food source.

Clockwise from top: Pyrenean chamois; in praise of the Andorran Pyrenees; a mountain lake and sign near the Refugi de Juclà. Previous page: surveying the landscape in the northeastern section of the trail

go wrong with a map to hand, thankfully, and the hours unspool in happy fashion. I pass hollows still thick with ice, as the peaks roar overhead and the sun beats down. I sleep well.

The forecast is poor for day four, which also happens to be the toughest stage. Such is life. The trail swirls and climbs through the Andorran northwest, with gargantuan, forest-striped views compensating for some punishing up-hills. I walk at a sharper pace than previous days – when the vulture appears, I'm half-delirious with joy-meets-fatigue – and make it to the final, high-perched

> "By the afternoon I'm crossing high grassland, where lizards dart across rocks, and wild thyme and micro-orchids squeeze out of cracks."

refuge just before the clouds unleash a three-hour downpour. Let me tell you, there's nothing like watching a mountain tempest when you're wearing clean socks and sipping tea. The final stage is long, but almost wholly downhill, descending more than 1000m (3281ft) to reach the point where I started. The relative ease of this last stretch gives the chance to reflect on the kilometres that I've clocked up over the past five days. Andorra's size makes it an easy place to overlook, even for seasoned outdoors-lovers, but you'd be pushed to find a loop walk of this distance that tops it for sheer natural finery. And yes, it's a tiny country – but you know what they say about good things and small packages. **BL**

ORIENTATION

Start/Finish // Escaldes-Engordany
Distance // 93km (58 miles)
Duration // Five days
Getting there // Other than driving, the simplest way to reach capital city Andorra La Vella is by direct bus from Toulouse or Barcelona. Andorra has no trains.
When to go // Late spring to early autumn. Early June to mid-July is a good window, as is September. Late July and August are warm, but often see afternoon thunderstorms.
More info // Visit www.coronallacs.com for a full route breakdown, with maps, as well as a booking portal. The tourist office website (www.visitandorra.com) also has information on the trail.
Things to know // Pre-hike, head to the Escaldes-Engordany tourist office on Plaça Santa Anna, to pick up a map and a trail passport (to be stamped in each refuge).

MORE LIKE THIS
BIG HIKES IN
SMALL COUNTRIES

LIECHTENSTEIN TRAIL, LIECHTENSTEIN

Unveiled in 2019, this cross-country (literally) trail spans the entire micronation of Liechtenstein, wending a wriggly path from south to north. It begins close to the Swiss border and finishes up adjacent to Austria, and these two neighbours give an indication of the kind of widescreen pastoral scenery you can expect. The ups and downs are manageable (the high point of the trail is just over 1100m/3609ft) and if you're feeling especially energetic, it's possible to march the whole thing in a day or two. Far better to take your time, though – the route passes through all 11 of the country's municipalities, taking in numberless historical and cultural sites, and gives the chance to learn more about this unique corner of the continent.

Start // Balzers
Finish // Schaanwald
Distance // 75km (47 miles)
More info // www.tourismus.li

MULLERTHAL TRAIL, LUXEMBOURG

Wealthy, wine-loving Luxembourg does things its own way. True to form, the Grand Duchy's best long-distance trail comprises three adjacent loops rather than a standard end-to-end hike. Focusing on the hilly Mullerthal Region in the east of the country, the trail offers a trio of roughly equidistant circuits taking in forests, castles and a fine assortment of canyons, valleys and waterfalls. There's a fair amount of uphill, but it tends to be short and sharp, and however you choose to tackle the trail you're unlikely to encounter crowds. Luxembourg often gets written off as boring, but there's plenty here that grabs the attention, not least the little abbey settlement of Echternach – the country's oldest town – where two of the loops begin and end.

Start/Finish // Echternach (Loops 1 and 2); Mullerthal (Loop 3)
Distance // 112km (70 miles)
More info // www.visitluxembourg.com

GOZO COASTAL TRAIL, MALTA

Gozo is the second-largest island in the Maltese archipelago (behind Malta itself) and has a more laid-back feel than its big brother. As its name suggests, this clockwise circular trail sticks largely to the coastline, placing the island's spectacular sea views centre-stage. It's split into four sections of between 11km and 16km (9 miles and 10 miles), the longest of these being the final and most testing part of the trail (although, this being Gozo, you won't be expending alpine levels of effort). One of the real joys of making the walk is the number of attractions encountered en-route, from old watchtowers and traditional villages to centuries-old chapels and quiet beaches. There are regular ferries between Malta and Gozo, and local advice is to make the walk between mid-September and mid-June, avoiding the more intense heat of high summer.

Start/Finish // Mġarr
Distance // 50km (31 miles)
More info // www.visitgozo.com

*Clockwise from top: the Galina
Falconry Centre, a detour from the
Liechtenstein Trail; a misty forest path
on the Mullerthal Trail; Mixta Cave
in Gozo*

A WINE WANDER
ALONG THE MOSELLE

*Hop between vineyards on a long-distance trail tracing the meandering Moselle River,
and discover the Roman remains and romantic ruined castles of this historic region.*

'Hail, river... Let show of vines lead on another pageant,
and let Bacchus' gifts attract our wandering gaze
where lofty ridge, far-stretching above scarped
slopes, and spur, and sunny hill-side with salient and
reentrant rise in a natural theatre overgrown with vines.' (Extract
from *Mosella* by Ausonius).

Well, perhaps I wouldn't put it in quite such florid terms –
though in fairness, those lines were originally penned in Latin by
a Gallic-Roman poet more than 16 centuries ago. And, I mused
from my perch overlooking the Moselle on a sun-soaked June
afternoon, they weren't too far off describing the scene I was
admiring on this most bibulous of German waterways. The vine-
striped slopes, the wooded hills, the small boats bobbing on the
river: all would have been familiar to Ausonius during his own
littoral mission in 368 CE. Our missions were quite different – he
was escorting an emperor's son west to the imperial capital of
Roman Gaul, Augusta Treverorum, while I was heading east from
that city, now called Trier – but we had two things in common:
our mode of transport and our love of wine.

Like Ausonius, I was exploring on foot, following the Moselsteig
– a waymarked trail that snakes 365km (227 miles) downstream
from the three-way France–Luxembourg–Germany border, keeping
the river company until its confluence with the Rhine at Koblenz.

I began my Moselle meander with a history lesson at the spot
where viticulture arrived with the Romans over two millennia ago.
Established by 16 BCE, Trier is reputedly the oldest city in Germany.
That imperial legacy lingers in the vast slabs of the *Römerbrücke*
(Roman bridge) and the blackened stone towers of the Porta
Nigra, the monumental city gate dating from 160 CE; it's evident in

the ruins of various baths and the now-grassy banks of the arena
where 20,000 spectators once roared at gladiatorial games. But
it's also apparent in the prolific Weinstuben (wine bars) serving the
fruity white rieslings that predominate here.

The scenic and historic splendour continued as I followed the
fulsome curves of this particularly serpentine river over subsequent
days. The Romans weren't alone in coveting this land; many a
hilltop is capped with a castle or fortress, most in photogenic ruins
following French assaults in the 17th or 18th century. So it was in
Bernkastel-Kues, my first major port of call, where Burg Landshut
– a bastion at the more battered end of the spectrum – stands

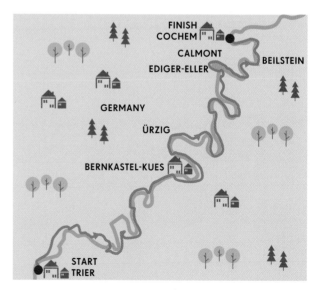

GERMAN WINE LEXICON

Prädikatswein is theoretically the best-quality German wine, with the highest level of natural grape sugar. Of this designation, Kabinett is light and often dry, Spätlese (late harvest) is richer and fuller-bodied, while Auslese is harvested later still and is often sweet. Beerenauslese and Trockenbeer-enauslese are dessert wines made from grapes with 'noble rot', while Eiswein is make from frozen grapes picked in winter. *Trocken* means very dry, *feinherb* is off-dry and *lieblich* is semi-sweet.

sentinel over an old town crammed with medieval-style timber-framed merchants' houses. And tourists: many of the honeypots along the river attract boatloads of visitors during the day, enjoying the culinary and alcoholic bounty as well as the heritage.

Fortunately, the trail affords plenty of opportunities for rising above the masses. Soon after leaving the town, I was climbing though woods of oak, beech, birch and pine, to a panoramic viewpoint from where I peered down at the vessels plying the glittering water, and at kestrels hovering above vertiginous hillsides striped with vines. And by vertiginous, I mean wince-inducingly precipitous – indeed, the vineyards at Calmont, a little farther north, are claimed to be the world's steepest.

But though you'll encounter plenty of hairpin bends and what might charitably be called 'undulating' terrain on this trail, the Moselsteig is rarely too testing – and you're never far from a refreshing wine-tasting opportunity. So it was that day: not far beyond Bernkastel-Kues I found myself waylaid at Kloster Machern, a former Cistercian monastery transformed into a

brewery, restaurant and (of course) wine cellar. And I quickly discovered that, in most villages along the route, every other building is daubed with a legend, in suitably gothic script, proclaiming a *Weingut* (winery) or *Weinprobe* (wine tasting) or *Weinverkauf* (wine for sale). Doorways festooned with wreaths or brooms advertise makeshift seasonal *Strausswirtschaften* or wine taverns, serving that family's own vintages and snacks. And every cultivatable square inch of land – plus much that, to the untrained eye, looks far too sheer and inaccessible to cultivate – is planted with vines. To paraphrase: you don't have to be wine-crazy to walk here – but it helps.

The following days settled into something of a routine, studded with familiar but persistently charming elements: hikes up to ridges blessed with plentiful benches and *Schutzhütte*, shady shelters with invariably delectable views; boozy lunches and tastings exploring the differences between Spätlese (late harvest) and Auslese (even later harvest) wines; rather slower afternoon ambles ending with a night in a charming village or

Clockwise from far left: approaching a ruined castle near Cochem; Moselle's famous bounty; rewards of the trail. Previous page: Bremm on the Moselle

"Every cultivatable square inch of land... is planted with vines."

medieval town overlooked by the regulation martial ruins. There were winsome communities such as Ediger-Eller and russet-hued hamlet Ürzig, embraced by the valley 'like a pearl in an oyster', as the local saying goes. There were stretches traversing emerald woods through which red squirrels scampered, and others crossing hillsides lined with dazzling yellow broom blossoms. Mostly, my route skirted rows of vines trained into the characteristic heart-shape that's the symbol of the region, and often overlooked by a statue of St Urban, patron saint of winemakers.

On my sample stretch of the Moselsteig, the best was saved for last. Beilstein, known to Germans as the 'Sleeping Beauty' village, is the most coherent and well-preserved of the lot; its medieval core packed with timbered, shonky-walled houses sandwiched between a hilltop Carmelite church and the obligatory skeletal stronghold. I approached along a slender, winding forest footpath that spat me out at the pentagonal castle tower, just as the soft light of the setting sun glinted off roof slates below, evoking a now-familiar Pavlovian response. A hike plus a castle plus a village plus a thirst... on this tempting river trail, it's a simple sum — and the correct answer's always riesling. Prost! **PB**

ORIENTATION

Start // Trier
Finish // Cochem
Distance // 214.5km (133 miles)
Duration // 8 to 14 days
Getting there // Trier is well connected by train. Cochem is a short train journey to Koblenz, where there are good connections across Germany and farther afield. Scheduled boat services connect several towns along the river.
When to go // May to early October.
What to wear // Comfortable hiking shoes or boots are advisable, along with a waterproof jacket.
Things to know // The complete Moselsteig route from Perl to Koblenz is 365km (227 miles) and takes 14 to 24 days. To mix things up, consider tackling some of the region's 1000km+ (620+ miles) of bike routes, including the well-surfaced Mosel Cycle Trail.
More info // www.mosellandtouristik.de

Opposite: the sun-baked vines of the
Douro Valley, Portugal

MORE LIKE THIS
WINE WALKS

VAUCLUSE, FRANCE

The Rhône region is hardly terra incognita for oenophile amblers, but away from the headline acts of Avignon and Châteauneuf-du-Pape, peaceful trails wind around the southwestern slopes of Mont Ventoux between timeless walled villages, castles and, naturally, vineyards. To taste the best of rural Rhône, tackle a moderate four-day route between winsome hilltop Venasque and Vaison-la-Romaine, the latter an attractive town blessed with Roman connections, as the name suggests. Hike via Mazan (location of the notorious libertine Marquis de Sade's château), castle-topped Le Barroux, crag-perched Crillon-le-Brave, and the sky-piercing white limestone outcrops known as the Dentelles de Montmirail looming over Gigondas – home to some of the finest wineries in the region. Throughout, you'll skirt vineyards and pass cellar doors where you can taste the famed Grenache and Syrah reds.
Start // Venasque
Finish // Vaison-la-Romaine
Distance // 65km (40 miles)
More info // www.ventouxprovence.fr

DOURO VALLEY, PORTUGAL

Few landscapes have been so shaped by wine as the valley of the Douro River, its hilly flanks etched into terraces over countless generations. Grapes have been cultivated here for over two millennia – a feat recognised in its Unesco World Heritage listing – and this is reputedly the oldest wine region in the world, demarcated in 1756. More to the point, it's a bacchanalian joy to explore on foot, following paths between and through vineyards and quintas (wine estates) where you can stop and sample the goods, bedding down each night in historic inns and whitewashed, stone-built manor houses. Trace a loop from the little riverside town of Pinhão – pausing to admire the beautiful azulejos (blue-tinted tilework) at the railway station – heading north to Sabrosa (birthplace of pioneering round-the-world navigator Ferdinand Magellan) and Alijó, then returning to the banks of the Douro via Vale de Mendiz.
Start/Finish // Pinhão
Distance // 51km (32 miles)
More info // www.visitportugal.com

PIEDMONT, ITALY

Hiking in this temptingly tasty northwestern Italian region is no truffle – I mean, trifle: the vines of Nebbiolo grapes stripe the foothills of the snow-capped Alps, ensuring steep gradients as well as a spectacular backdrop. But the mist-softened hills known as Le Langhe reward your efforts with gorgeous medieval hilltop towns and villages, delectable local cuisine and ample helpings of Barolo, a dry red tipple dubbed the 'King of Wine'. A tangle of trails laces the countryside south of gourmet capital Alba, offering diverse hiking options; a wine-lover's wander might lead from Roddi, guarded by its compact castle, to Cortemilia via Vergne, Barolo, Monforte d'Alba, Cissone and Cravanzana, via viticulture museums, hazelnut groves, frescoed stone villages and oakwoods where the region's famed white truffles grow.
Start // Roddi
Finish // Cortemilia
Distance // 77km (48 miles)
More info // www.piedmonttravel guide.com

OVER THE PYRENEES ON THE CHEMIN DE LA LIBERTÉ

Take this challenging hike through the heart of the French and Spanish Pyrenees, and into an incredible, and little-known, chapter of history.

I'd reached that point in making my latest documentary where all the joy had gone. It always comes, but I'm never ready for it. I'd been locked in edit rooms for days on end, and buried in books about WWII in Burma that had once set my mind alight, but now sent it to sleep. A filmmaker friend recognised this very particular malaise and suggested I come for a walk. This was no ordinary walk, however. It was a walk through WWII history, and just the sort of remarkable and little-known chapter of that story that gets my blood pumping.

Not as much as the walk itself would, it turned out. In signing up with six others for the Chemin de la Liberté (The Freedom Trail), which winds through the Pyrenees mountain range from southwest France into northeast Spain, I was committing to four days and 50km (31 miles) of punishing up and down hill-climbs topping out at 2200m (7218ft). It was an experience I would gladly repeat, as do many others from across Europe in what's become an annual pilgrimage of remembrance each July.

This gruelling yet stunning hiking trail gets its name from the part it played as an escape route for thousands of Allied servicemen and women fleeing Nazi-occupied Europe to neutral Spain. These hardened special forces soldiers, leftover troops who'd missed the Dunkirk evacuation, and airmen who'd been shot from their planes weren't the only ones to use it, however. They were joined by many thousands of Jews and French citizens for whom continued life under the Nazi occupation was not an option.

It was one of the toughest routes open to those fleeing capture and execution, which is why tens of thousands took it – in its hardship lay the greatest hopes of avoiding detection. Many would risk this punishing journey in the depths of winter and with little

food or clothing, sometimes with small children in their arms. The bitter Pyrenean weather would sadly claim the lives of many of those for whom all other options had been exhausted, which is why since 1994 this trail has been officially designated a memorial.

Those that did survive owed their lives to the *passeurs* (local guides) who stepped up to help the escapees in their most desperate hours of need. In offering their help, the *passeurs* – often local farmers, shepherds, miners or smugglers who knew the secret paths through this forbidding terrain – acted with full knowledge they were putting their own lives, and the lives of their families, at risk. Those caught helping, or even suspected of

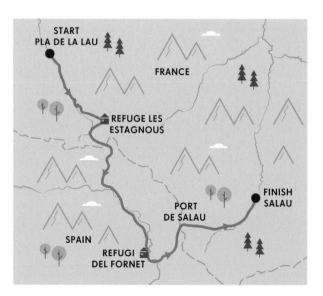

helping, people to flee the regime were shot on sight. Historians guess that almost 1000 *passeurs* paid the ultimate price for their willingness to help others.

We often talk about walking through history, but there can be few places on Earth where we get so close to the experience of those in whose footsteps and mindsets we're trying to retrace. Even on a full belly and in the most advanced hiking gear, this is not a walk for the faint-hearted. Relentless uphills for five to six hours, where your world reduces to the boots of the hiker in front, are followed by punishing downhills of similar length where the knees (or at least mine) start to audibly squeal. The set of poles I'd rejected from our guide, Will, on day one were gladly accepted on day two. Having double the amount of legs soon eases the worst of the grind.

That allowed me at last to look up, to see mountain vistas I will never forget. Ahead of us was Spain, behind us France, and somewhere just visible in the distance to my left was the quirky microstate of Andorra nestled in its ring of snow-capped peaks. I'm here on a balmy September day, and in the midday sun my sweat glands are in overdrive under my thin thermal shirt. Will points out a small mountain lake, eerily still, where my companions and I strip off for a dip in the glacial water. It flushes out the industrial quantities of lactic acid in our muscles, and we're reluctant to leave. There isn't a cloud in the sky, and the years drop away to leave a childlike contentment as we drip dry in the sunshine on the soft mountain grass.

> *"Even on a full belly and in the most advanced hiking gear, this is not a walk for the faint-hearted."*

As soon as the sun dips behind the peaks the temperature plummets however, and the question of how large patches of snow and ice have survived the fierce midday sun is soon answered. Luckily – unlike for those who took this path during the war – waiting for us each night are cosy refuges where huge dishes of the heartiest Pyrenean cuisine are gratefully inhaled alongside a medicinal glass of rich red wine (or three). Then it's off to the cosy little bunkbeds, where there's a race to get to sleep before the symphony of snoring begins. Earplugs are highly recommended...

As we crossed back into France from Spain on our final day, the morning thaw came with a sudden revelation. Three days of solid hiking, fantastic company, hearty food and astounding views had been just the tonic to relight my passion. Rarely in life today do we get the chance to completely disconnect from our technology, and reconnect with the things and people that matter. It was a sense of the peace and freedom that so many had fought and died for in WWII, and for whom this trail will stand as a proud testament for generations to come. **AB**

FREEDOM TRAIL MUSEUM

The museum for Le Chemin de la Liberté, located just outside St Girons, is highly recommnded. There you will find a permanent exhibition covering all aspects of the trail's history, including profiles and first-hand accounts of escapees and of the *passeurs* who risked their lives to help them. The museum opens Monday to Friday 2pm to 4.30pm.

Clockwise from top: the descent from Mt Valier; refuelling Pyrenees-style; evening at Refuge les Estagnous. Previous page: contemplating an extreme escape route

ORIENTATION

Start // Pla de la Lau
Finish // Salau
Distance // 46km (29 miles)
Duration // Three days
Getting there // Trains are available from Paris and Toulouse to Saint Martory, then take private transport.
When to go // Mid-June to September.
What to pack // Sturdy above-ankle hiking boots, walking poles, layers for the changing daily temperatures, waterproof jacket, small towel, earplugs.
Where to stay // Refuge les Estagnous and Refugi del Fornet offer basic accommodation and meals. Book in advance.
Where to eat // This is remote mountain hiking. Ensure you have enough food and water for each day of hiking.
Tours // Pyrenees Adventure Company offers an all-inclusive two- to four-day walking tour (www.pyreneesadventure.com).
More info // www.chemindelaliberte.fr

Opposite from top: remnants of a WWI battle on the peak of Mt Krn in the Julian Alps; visitors walk among the graves of Australian soldiers killed during the Gallipoli Campaign in Anzac Cove

MORE LIKE THIS
FRONT-LINE FORAYS

WESTERN FRONT WAY, BELGIUM/ FRANCE

In 1915 a young British soldier called Alexander Gillespie wrote a letter home from the WWI trenches, 'When peace comes, our government might combine with the French government to make one long avenue between the lines from the Vosges to the sea...'. He was killed in battle a few days later. But his legacy now lives on, in the nascent Western Front Way. Still under construction, it will be as Gillespie suggested: a waymarked path for peace and unity from the French–Swiss border to Nieuwpoort, on the North Sea. It will link a series of 200-plus plaques in towns, villages and at significant sites en route, such as the Somme, Poppy Country, Arras, Vimy Ridge and Verdun, as well as wildlife-rich landscapes, charming towns and delicious local cuisine.
Start // Pfetterhouse
Finish // Nieuwpoort
Distance // Approx 1000km (620 miles)
More info // www.thewesternfront way.com

ANZAC WALK, TURKEY

Around 100,000 British, Australian, New Zealander and Ottoman troops lost their lives in the short, bloody battle for Turkey's rugged Gallipoli Peninsula, and thus domination of the Hellespont strait to Istanbul. The near-circular Anzac Walk links 14 locations where Australian soldiers fought and died during this WWI conflict, starting at North Beach (site of a major Allied base) and finishing at the graveyard at Walker's Ridge. En route it passes infamous Anzac Cove, where most Australian troops first set foot on Gallipoli. It ventures into Shrapnel Valley, a conduit that became notorious for Turkish snipers. And it follows Artillery Road, along which some of the bloodiest encounters took place: the cemeteries of Lone Pine, Johnston's Jolly and Nek, as well as several memorials to the fallen Turks, pay homage to both sides.
Start // North Beach
Finish // Walker's Ridge
Distance // Approx 6km (3.5 miles)
More info // www.anzacportal.dva. gov.au

WALK OF PEACE, SLOVENIA/ITALY

The Walk of Peace trail, which winds from the Alps to the Adriatic, follows the Isonzo Front, the former frontline where Italian and Ottoman forces clashed during WWI. The route, which is broken down into 11 stages, is spectacular, sneaking through mountainous Triglav National Park, wending along the emerald-hued Soča River, traversing Slovenia's vine-streaked wine country and cutting across cavern-riddled karst landscapes to eventually meet the sea. But it is also littered with evidence of its brutal past – you'll find cave hideouts and command posts, ruined battlements and underground bunkers, military cemeteries and memorial churches. There are also outdoor museums – for instance, climb up to ridgetop Kolovrat to walk along its well-preserved tunnels and trenches, with sweeping (and once strategic) views over the Friuli Plains and the Julian Alps.
Start // Log pod Mangartom
Finish // Trieste
Distance // 230km (143 miles)
More info // www.potmiru.si

A HOP-ON, HOP-OFF TOUR OF THE HEART OF WALES LINE

A rural trainline has trundled through Mid-Wales for over 150 years; now, Sarah Baxter finds a walking route shadowing its tracks and a wonderfully wild rail ramble.

There's a touch of the fairy tale about the Heart of Wales Line railway. Standing on one of its platforms, listening to the reel of exotic-sounding stops – Pontarddulais, Pantyffynnon, Rhydaman; Llandeilo, Llangadog, Llangammarch; Cilmeri, Cnwclas, Tref-Y-Clawdd – seemed less public announcement than magic spell; a long, vowel-heavy conjuration. The line is, one local had told me, a bit *Alice in Wonderland*. And I was about to head down the rabbit hole, ticket in hand, walking boots laced.

This rural railway connecting Swansea and Shrewsbury opened in 1868 to move coal, livestock and people around the gloriously green and lumpy valleys of Mid-Wales. Many similar British lines were axed in the 1960s but the Heart of Wales Line survived, partly because it ran through several marginal constituencies that no politician was willing to risk upsetting. And so it endures. A slow travel anomaly, with 30-odd stations – 16 of which are stick-your-arm-out request stops – linking old spa towns, remote villages, remoter hamlets, tidal wetlands, wild uplands, Norman castles, the global epicentre of weird sport, and field upon field of sheep.

Due to the railway's wilderness-probing nature, it's always been handy for walkers eager to access the countryside. But, to mark the line's 150th birthday, a group of ramblers got together to go one better, creating the Heart of Wales Line Trail. Running from Llanelli, on the Loughor estuary, to the Shropshire market town of Craven Arms, the walking route wiggles around and about the train tracks, linking to all but four of its stations, enabling easy hop-on, hop-off rail rambles, or one great through-hike for trainspotters.

I was doing the former, which meant lots of varied terrain and lots of poring over maps and timetables. The train only runs a few times a day, so you need to do a bit of planning in order not to get

stranded; such scheduling pressures certainly add a bit of extra excitement to a fine day's walk.

It was lovely to start by the water's edge, an easy, flat amble from Llanelli, along the Millennium Coastal Path, accompanied by sea-salt breezes, noisy wading birds and views across to the Gower Peninsula. There was no unnecessary drama either: I made it to Bynea station in plenty of time for the train. And once aboard I told the conductor I wanted to jump off at Pontarddulais, a request stop.

Pontarddulais looked fairly nondescript but I was there on good advice. Professor Les Lumsden – the main man responsible for

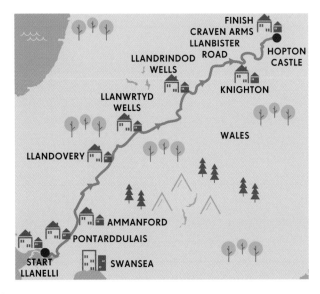

devising the Heart of Wales Line Trail – said the stretch from here to Ammanford was one of the biggest surprises: 'wild and wonderful.' So I picked up the waymarks from the station and, before long, was climbing up onto the Graig Fawr ridge, hop-skipping on a stony, then muddy track. I exchanged nods with a flat-capped dog-walker but otherwise saw no one. There were huge views: down the green valley to the west, towards the Brecon Beacons to the east, the glittering estuary behind. The bounce in my stride wasn't just due to the spongy tussocks.

I spent the night, thanks to another train hop, in lovely Llandovery, where the station is now a community cafe – the ideal place to pick up local gossip and homemade Welsh cakes. And I was up at the crack of dawn to catch the first train out the next morning, an atmospheric ride into the innards of Wales, via the 18-arch Cynghordy Viaduct and the near-kilometre-long Sugar Loaf tunnel. Everything out of the window seemed wilder and weirder now. Not least the former Victorian spa town of Llanwrtyd Wells, which has refashioned itself as the World Capital of Bog Snorkelling. I got off for a circular stroll along the River Irfon and up onto the moor, where it was just me and the red kites.

Over the next few days, the train and the trail opened up a whole host of new adventures. There was Builth Road station, with its access to the banks of the gurgling River Wye. There was Llandrindod Wells, from where I strolled past its famed mineral springs and the remains of Cefnllys Castle. And there was lonely Llanbister Road, a middle-of-nowhere platform that I might have ignored had Les not told me this was the gateway to his favourite section. I got a little lost from here, wandering the wild and windy hillsides, and ended up popping out at Llangynllo station rather than Knucklas, sadly missing the latter's show-stopping 13-arch viaduct.

I spent my last night in Knighton, just about still in Wales, though my final walk soon took me over a bridge straddling the border and

WORM-CHARMING, ANYONE?

Tucked beneath the Cambrian Mountains, the former spa resort of Llanwrtyd Wells has reinvented itself as silly-sport central. In 1985, it hosted the first World Bog Snorkelling Championships; in August 2012 it held its inaugural World Alternative Games, a now biannual olympiad of oddities encompassing gravy wrestling, worm charming and finger jousting. The japes continue year-round, with other highlights including the Welsh Open Stoneskimming Championships and the Man versus Horse Marathon.

Clockwise from left: Gosen Chapel and Cynghordy Viaduct with its 18 arches; on the trail in Shropshire; bog snorkelling at the World Alternative Games; Welsh cakes. Previous page: heading out on the Heart of Wales Line

> *"The line is... a bit Alice in Wonderland. And I was about to head down the rabbit hole, ticket in hand, walking boots laced."*

into Shropshire, England. The morning was spent following Offa's Dyke, a medieval earthwork with an excellent National Trail of its own (one for another day). Climbing uphill, I traced the ancient bank-and-ditch remains – now unceremoniously spattered with sheep poo – before picking up an old drovers' road that sliced across the misty hills; the Iron Age hill fort of Caer Caradoc loomed large to the north. It was almost a shock to descend to the pretty neatness of Bucknell, with its church, half-timbered houses and, of course, station. From here, I had just enough time for a few more miles, just enough time to continue to 13th-century Hopton Castle. And, once there, I settled onto a bench at deserted Hopton Heath station (another request stop) and got ready to stick my arm out for my final train. **SB**

ORIENTATION

Start // Llanelli
Finish // Craven Arms
Distance // 229km (142 miles)
Duration // 10 to 12 days for the full through-hike, or as little as two or three days if using the train.
Getting there // Both Llanelli and Craven Arms are, of course, served by the Heart of Wales Line, which runs between the larger hubs of Swansea and Shrewsbury.
When to go // Spring and summer (March to August) are the best times. The weather is usually warmer and drier and, because the Welsh Government offers free travel on the Heart of Wales Line to holders of concessionary passes between 1 October and 31 March, trains tend to be less busy outside these months.
More info // For timetables and info, see www.heart-of-wales.co.uk. There is a guidebook to the route published by Kittiwake Books (www.kittiwake-books.co.uk).

*Opposite: walking beneath the
spectacular Landwasser Viaduct*

MORE LIKE THIS
RAIL TRAILS

VENNBAHN, BELGIUM/GERMANY/LUXEMBOURG

From 1885 to 1989 the Vennbahn railway
linked the German town of Aachen to
Ulflingen (now Troisvierges) in Luxembourg,
passing through Belgium en route. Now,
the abandoned line has been converted
into one of the continent's longest traffic-
free bike and hike rail trails. From Unesco-
listed Aachen, the route zigzags across
the German–Belgium border, through
forest, fens, moorland and woodland. It
visits historic towns – such as magnificent
Monschau with its half-timbered houses
– and takes in a range of old railway
paraphernalia, from disused stations to the
Von Korff Viaduct and a tunnel that's been
turned into a bat-spotting adventure trail.
The final stages wend via the Ardennes
foothills and ruined Reuland Castle before
finishing at Troisvierges's historic terminus:
it was here, in August 1914, that German
soldiers first arrived in Luxembourg, the
start of over four years of occupation.
Start // Aachen, Germany
Finish // Troisvierges, Luxembourg
Distance // 125km (78 miles)
More info // www.vennbahn.eu

HERITAGE TRAIL, ENGLAND

Created by the East Lancashire Long
Distance Walkers Association, the Heritage
Trail uses a mix of riverside ways, towpaths,
green lanes, packhorse routes and old
farm tracks to connect the region's three
preserved steam railways – the East
Lancashire, the Keighley & Worth Valley,
and the Embsay & Bolton Abbey lines.
Choose to walk the route in a linear fashion
(87km/54 miles) or piece together 16 linked
loops (totalling 109km/68 miles). Either way,
the trail showcases both the rural splendour
and industrial history of these parts of
Lancashire and West Yorkshire. Highlights
include delving into Gorpley Clough Woods,
picking up the Rochdale Canal, ascending
Top of Stair (at 425m/1394ft, the route's
highest point), traversing heather-cloaked
Farnhill Moor and visiting Haworth (with
its Brontë connections). There are plenty of
train-spotting opportunities too.
Start // Ramsbottom
Finish // Embsay
Distance // 87–109km (54–68 miles)
More info // www.ldwa.org.uk;
Heritage Trail guidebook available from
Sigma Press (www.sigmapress.co.uk)

VIA ALBULA/BERNINA, SWITZERLAND/ITALY

With 55 tunnels, 196 bridges and a 2253m
(7392ft) mountain pass to surmount, the
Unesco-listed Albula/Bernina Rhaetian
Railway is an astonishing feat of transport
engineering. It's also a great walk: a hiking
trail around and alongside the tracks allows
for up-close encounters with its mighty
viaducts and historic stations. The hike
starts north of the Alps, climbing through
the Albula Valley and the Upper Engadine
high plateau to St Moritz, via the looming
Landwasser Viaduct and Bergün's railway
museum and Bahnerlebnisweg (Railway
Experience Trail). The southern sections
continue over the Bernina Pass, wending
via the Stazerwald forest, Morteratsch
Glacier and the lovely lake-dotted Val
Poschiavo to hop the border and reach the
Italian town of Tirano. And if your legs tire
at any point, it's easy to hop on the train.
Start // Thusis, Switzerland
Finish // Tirano, Italy
Distance // 131km (81 miles)
More info // www.rhb.ch

AUSTRIA'S BEST DAY HIKE: PINZGAUER SPAZIERGANG

With front-row views of the sky-high peaks and glaciers of Hohe Tauern National Park, this day-long ridge hike has views to make you yodel out loud.

The weather gods have answered my prayers. You need a clear day for the Pinzgauer Spaziergang, locals told me, with knowing eyebrows raised, as dark clouds bubbled on the horizon, threatening a storm. Yet, during the night, rain had rinsed the Alps clean, bringing a real beauty of an early summer's day, and a flawless blue sky rendering the mountains in stark relief, peaks lifting their snowy caps towards the heavens, and wildflowers erupting on pastures where doe-eyed cows were swinging their heavy bells.

While you can swoon over views of the Hohe Tauern range from the shores of Zell am See, the crowds can be distracting,

so it isn't until you rise above it all that you can truly appreciate the silent grace of these mountains. I take the cable car up to Schmittenhöhe, 1965m (6447ft) above sea level, where the Kitzbühel and Hohe Tauern Alps fan out magisterially before me: fold after wooded fold, peak after pearl-white peak, glacier after glacier. Despite the first pink blush of alpenrosen on the slopes, there is still the crispness of snow in the air. I feel that frisson of excitement that comes with the first steps taken on what I know will be a hike to remember.

Rightfully billed as one of Austria's most spectacular day hikes, the Pinzgauer Spaziergang is the pot of gold at the end of the

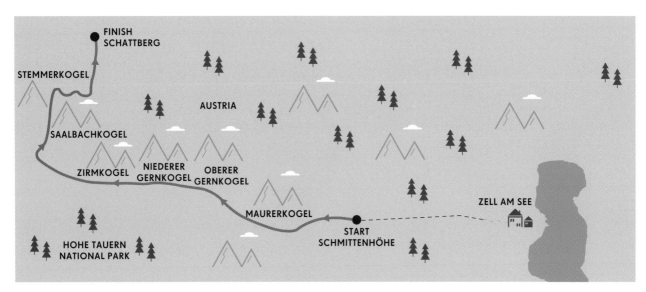

AUSTRIA'S GREATEST ALPINE DRIVE

If you have your own wheels, drive over to Bruck, the starting point for one of Europe's most unforgettable road trips: the Grossglockner High Alpine Road, now on the tentative list of Unesco World Heritage sites. Buckle up for 48km (30 miles) of head-spinning, wow-what-a-mountain road trip. Pick a fine day to make the most of the views of glacier-capped peaks, waterfalls and jewel-coloured lakes as you crunch gears on the hairpin bends. www.gross glockner.at

"I feel that frisson of excitement that comes with the first steps taken on what I know will be a hike to remember."

Clockwise from top left: enjoying a grassy bank overlooked by Grossglockner; the peak of Grossglockner; alpenrosen in bloom; Previous page: Hohe Tauern National Park

Hohe Tauern National Park rainbow. Though the terrain is high, anyone with a sense of adventure, solid walking boots and a decent level of fitness can give it a go. Indeed, the walk eases me in gently as it winds down through pastures, spurring me on as the view opens up of the brilliantly glittering Zeller See far below, and the glacier-encrusted Hohe Tauern range beyond. The trail narrows as it passes through moors flecked with silky cottongrass and threads up through forest, passing Alpine tarns that shine like jewels in the sharp morning light.

I head on through meadows bursting into flower and make a short, painless ascent to the cross-topped summit of 2076m (6811ft) Maurerkogel. It's as fine a picnic spot as any: to the north I can see the distinctive limestone turrets and pinnacles of the Kaisergebirge massif and the pale-grey Steinernes Meer karst plateau rippling across to Bavaria in Germany. To the south, my gaze is drawn to a parade of cloud-piercing peaks guarding the horizon: Austria's crowning glory Grossglockner, a whopping great bell of a mountain, 3798m (12,461ft) high, the Kitzsteinhorn and its

glacier, the mighty fang of Granatspitze and the pyramid-shaped Grossvenediger. I could linger all day but the path beckons.

The trail becomes lovelier still as I press on, following a beautiful balcony trail that tightly hugs the contours of Oberer-Gernkogel and gently mounts the grassy summit of Niederer-Gernkogel, where more phenomenal views of the mountainscape await. But I crave more of a challenge and so summon up the strength for an hour-long detour, climbing up to 2215m (7267ft) Zirmkogel. The steep track demands full concentration and surefootedness, and I feel as though I have earned the views that unfold as I crest the rocky summit. Beyond the burnished high moors, peaks rumple the horizon as far as the eye can see, from the eternally snow-capped giants of Hohe Tauern to the more jagged peaks of the Kitzbühel and Bavarian Alps.

Back on the Pinzgauer Spaziergang, the trail gets rockier as it picks its way through high meadows and mountains mottled gold and green like tortoiseshell. I stop to catch my breath at a small hut near a wisp of a stream. It is a brief respite before the

path begins once again to steepen, this time climbing steadily up to Klingertörl saddle, where I pause to take in the sensational panorama of the Northern Limestone Alps. Mountain bikers blaze on past, but I relish the slow pace of exploring the trail by foot, wandering on in quiet exhilaration.

I edge around the base of cliffs that sweep down from the slopes of 2249m (7379ft) Hochkogel, a prominent ridge that nevertheless appears dwarfed by the grand scale of its backdrop. It is a short descent from here to the small lake and Seetörl, where an ink-blue lake creates a perfect mirror image of the surrounding mountains.

As the hike nears its conclusion, it is easy to become blasé, but there are a couple of moderately challenging curveballs to surprise me towards the end. First up, an ascent of 2092m (6864ft) Saalbachkogel, and then, just when I think I am on the home run, a climb up to 2123m (6965ft) Stemmerkogel. It would be possible to skirt the slopes of these fin-shaped mountains, but the temptation to stand at their summits proves irresistible.

Spaziergang in German translates as a gentle stroll, but as hardcore as the Austrians are when it comes to the outdoors, the Pinzgauer Spaziergang is no mere walk in the park. The descent down the ridge now to Schattberg, however, really is a breeze. The light is beginning to fade and I'm anxious that I don't have long before I must make a mad dash to catch the gondola down to Saalbach. But for now, I savour the final precious moments on the trail, as the last light of day touches the peaks like a caress. **KW**

ORIENTATION

Start // Schmittenhöhe (Zell am See)
Finish // Schattberg (Saalbach)
Distance // 19km (12 miles)
Duration // Five to six hours
Getting there // Zell am See has good connections to the Austrian rail network, with hourly trains to destinations including Salzburg. See www.oebb.at. For cable cars serving Schmittenhöhe and Schattberg, see www.schmitten.at and www.saalbach.com respectively.
When to go // June to September.
Where to stay & eat // Take plenty of water and snacks as there is nothing en route. Hotels, guesthouses and restaurants are plentiful in lakeside Zell am See.
What to wear // Bring a fleece, waterproofs and sturdy walking boots, plus a hat and sunscreen.
More info // www.zellamsee-kaprun.com; www.hohetauern.at

Opposite from top: views of Kamnik
Hut and the Kamnik-Savinja Alps
from Kamniško Sedlo; the rugged route
to Schneibstein

MORE LIKE THIS
ALPINE RIDGE TRAILS

FAULHORNWEG, SWITZERLAND

The ultimate day hike in the Swiss Alps? The astoundingly beautiful Faulhornweg is a hot contender. A vintage cogwheel train hauls you up to 1967m (6453ft) Schynige Platte, the trailhead for a ridge hike that keeps you constantly on a high. The trail drifts over rolling pastures then contours scree slopes on the western-flank of gnarly Loucherhorn, continuing to dip and rise before reaching the boulder-strewn pass of Egg at 2067m (6781ft). This opens northeastward into the high moors of the Sägistal, where a lake makes an aquamarine splash. Push on through a rocky gully to the saddle-top mountain hut of Berghaus Männdlenen. From here, the trail makes a steep traverse to the ridge of Winteregg, before surmounting the 2681m (8796ft) peak of Faulhorn, which opens up a 360° panorama of glacier-capped Eiger, Mönch and Jungfrau. Listen for whistling marmots as you descend to the grassy basin of Bachalpsee, then down to the gondola lift at First.
Start // Schynige Platte
Finish // First
Distance // 16km (10 miles)
More info // www.jungfrau.ch

KAMNIŠKO SEDLO, SLOVENIA

If you are up for a challenge, this half-day hike in northern Slovenia's limestone Kamnik-Savinja Alps, covering 1263m (4144ft) of vertical, has climbs to quicken the pulse and views to make the heart sing. The steepish trail demands a good level of fitness, weaving through high meadows and rocky, root-strewn forest, and traversing scree slopes where vertical rock walls fling up on all sides. The craggy twin peaks of Brana 2253m (7392ft) and Planjava 2392m (7848ft) loom above. From the saddle above the Kamnik Hut (Kamniška koča), you're rewarded with tremendous views of the Alpine valley of Logarska dolina below, and Austria and Ljubljana beyond. Bring water and snacks as there is nothing en route until you reach the Kamnik Hut (open June to September).
Start // Kamniška Bistrica Hut
Finish // Kamnik Hut
Distance // 5.4km (3.4 miles)
More info // www.visitljubljana.com

SCHNEIBSTEIN, GERMANY

The Northern Limestone Alps provide a ruggedly dramatic backdrop for this high-level trek to 2276m (7467ft) Schneibstein, one of the most prominent peaks in the Hagengebirge range of the Berchtesgaden Alps. Grazing the German–Austrian border, the trail starts at Hinterbrand, above the sublimely lovely mountain lake of Königssee near Berchtesgaden, and makes an initial gentle ascent before steepening to climb through meadows, forests and up rocky slopes. Keep an eye out for chamois and ibex at Seeleinsee, a turquoise teardrop of a lake rimmed by mountains. The trail then rises through a wild valley and crests the Windscharte saddle up to the cross-topped summit of Schneibstein. Though technically undemanding and well marked, there's plenty of vertical to negotiate on the hike, so get an early start.
Start // Hinterbrand
Finish // Jennerbahn
Distance // 9km (5.5 miles)
More info // www.berchtesgaden.de

THROUGH THE VILLAGES OF THE ALPUJARRAS

*A winding mountain traverse through Spain's pastoral Alpujarras region
that dips into a handful of craft-producing Moorish-Spanish villages en route.*

t might have only been early February but, in the aromatic
pastures of southern Spain, a premature whiff of spring
was hanging in the air. Carrying a light overnight pack, I
traversed a narrow path as it contoured a wide kink in the
mountains, making for a cluster of white houses grafted onto a
hillside in the distance. This was the village of Trevélez, famous
for its delicate air-cured hams that mature on the cool southern
slopes of Mulhacén, mainland Spain's highest peak. Budget
permitting, I resolved to find a guesthouse in the village's tight
coil of streets, and fall asleep in the dreamy rural atmosphere of
eastern Andalucía.

At a lonely path junction, a red-and-white signpost inscribed
with the initials GR7 confirmed that I was following the correct
route. The so-called 'Gran Recorrido 7', is a 1900km (1181-mile)
footpath across Spain stretching from Tarifa at the jaws of the
Mediterranean to the Pyrenees on the border with France. With
three days at my disposal, I was tackling a bite-sized 69km (43-
mile) portion of it in the unseasonably balmy Alpujarras.

The Alpujarras is the communal name given to a string of white
villages that cling like snowfields to the fertile southern slopes of
the Sierra Nevada. Isolated until the mid 20th century, the region
keeps one foot in the rural Spanish present and the other in a feistier

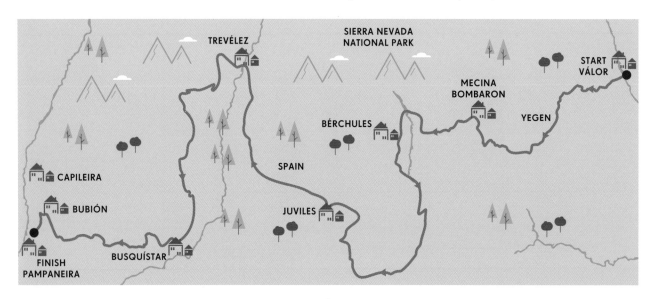

Moorish past. In contrast to other areas of Spain, the Moors lingered in the Alpujarras long after the fall of Granada in 1492, staging sporadic uprisings against the country's uncompromising Catholic monarchs until the early 1570s. Even today, the villages' flat-roofed houses and narrow winding streets appear to have more in common with northern Morocco than southern Spain.

I had started my trek one day earlier in the village of Válor, three hours east of Granada via a bumpy rural bus ride. Installed in a low-key guesthouse, I hit the town for a pre-trek meal. The place to dine, I was told, was Restaurante Aben Humeya named after a rebellious Morisco (a Muslim forcibly converted to Christianity) who waged a three-year guerrilla war against the Spanish in the 1560s. Skimming a menu of local standards such as partridge and rabbit, I opted for the protein-heavy *plato alpujarreño* consisting of eggs and potatoes anchored with *mucho* meat.

I could still feel the weight of my dinner the next morning as I waved goodbye to my accommodating guesthouse and set off on the undulating GR7 towards Yegen, population 440, the next settlement to the west.

While displaying subtle individual characteristics, the villages of the Alpujarras share a common Spanish-Moorish heritage enshrined in simple cube-like houses, diminutive Mudéjar churches (many of them converted from former mosques) and longstanding craft-making traditions.

My first stop Yegen is notable for being the one-time home of British writer, Gerald Brennan who lived there in the 1920s and quickly became infatuated with life in Spain. It's a love affair that has bitten many Northern Europeans in the years since. Some have moved to the Alpujarras to run guesthouses and farms; others have opted to chill out in off-the-grid hippy communities such as Beneficio near Órgiva.

Yegen, which has a street named after Brennan, felt pleasantly soporific. Indeed, up to this point, I had yet to see another hiker on the trail. Despite its impressive length and status as a segment of Europe's E4 route running from Spain to Greece, the GR7 is no Camino de Santiago, a bonus for anyone who comes here looking for tranquility and voluntary social distancing.

Between the villages, I quietly absorbed a kaleidoscope of quintessential Alpujarras scenery: terraced fields intermingled with olive groves, tumbledown farms overlooking scrubby mountain pastures, and noble bulls silhouetted on rocky hillsides. On the edge of Mecina Bombarón, 6km (3.7 miles) west of Yegen, I was held up by a herd of goats briefly blocking the road.

Every so often the slopes were bisected by deep gorges through which the path had to divert in long serpentine curves. Over the next two days, the mountain villages got increasingly spectacular. Bérchules was adorned with attractive stone fountains, handy for refilling water. Juviles hid the remains of an 8th-century Moorish fortress. Whitewashed Trevélez, where I ended day two, is the second highest municipality in Spain. From a distance, its white houses could be mistaken for a glacier sliding down the mountainside.

HOMEMADE ALPUJARRAS

A sustainable ethos runs through the Alpujarras and despite, their diminutive size, most of the villages sell locally made cheese, honey, *jamón serrano* (cured ham), olive oil and wine. Pampaneira even has a mini chocolate factory. Longstanding artisan shops are ubiquitous. Capileira specialises in leather goods. Pampaneira weaves coarse rugs. Further east, the Busquístar and La Taha regions are renowned for their ceramics.

Clockwise from top: handmade rugs on sale in Pampaneira; the white village of Capileira near the end of the trail; cured hams in Trevélez. Previous page: autumn colours in Bubión

"The region keeps one foot in the rural Spanish present and the other in a feistier Moorish past."

On my third walking day, I rejoined the GR7 as it progressed gently downhill from Trevélez to Busquístar. Beyond lay La Taha, a knot of seven tiny hamlets where hedgerows lined narrow lanes, and the chestnut trees looked older than the houses. Despite its bucolic airs, I lingered only briefly before pressing on through pine woods to a high promontory overlooking the Barranco de Poqueira, the Alpujarras' most spectacular and well-known gorge. Down below lay my finish-line: the three whitewashed villages of Pampaneira, Bubión and Capileira, stacked up one above the other in a steep-sided valley with the snow-covered peaks of the Sierra Nevada standing sentinel. I admired the scene for a few minutes – low cloud hanging above the flat-roofed houses, a rainbow rising serendipitously above a church tower – before descending into Capileira where well-stocked craft shops were doing a respectable business with early-season tourists. With no room for thick rugs or Mudéjar cabinets in my overnight bag, I limited myself to casual browsing before booking a room in a hotel opposite the church. Tomorrow I'd take the bus to provincial capital Granada, I mused, or maybe I'd just keep on following the unfolding drama of the GR7 for another day or two. **BS**

ORIENTATION

Start // Válor
Finish // Pampaneira
Distance // 69km (43 miles)
Duration // Three days
Getting there // Buses run two to three times daily between Granada and Válor/Pampaneira.
When to go // Avoid peak summer and go February to June and September to November.
What to wear // Light layers, walking boots or runners.
Where to stay // Most villages en route have *hostales* (small, family-run hotels) and/or B&Bs.
Where to eat // Village restaurants are good quality.
Things to know // The route is mostly on mountain paths with some paved roads in the villages. As the walk is mainly a traverse, there are no difficult ascents or descents.
More info // *Walking the GR7 in Andalucia* by Kirstie Shirra (Cicerone Guides, 2010); www.treksierranevada.com.

Opposite from top: Lake Como;
beachside village in Cabo de Gata

MORE LIKE THIS
VILLAGE-TO-VILLAGE HIKES

CABO DE GATA, SPAIN

In Andalucia's arid southeastern corner, the coast has been protected from Costa del Sol–style development and retains a unique Spanish-meets-Spaghetti-Western feel. Quiet villages of simple white houses are connected by a network of trails. The finest section is the 28km (17-mile) section between San Miguel de Cabo de Gata and La Isleta del Moro, best spread over two days with an overnight in the seaside nexus of San José.

Heading east out of San Miguel takes you past bird-rich salt flats (home to pink flamingos) to a headland topped by a lighthouse and an old lookout tower with superb panoramas. Pristine beaches with interesting lava and fossil formations nestle in secluded coves nearby. Beyond San José, the route partly follows old mining roads and skirts the ancient volcano of El Fraile on the way to the tiny beach settlements of Los Escullos and La Isleta del Moro.

Start // San Miguel de Cabo de Gata
Finish // La Isleta del Moro
Distance // 28km (17 miles)
More info // www.cabogataalmeria.com

TEST WAY, ENGLAND

Starting amid grassy downs on the cusp of Hampshire and Berkshire, the Test Way follows the River Test through chalky hills, water meadows and peaceful English villages to its confluence with Southampton Water on the south coast. The early stages of the walk skirt Watership Down (famous for the Richard Adams novel) and Combe Gibbet (a former execution site) before merging with the course of an old railway line near the upper-crust village of Stockbridge. The waymarked path dips into numerous smaller villages. Wherwell with its crooked lines of thatched cottages is a highlight. Far grander is Mottisfont Hall, where you can take afternoon tea; and Broadlands, the former estate of Lord Mountbatten, the last Viceroy of India. The market town of Romsey with its Norman abbey and 18th-century watermill makes a great rest stop. The clear, mellow Test river, famous for its trout fishing, remains your companion throughout.

Start // Walbury Hill
Finish // Eling
Distance // 71km (44 miles)
More info // www.hants.gov.uk

GREENWAY DEL LAGO DI COMO, ITALY

Following an old Roman road, the so-called Antica Strada Regina, that once linked Milan and Switzerland, this wandering route winds its way along the western shores of Lake Como in northern Italy. Using waterside esplanades and quiet backroads, it mostly avoids the lake's traffic-choked highway and dips into plenty of *bellissima* villages along its course.

Beginning in Colonno and tracking north, the path skirts manicured gardens and passes close to at least two grandiose villas: Villa Carlotta and Villa del Balbianello (both open to visitors). Minor climbs are rewarded with views over red-tiled roofs and Alpine peaks. The trail is paved throughout and generally well-marked. Most of the attractive villages merge into one another, meaning you are never far from a cafe or gelateria. Descending to the lake at Tremezzo, the last stretch tracks alongside the water in front of rich art nouveau facades.

Start // Colonno
Finish // Cadenabbia
Distance // 10km (6.2 miles)
More info // www.greenwaylagodi como.com

A WINTER TRAVERSE OF THE GREAT ST BERNARD PASS

Oliver Smith dons snowshoes to cross the Swiss–Italian border over a storied mountain pass, and meets the brave souls who watch over travellers on the road.

It takes around five minutes to drive through the Great St Bernard Tunnel. Five minutes to drive 5km (3 miles) underneath the Alps and cross the border between Switzerland and Italy as you go – piazzas and pizzerias on one side, timber chalets and watch emporiums on the other. It is just about enough time for a motorist to hum along to Puccini's *Nessun Dorma*, or attempt some light yodelling.

However, there is an older route that runs directly over the heads of motorists in the tunnel: up above the sunroof, up above the strata of metamorphic rocks and a crust of ice and snow, high among the summits where the air is thin and the passing airliners don't seem so very far away. This route is the Great St Bernard Pass, a frozen highway counting as one of the most treacherous and storied trails in Europe.

'Summer and winter are two different worlds up there,' explains Eric Berclaz, leaning on his ski poles at the foot of the pass. 'Summer is not a problem. In winter, you need to know what you are doing.'

Eric is my guide for the ascent, and it is also his job to help decide when the Great St Bernard Pass is able to open to motorists for the summer season. 'Summer' in the loosest sense of the word. For just two or three months of the year, the snow melts enough for tourists to drive to the top, admire the view and maybe buy a souvenir fridge magnet from a kiosk. From September to June, the Great St Bernard Pass is plunged into a near-permanent state of Narnia: the road buried deep in snow, shivering in temperatures that sink to -30°C (-22°F) while holidaymakers on the Mediterranean siesta on the beach not so far away. During this time, the only way to cross the pass is on skis or snowshoes.

I strap into my snowshoes for the three-hour hike to the top. It soon feels like an exercise in time travel. In the valley below, spring is arriving: wildflowers grow in the meadows and people are wearing shorts. The Great St Bernard Pass, meanwhile, is lagging a few months behind in bleak midwinter. The snowdrifts become deeper with every step. Everything is still, but for the croak of ravens and the hum of overhead power cables. A few skiers and snowboarders whoosh past.

Today, like much of the Alps, the Great St Bernard Pass is a place for recreation. But before the tunnel was built in the 1960s, travellers between the Italian plains and northern Europe had

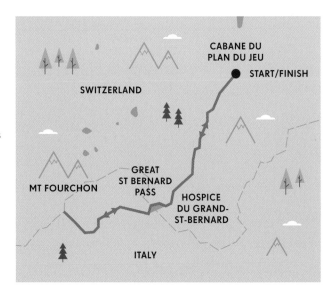

little choice but to come this way. Pilgrims on the Via Francigena crossed on their way from Canterbury to Rome. Napoleon led a 40,000-strong army over the mountains, the soldiers hauling their cannons up the mountainside (the man himself sliding down on his tiny backside). Everyone from Roman legions to counterfeit cigarette smugglers traversed the Great St Bernard Pass. And there were also wayfarers who climbed into the mountain mists, and never came back down again.

Snowflakes glide through the air as Eric and I arrive at the top of the pass. Out of the wilderness there emerges a grand doorway hung with icicles, and windows half-submerged in the drifts. We have arrived at the Hospice du Grand-St-Bernard, a religious hostel that has stood at the highest point of the pass since the 11th century. Its robe-clad holy men and gigantic St Bernard dogs gained fame as a mountain-rescue double act: fishing passers-by out of avalanches, guiding them through fog to the safety of the hospice. Still run by the Catholic Church, the institution exists for the same purpose today: to welcome and protect passers-by.

Today, the St Bernard dogs live in an institute on the floor of the valley, but the two-legged community still thrives at the top of the pass. Three canons and several housekeeping volunteers supply about 50 visitors with clean beds and three generous meals a day

"The A-listers of the Alps assemble on the horizon... the ridge of Gran Paradiso... the perfect pyramid of the Matterhorn."

LEGACY OF ST BERNARD

St Bernard de Menthon (c 1020–1081) was a medieval priest who built a stone shelter for travellers in the Alps. In time, this shelter grew into a small community, with no members more famous than the giant St Bernard dogs, whose thick fur, large paws, strong limbs and sensitive smell made them ideal for rescue missions. St Bernards were used to uncover lost souls in the snow until the 1950s, when helicopters replaced the doe-eyed woofers.

Clockwise from top: up and over the border; essential kit; plaque at the hospice; a guide points the way. Previous page: the beauty of the pass

in one of the most hostile wildernesses in Europe. The front door is open to everyone, regardless of their religion. In 1000 years the door has never been locked.

Packing a sandwich and an apple, I set out on a day trip to Mt Fourchon, the shark-fin-shaped peak that's visible from the kitchen window of the hospice. The trail leads across the Italian border, past sentry posts locked for the winter, and little road signs peeking above the snowline: 'STOP' and 'PASSPORTS'. Hours pass. A northerly wind gathers strength. Distant walkers shrink to tiny dots. As I draw closer to Fourchon, the A-listers of the Alps assemble on the horizon. To the south is the ridge of Gran Paradiso – the tallest peak entirely within Italy, where a little statue of the Virgin Mary stands on the summit praying to the sky. To the east the mass of Grand Combin and the perfect pyramid of the Matterhorn. Back to the north is the beginning of the pass; once the site of a temple to Jupiter, where Romans came to worship the god of lightning.

And beside it is a vast statue of St Bernard himself, his back turned to the mountains and his outstretched bronze hand pointing travellers home to the hospice. Guests return one by one as the sun sinks over the Mont Blanc massif, colouring the snow rosy pink on its way.

Since the building of a tunnel, the hospice is no longer a necessary staging post, and yet thousands of visitors still make the journey every winter. Some people come to conquer a mountain, a few to look for Jesus Christ walking barefoot in the snowdrifts. Many come to be above the world below, here where the air is crisp and the views stretch forever. **OS**

ORIENTATION

Start/Finish // Bourg St Pierre
Distance // About 8km (5 miles) one way
Duration // Three hours
Getting there // It's a two-hour drive from Geneva.
Where to stay // Before the ascent, at Cabane du Plan du Jeu (www.vicheres.ch), or luxurious options in Marigny.
When to go // Snow is on the ground from December to May.
What to pack // Walking boots for snowshoes to lock around; winter boots will be comfier, but sturdy three-season boots are sufficient. Pack waterproof clothing, sunglasses and high-factor sun cream, with avalanche transmitters advisable.
Tours // www.swissmountainleader.com and www.alpinetreks. com offer two-day treks, overnighting at the Hospice du Grand-St-Bernard.
Things to know // Check your travel insurance covers you for Alpine snowshoeing – Swiss mountain-rescue services charge (a lot) for call-outs.
More info // www.saint-bernard.ch

Opposite: wild ibex in the Gran Paradiso National Park

MORE LIKE THIS
TECHNICAL WINTER HIKES

GRAN PARADISO, ITALY

An ascent of Italy's highest peak (excluding Mont Blanc, which has its head and one foot in France) begins with a hike through the country's oldest National Park. It's not a super-technical climb, but you do require technical equipment (rope, crampons, helmet, ice axe) and a guide if inexperienced in the mountains. The path wends through woodlands before emerging from the trees and gaining height via a series of steep switchbacks, washed by waterfalls and populated by mischievous marmots. At the snowline at 2735m (8973ft) you reach Rifugio Vittorio Emanuele II, your overnight nest. The hard hike to the 4061m (13,323ft) summit begins under torchlight after a 4.30am breakfast. Several routes, one involving via ferrata, lead to the top, where, attached to your guide/climbing buddy by an umbilicus of rope, you squirm towards the apex of Italy and a meeting with Madonna (Virgin Mary statue, not the pop star).
Start/Finish // Gran Paradiso National Park
Distance // 17km (10.5 miles)
More info // www.parks.it

VAL BADIA, ITALIAN DOLOMITES

Many mountains lay claim to having inspired Tolkien's Middle Earth fantasies, but in South Tyrol's Val Badia you can believe the hype. These sheer walls of pale limestone thrust up like natural fortifications, blushing pink with the setting sun. If they look formidable in summer, in winter they are pure wonderland. Linking the mountain villages of San Cassiano and Badia, this 4½-hour snowshoe hike is an enchanting stomp through white-frosted meadows and larch forests, heading north until it reaches the 600-year-old Santa Croce (La Crusc) pilgrimage church at 2047m (6716ft).
From here, you're treated to sensational views of the rocky ramparts of the Sasso di Santa Croce massif and 3343m (10,968ft) Marmolada, the highest peak in the Dolomites. From here, the trail swings west and down through pastures and woods to the hamlet of Oies and Badia. You can go solo or with a guide.
Start // San Cassiano
Finish // Badia
Distance // 11.5km (7.1 miles)
More info // www.altabadia.org; www. altabadiaguides.com.

KOROUOMA CANYON, FINLAND

When it snows in the Korouoma Canyon in Southern Lapland hikers can step into a real-life fairy-tale. While the 5km (3-mile) circular trail is pretty, consider skiing or snowshoeing the two-day trail in its entirety to really experience the silent, frozen majesty of this gorge, which was formed by a fracture in the bedrock millions of years ago. Passing icy lakes, snow-daubed spruce forest where wolves, wolverine, reindeer and elk roam, and a trio of sensational frozen waterfalls – Jaska Jokunen (Charlie Brown), Ruskea Virta (the Brown River) and Mammuttiputous (the Mammoth Fall) – the path is utterly silent but for the squeak of fresh powdery snow underfoot. It feels properly remote, too, especially when you stop for a campfire or stay overnight at a rustic log shelter, such as Pajupuro Open Wilderness Hut. Orange paint splashes mark the way but you'll also need a GPS, map and compass or a reliable guide.
Start // Koivuköngäs
Finish // Lapiosalmi
Distance // 30km (19 miles)
More info // www.nationalparks.fi/ korouoma

CORSICA'S GR20

Cross the mountainous island of Corsica on foot along France's most famous — and challenging — long-distance route.

I t's late in the afternoon in the granite mountains of Corsica. Barren peaks surround me in all directions: great pinnacles of rock rising like needles from the valley floor, far, far below. The setting sun is tinting the mountains orange, like poker tips heated in the fires of a blacksmith's forge. A faint salt tang drifts on the evening breeze — a reminder that even here, high in the mountains, in Corsica the Mediterranean is never far away. In the distance, I hear the tinkle of goat bells — a sign the next refuge is close by.

I'm exhausted. Deeply, soul-sappingly exhausted. My legs feel like breeze blocks. My calves, shoulders and back are ablaze. I've been on the GR20 for fifteen days, averaging six to seven hours a day. I've climbed alpine peaks and plunged into deserted valleys. I've stayed at lonely mountain huts, camped on barren hillsides, bivvied in the open under clear black skies. I've walked windy ridges, scrambled up chains, climbed ladders via ferrata-style. I've hiked harder than I've ever hiked before, and if I'm honest, I'm not sure how much further I can go. But here in the mountains of Bavella, I'm less than a day's walk from trail's end — and no matter how much my body creaks and aches, I can't help feeling a stab of melancholy that my cross-Corsican pilgrimage is nearly over.

The GR20 is generally considered to be one of Europe's hardest hikes. Covering approximately 180km (112 miles) and around 10,000m (32,808ft) of ascent — higher than Everest — it traverses the spiny backbone of mountains that run across the centre of Corsica (the Granite Island, as British author Dorothy Carrington christened it in her classic 1971 travelogue). Along the way, it passes through a bewildering range of terrains — from wind-whipped peaks to barren granite plateaus, farming valleys to

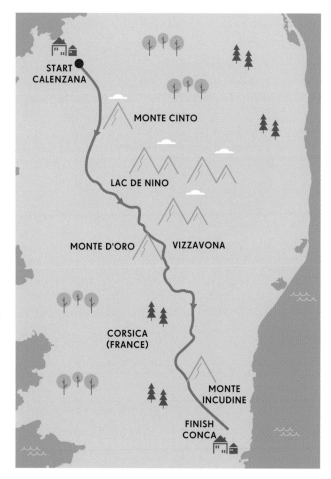

MAQUIS

Maquis covers around 20% of the Corsican landscape. Consisting of wild shrubs such as thyme, myrtle, cistus, broom, rosemary, honeysuckle and heather, these hardy, heavily scented plants have traditionally been used in Corsican cooking and folk medicine for centuries. The maquis is notoriously tough, able to thrive even in the island's harsh, sun-baked climate: during WWII, the French Resistance named themselves after the maquis as a sign of their own endurance, fortitude and stubborn will to survive.

Clockwise from top left: a Genoese stone bridge high in the Corsican mountains; campsite on the trail; a scrambling descent. Previous page: setting out on the GR20

alpine meadows, fragrant pine forests to maquis-cloaked moors. Lasting sixteen gruelling days, the GR20 has been known to reduce even the hardiest of hikers to tears of exhaustion. This is not a walk to take on lightly – but for those brave enough to tackle it, the 'Fra li Monti' ('the way across the mountains', as it's known in Corsican) represents the ultimate test of a hiker's mettle.

Corsica's legendary cross-island trek dates back to the 1950s. The route was devised by Jean Loiseau, a local architect, and developed further in the 1960s by Guy Degos, an engineer. Initially, only a handful of people ventured along it, but the formation of the Parc Naturel Régional de Corse in 1972 led to an explosion in popularity. It's now one of France's flagship *grandes randonnées*, or great walks (the 20 refers to the island's old postcode). Today, around 20,000 people hike the GR20 every year. Those who complete it even qualify for a special certificate.

Most people follow the route north–south, beginning in the small village of Calenzana and ending in Conca. It can be done in the opposite direction, but the northern sections are the hardest and most technical, so most people prefer to take them on when their legs still feel relatively fresh. The village of Vizzavona marks the halfway point; from here, the trail gets slightly easier, winding on gradually all the way to Corsica's southeast coast.

'Easy' is not a word that you're likely to hear very much on the GR20, however. This trail is tough. Seriously tough. At

some points, you'll be hauling yourself up on chains fixed into the mountainsides; at others, you'll be teetering on knife-edge ridges with sheer, buttock-clenching drops on either side. There are technical scrambles over plains of unstable scree; long, leg-sapping hauls along valleys that feel far from civilisation; dispiriting days when the wind gets up, the clouds roll in and you're soaked to the skin by one of Corsica's torrential summer storms. You'll be sleeping rough – either in basic bunks in the refuges, or camping wild – with no electricity, no phone signal and no prospect of a hot shower. There will be days when you feel you can't walk another step, but thankfully the next mountain refuge is never far away – along with its promise of a hot, home-cooked meal and a cold Pietra beer.

The refuges, or mountain huts, are a big part of what makes the GR20 possible. There's one at the end of every stage, staffed between June and September. Here, hikers can stock up on food, fresh water and supplies, and bunk down for the night with their

fellow hikers. Just as importantly, the refuges offer companionship after lonely days on the trail: the chance to swap stories and feel the sense of fraternity that will be familiar to any long-distance hiker.

One night, I hear a story from two hikers who bought fresh goat's milk and tangy *brocciu* cheese from a shepherd near the Lac de Nino. Another tells how they were woken up in the middle of the night by an inquisitive wild boar who was raiding their food stash. In return, I recount my own stories. Watching hawks soaring around the slopes of Monte d'Oro. Skinny-dipping in the glacial waters of Lac de Nino. Hollering from the top of one of Corsica's highest summits, Monte Incudine. Watching shooting stars as I bivvied on the meadows near Vizzavona.

> ## "The GR20 has been known to reduce even the hardiest of hikers to tears of exhaustion."

Settling into my sleeping bag on my last night on the trail, savouring the scent of pine sap in the cool night air, I realise that's one of the most special things about the GR20. Though everyone follows the same route, every hiker returns with their own set of stories about this wild, strange and fascinating island. The Île de Beauté never fails to live up to its name. **OB**

ORIENTATION

Start // Calenzana
Finish // Conca
Distance // 180km (112 miles)
Duration // 15 to 16 days
Getting there // There are regular ferries to Bastia and Ajaccio from Nice, Marseille and Toulon. Local buses run to Calenzana and Conca.
When to go // Refuges are open from June to October. Consider later in the season to avoid the heat and crowds.
What to wear // High-ankle hiking boots and breathable clothes are essential. Pack a waterproof jacket and trousers.
What to pack // IGN trail maps, walking poles, portable stove and spare gas, good quality mountain tent.
Where to stay and eat // Refuges offer dorm beds and meals. Book in advance at www.pnr-resa.corsica. There is no access to electricity or hot water. Alternatively, camp.
More info // www.pnr.corsica; www.le-gr20.fr

Opposite from top: looking out from a ridge on Mt Reinebringen in the Lofoten Islands; on the way to Mt Teide

MORE LIKE THIS
EPIC ISLAND HIKES

LONG CROSSING OF THE LOFOTEN ISLANDS, NORWAY

When it comes to Instagrammable peaks and sea-to-sky vistas, it's hard to top Norway's Lofoten Islands, the rugged Arctic archipelago that reaches out into the Norwegian Sea like an exploratory finger. Located inside the Arctic Circle, the islands are blanketed by ice and snow in winter, but in summer, their jagged peaks make for mind-blowing hiking. The 9km (5.5-mile) hike from Ryten to Kvalvika Beach on Moskenesøya is a classic, and not quite as calf-shredding as many of the islands' hikes – but if you're up for something more taxing, you could tackle the legendary Long Crossing, a 160km (99-mile) rollercoaster route right down through the archipelago.
Start // Village of Å
Finish // Delp
Distance // 160km (99 miles)
More info // www.rando-lofoten.net

MT TEIDE, TENERIFE, SPAIN

At 3718m (12,198ft), Spain's highest mountain is an enjoyable and surprisingly rigorous summer challenge, but outside high season, when the Parque Nacional del Teide's four million or so annual visitors trickle down to manageable numbers, it comes into its own – particularly in early spring, when the lower slopes start to bloom in flowers and, if you're lucky, the summit area still has a hat of snow. The ascent to the volcano's peak is the real challenge, especially if you opt for the very tough six-hour hike, but if weather or lung-power make this impossible, the cable car will still give you the views, and the park's 190 sq km (73 sq miles) plenty of other enjoyable hikes. The Unesco site protects nearly 1000 Guanche archaeological sites and contains examples of 80% of the world's different forms of volcanic formations, as well as 14 plants found nowhere else on earth.
Start // Montaña Blanca
Finish // Peak of El Teide
Distance // 16km (10 miles)
More info // www.telefericoteide.com

SAMOTHRAKI, GREECE

Samothraki is not your typical Greek island. Rocky, mountainous and rural, the island rises 1611m (5285ft) out of the Mediterranean, making it the third-highest Greek island after Crete and Evia. The island's highest point is Mt Sàos, known to locals as Mt Fengari – the Mountain of the Moon – so called since it's said to be tall enough to block out the moon's light. The island has many hikes, from relatively easy routes like the Fonias Trail to lung-busters such as the ascent of Mt Marmaras. You can also hike to the ruins of the island's most famous archaeological site, the Sanctuary of the Great Gods, a complex of ruined temples, shrines and amphitheatres. A 2.5m (8.2ft) statue of Nike was discovered here in 1863: now known as the *Winged Victory of Samothrace*, it's one of the Louvre museum's most prized exhibits.
More info // www.samothraki-tourism.gr

SHETLAND'S NESS OF HILLSWICK CIRCUIT

Stuart Maconie takes a circular walk in the most beautiful and dramatic corner of Britain's wildest, most northerly outpost.

Shetland is different. More Scandinavia than Scotland, more seabirds than shortbread, a wild lonely magnificent place that gets under the skin and lingers in the mind. I fell hard for it on my first trip and now come back as often as I can. Something about it won't let you go, or me at least. It may not be quite Ultima Thule, the old travellers' name for the northern edge of the world, but on a quiet midsummer white night (or 'simmer dim' as the locals call it), as the fulmar, kittiwakes and puffins wheel and dart along the cliffs, when you realise you are closer to Bergen than Edinburgh, nearer to Oslo's parliament than Westminster, the traffic and lights and bustle of all of them seem a very long way away.

Shetland is actually a group of over a hundred islands, of which only 15 are inhabited, none more than 5km (3 miles) from the sea and each with its own character and charm. There's the dark and brooding Foula to the west, tiny Mousa with its ancient broch or tower to the east. The attractive isles of Whalsay, Bressay and Fetlar, the 'garden of Shetland' – all worth the short ferry trips. Yell and Unst are the most northerly, with the latter being the inspiration for Robert Louis Stevenson's *Treasure Island.* The whole Shetland archipelago culminates in the jagged northern stacks of Muckle Flugga with its lofty lighthouse.

The Northmavine peninsula is almost a separate island. But not quite, as a narrow isthmus called the Mavis Grind connects it to the Shetland mainland. It's just over 30.5m (100ft) long at its narrowest and the only place in the UK where you could conceivably skim a stone from the North Sea to the Atlantic. The Vikings would drag their boats across it as a neat shortcut and it's often used as such by the local otters too. This is my favourite

part of Shetland, austere but beautiful, vast yet charming and magical, serene and mysterious, but vibrant with lively communities in its many villages.

One of these is Hillswick and our walk begins here, before taking in the entire circuit of the diamond-shaped peninsular headland that hangs like a bunch of grapes into the gleaming blue waters of the Atlantic Ocean. Initially unseen from Hillswick, as the walk progresses along the coast of the Ness, more and more of the stunning Shetland landscapes and seascapes are revealed: dramatic sea stacks, hidden coves, soaring cliffs and the Ness' huge, silent interior moorland.

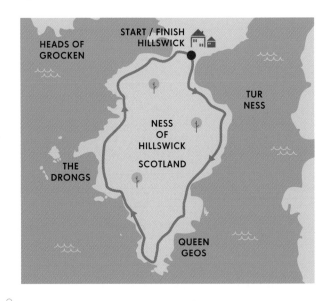

Hillswick was developed in the 1700s as a fishing station and is today a cluster of houses, a shop, an art gallery, a doctor's surgery and the St Magnus Bay Hotel, built in 1900 by the company who then operated steamer ferries from the Scottish mainland to Orkney and Shetland. They've long ceased, but the St Magnus Bay Hotel still thrives and you can sample its warm welcome and excellent food and drink at the walk's end. On that point, many guidebooks plot the walk from here anti-clockwise around the Ness. But we're heading clockwise as I think this way the scenery and ambiance improves and reveals more with every step. And this way the St Magnus is waiting as a reward.

Your first steps, though, are breathtaking enough. Walk down the shingle beach to pass the Manse house on your right and on to Tur Ness. This stretch of the coastline is dotted and scored with bays and inlets, with some striking exposed rock strata, increasing in drama as height is gained gently. If you have the time and inclination to detour inland from here, overlooking the Loch of Niddister is evidence of human settlement from different ages. Neolithic people dwelt here five millennia ago, and much later this was a thriving crofting township, now all but vanished.

Continue carefully round the coast, absorbing the amazing and constantly opening views, but taking care to keep a distance from the cliff edge. This can be a dangerous place in fog or high winds

> "More and more of the stunning Shetland landscapes and seascapes are revealed: dramatic sea stacks, hidden coves, soaring cliffs and the Ness' huge, silent interior moorland."

and as you reach Queen's Geo, you'll see a line of posts hammered in to help the lighthouse staff reach the building safely in poor conditions. The lighthouse itself marks the peninsula's southern tip and from here things become even more dramatic. The next half hour is awe-inspiring. Sheer and rugged cliffs fall away, Foula, Fitful Head and the Ve Skerries can be seen on the horizon. To the northeast are the spectacular rock architecture of the Drongs, Eshaness and the Heads of Grocken. In high winds, this can get pretty bracing and you should keep well away from the cliff edges in such conditions but on a fine, clear day – the best for this walk – you will be rewarded with haunting seascapes and an always-changing ballet of water and sky. If you are very lucky, you may even see orcas playing in the waves. As you turn towards Hillswick, Shetland's highest point, the huge lonely dome of Ronas Hill looms across to the north. Down below nestles Hillswick itself. From here the going can get a little squelchy after rain, but generally it's a long but easy and frequently exhilarating stomp down surrounded by scenery you will never forget. **SM**

BIRDS OF ANOTHER NAME

For birdwatchers, Shetland is paradise. As well as being a stopover for migrating Arctic species, there are vast seabird-breeding colonies. Be aware that every bird seems to have its own name here: rain geese are red-throated divers, bonxies are great skuas, and alamooties are storm petrels.

Opposite, clockwise from top: crossing the open moorland of the Ness; St Magnus Bay Hotel waits at trail's end; a puffin landing. Previous page: the Drongs sea stacks at sunset

ORIENTATION

Start/Finish // Hillswick, Shetland
Distance // 8km (5 miles)
Duration // Five hours
Getting there // Hillswick is a 45-minute drive from Lerwick, Shetland's main town and port.
When to go // April to May for wildflowers, and mid-June for the white nights.
What to pack // Waterproofs and sturdy walking boots, plus midge repellent.
Where to stay // St Magnus Bay Hotel in Hillswick, or local home rentals.
Where to eat // An evening meal at St Magnus Bay Hotel is a fantastic end to the hike. Alternatively, there is a good fish and chip shop in Brae.
More info // www.shetland.org

Opposite from top: the Old Man of Hoy; light catching the landslipped escarpment of the Quiraing on the Isle of Skye

MORE LIKE THIS
DAY HIKES ON SCOTTISH ISLANDS

THE QUIRAING, ISLE OF SKYE

Skye offers some of the finest – and, in places, the roughest and most difficult – walking in Scotland. In the Trotternish Peninsula in the north of the island the dramatic basalt escarpment known as the Quiraing is a photographer's (and hiker's) dream: its impressive land-slipped cliffs and pinnacles constitute one of Skye's most remarkable landscapes.

From a parking area at the highest point of the minor road between Staffin and Uig, you can walk north to the Quiraing on this relatively short loop. Be aware that, while short, the walk is rough and involves coming close to some precipitous cliffs (the walk is not advisable in high wind) and scrambling a bank of scree. Sights on the walk include The Prison, a rock resembling a fortress; The Needle, a 37m (120ft) pinnacle; and The Table, a flat, grassy plateau. Throughout, take in the sensational views of the untamed and other-worldly landscape of the Trotternish.

Start/Finish // The Quiraing car park
Distance // 6.8km (4.2 miles)
More info // www.isleofskye.com;
www.walkinghighlands.co.uk

OLD MAN OF HOY, ORKNEY

Orkney's second-largest island, Hoy (meaning 'High Island'), got the lion's share of this archipelago's scenic beauty. The northern part of the island offers spectacular coastal scenery, including some of Britain's highest vertical cliffs and the 137m (450ft) rock stack known as the Old Man of Hoy.

This popular walk climbs steeply westward from Rackwick Bay, then curves northwards, descending gradually to the edge of the cliffs opposite the Old Man of Hoy. From the top of the cliffs take in the full height of The Old Man, and keep a look out for rock climbers. The stack was first scaled in 1966 and has become a magnet for adventurers. For a worthwhile extension to this walk, continue along the cliff path to St John's Head, at 335m (1099ft) the highest vertical cliff in the UK.

Start/Finish // Rackwick Bay car park
Distance // 9.3km (5.6 miles)
More info // www.orkney.com;
www.walkinghighlands.co.uk

SGURR OF EIGG, ISLE OF EIGG

The Isle of Eigg takes its name from the Old Norse egg (edge), a reference to the Sgurr of Eigg, an impressive 393m (1289ft) mini-mountain that towers over the island's port of Galmisdale. Ringed by vertical cliffs on three sides, it's composed of pitchstone lava with columnar jointing similar to that seen on the Isle of Staffa and at Giant's Causeway in Northern Ireland.

Allow three to four hours for the climb to the summit, which begins on the stony road leading up from the pier. On a fine day the views from the top are magnificent – Rum and Skye to the north, Much and Coll to the south, Ardnamurchan Lighthouse to the southeast and Ben Nevis shouldering above the eastern horizon. Take binoculars – on a calm summer's day there's a good chance of seeing minke whales feeding down below in the Sound of Muck.

Start/Finish // Eigg ferry pier
Distance // 8km (5 miles)
More info // www.isleofeigg.org;
www.walkinghighlands.co.uk

SOUTHEASTERN EUROPE

THE
MENALON TRAIL

Bucolic landscapes and gushing springs, ancient ruins, stunning monasteries, Greek revolutionaries and mythological creatures. The Menalon Trail is Arcadian in every sense.

'm trying to shove a map into my over-stuffed daypack when Nena, my genial host, offers me 'just one tiny thing more'. Hardly small, it's a bag of breakfast remains: fresh bread, feta cheese and handfuls of homemade *koulourakia* (sweet biscuits). I protest. Nena is emphatic: 'These are for Pan.' She is alluding to the Greek mythical god – half man and half goat – who was renowned for his lusty appetite and lecherous dalliances with nymphs.

For anything is possible here in Arkadia, the fabled realm of Pan, and contemporary region in the Peloponnese. Poet Virgil was the first to record Arkadia as a lost idyll. Later, painters including Titian, Poussin and Watteau depicted Arkadia as pastoral landscapes, where shepherds, surrounded by flirtatious nymphs and satyrs (woodland creatures), gazed meditatively across trees and meadows. Pan frequently appears in these over-sentimental scenes with a reed flute, the pan pipes.

I'm about to enter this bucolic scenery on the region's five-day hike along the Menalon Trail. It's a 75km (47-mile) journey along former

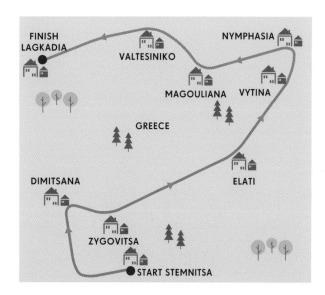

mule paths that head along the Menalon massif, the Mylaion River and Gortynian Mountains. Joining nine historic villages – Stemnitsa, Dimitsana, Zygovisti, Elati, Vytina, Nymfasia, Magouliana, Valtessiniko, and Lagadia – the route comprises eight sections that range from 4.2km (2.6 miles) to 15km (9 miles), the longest trail.

To access the trailhead I head down the steep steps from the charming guesthouse, *Mpelleiko*, a converted 16th-century home perched above Stemnitsa, a handsome village of around 200 people. After the Greek Revolution in 1821, Stemnitsa was the seat of the temporary government of the liberated Peloponnese.

The first leg, to Dimitsana, follows the trail that drops down into the Lousios Gorge, a beautiful, forested ravine lined with walnut and oak trees. A stream gushes in the river bed below. Nearly two hours into the walk I reach the short detour to the 16th-century Prodromos Monastery, an elongated building that's tucked into a hollow of an overhanging cliff ledge. A spicy-sweet aroma of incense envelopes me. Inside, a monk offers me *loukoumi* (the Greek version of Turkish Delight) and water. Back on the track, it's another steep climb to the extraordinary cliff-side Filosofou Monasteries, before dropping down to the river. Around me, thick foliage creates the perfect shade.

Church bells ring the hour when I arrive in Dimitsana, the birthplace of influential revolutionaries who waged the Greek War of Independence against the Ottoman Empire between 1821 and 1830. I stop outside the homes of Bishop Palaion Patras Germanos and Patriarch Grigorius V, two famous Greek revolutionaries. Elsewhere, the village library holds over 5000 books, manuscripts and documents from the 16th and 17th centuries.

The village square has a sign, a copy of the official trail map, outlining the Menalon Trail and the route's many highlights. Dimitsana to Zygovisti, an easy 4.2km (2.6-mile) stroll through fields, has the St Apostoli Monastery. The proud village of Zygovitsi is home to The Immortal Body memorial, a tribute to the 197 locals who formed the guard of Kolokotronis, Greece's most prominent independence leader. Zygovisti to Elati, the toughest section, has a steep hike up the Bilali Pass. The partially paved trail from Elati to Vytina is one of the shorter, and most beautiful, legs. It cuts through the lush Mylaon river valley. Oaks and spruce forests are the features of Nympasia to Magouliana and Magouliana to Valtesiniko, as well as the wonderful Kernitsas Monastery. The final trail, Valtesiniko to Lagkadia, passes the ruins of a Byzantine fortress.

My head is spinning with what lays ahead and I stop at a tavern to unwind. I sip on *krasí* (wine) and devour a plate of rooster with *hilopites* (egg pasta squares), a regional specialty.

Each day brings new sights and aromas, landmarks and legends. Ancient ruins. Abandoned windmills. Historic stone water fountains (useful for filling up). By now, I am less anxious about recalling what site is where. Instead, like the shepherds in the Arcadian canvases, I give in to the serene surrounds. And it's worth it.

Around me, sparrows chirp and nightingales sing. Occasionally, a partridge darts off into the foliage. A hawk soars overhead. Eagles, too. (Incredibly, few people pass, except for a couple of hikers and

HOW TO HIKE THE MENALON TRAIL

Each trail section can be completed on its own, meaning you can dip in and out as you wish, or join some of the shorter legs. Not all villages offer accommodation. Many hikers stay in one or two villages for the entire trail and use local taxis to shuttle between their accommodation and entry/exit points, and transfer luggage. If you decide to bail out, you can organize a taxi where the main road intersects the path. Trail indicators are generally clear, although a GPS is worthwhile.

Clockwise from top: the cliff-edge Prodromos Monastery; traditional dancing in Stemnitsa; carnations growing wild on the trail. Previous page: the Arcadian landscape near Prodromos Monastery

a group making a pilgrimage to some of the local monasteries.) And the wildflowers? Tulips, orchids and anemones. Herbs – sage and mint, oregano and chamomile – fill the air.

By the final day, I'm lost in relaxed thought. Near the trail's completion, I emerge from the foliage. Ahead, I can distinguish a silhouette: legs of a goat, body of a man. It's Pan, the region's mythological being! For a brief moment, I'm startled by the illusion.

> "Tulips, orchids and anenomes. Herbs – sage and mint, oregano and chamomile – fill the air."

I am brought to my senses by a dog that's standing guard across the track. It belongs to a shepherd, the very figure in front of me. He is surveying his goat herd. But from my approach – where a goat is positioned directly in front of the man – it appears the perfect outline of Pan himself.

As I pass the shepherd I proffer my two remaining, crumpled biscuits. Out of politeness, he accepts them. 'Efharisto' (thank you), he mutters.

During the trail's final kilometre to Lagkadia, it dawns on me that the Menalon Trail is indeed legendary. I've truly experienced Arcadia. And, true to Nena's prophecy, I've sated Pan's appetite. Albeit not in the classical way. **KA**

ORIENTATION

Start // Stemnitsa
Finish // Lagkadia
Distance // 75km (47 miles)
Duration // Five days
Getting there // Buses from Athens to Tripoli from where you must change to a public bus (twice weekly) to Stemnitsa. By car from Athens, head to Tripoli and then to Stemnitsa.
When to go // March to October.
What to wear // Sturdy hiking shoes, sun hat, hiking poles, clothing layers. Note: the monasteries require long trousers or skirts (skirts provided at entry, if required).
What to pack // Water bottle, sunblock, insect repellent, light rain gear, GPS.
Where to stay and eat // Several of the route's villages offer rooms, and they all have excellent places to eat.
More info // www.menalontrail.eu. The Menalon Trail Topoguide app provides offline maps and points of interest.

*Clockwise from top: the ruins of
Aggstein Castle on the Danube
River in Wachau; the extraordinary
monastery-topped pinnacles of
Meteora; frescoes in Velika Remeta
Monastery, Fruška Gora*

MORE LIKE THIS
MONASTERY HIKES

WACHAU WORLD HERITAGE TRAIL, AUSTRIA

This 180km (112-mile) trail, located within
the Danube Valley and the Unesco World
Heritage Wachau Valley wine district,
passes through 13 villages (14 sections).
The start/end points are Dürnstein and
WeiBenkirchen and you can hike it in either
direction or complete individual sections.
Dürnstein is home to the Melk Abbey,
known for its distinctive blue monastery
domes. The trail heads through forested
slopes of the river valley, and through
charming, medieval wine-making villages.
Ancient fortresses, perched on mountain
ridges, provide extraordinary views of the
valley's vineyards, sublime apricot orchards
(famous for their blossoms) and, of course,
the famous Danube River.
Start // Dürnstein
Finish // WeiBenkirchen
Distance // 180km (112 miles)
**More info // www.lower-austria.info/
world-heritage-trail-wachau**

FRUŠKA GORA, SERBIA

Fruška Gora, Serbia's oldest national park,
covers 266 sq km (103 sq miles) of rolling
hills and forest. The region's highlights
are the monasteries that were constructed
between the 15th and 18th centuries. Of
the 35 original monasteries, 17 remain
and they're open to visitors. Most of the
park's 19 marked hiking trails head to the
monasteries that are scattered throughout
the park; unfortunately, no single circuit
encompasses them all. The walking level is
moderate (think hills, not mountain peaks).
Hikes in Fruška Gora vary enormously,
from a short 3.9km (2.4-mile) route
connecting Velika Remeta and Grgeteg
Monasteries, to a longer 16km (10-mile)
loop route between Beočin Monastery
and Crveni čot, the park's highest peak
(539m/1768ft). Some tracks head deep into
forests of beech and linden trees, while
others head over pastures, along orchards
and vineyards and to secluded villages.
Start/Finish // Varies
Distance // Various
More info // www.serbia.com

METEORA, GREECE

The monasteries of Meteora, in central
Greece, perch above extraordinary rock
pinnacles (at yes, meteoric heights) and
are one of the world's most spectacular
sights. Hermit monks first lived in the
scattered caves in the 11th century. These
days, visitors can visit six of the active
monasteries. The best way to visit is
on foot, via the network of hundreds of
monopati (footpaths) that head up to and
down from the monasteries. The tracks are
not signed, but the routes are clear, and
the landmarks – the rocks – are visible. The
tracks pass through fields of wildflowers,
and olive groves dotted with massive
boulders. Foliage provides shade in some
(but not all) instances.
**Start/Finish // Kalambaka or Kastraki,
Meteora's two villages**
Distance // Various
**More info // For a map of the area, see
Visit Meteora (www.visitmeteora.travel)**

THE ROOF OF MONTENEGRO: BOBOTOV KUK

A hike to the top of Montenegro's highest mountain rewards with views of three Balkan nations –
and the hike down promises glacial lakes and the brooding landscape of Durmitor National Park.

'Here in Durmitor, we call our lakes Gorske Oči – the eyes of the mountain,' explains my guide Slavko Borozan, as he emerges from the forest beside a glinting turquoise lake, ringed by a circlet of pines. 'It's a good name. Sometimes, it feels as though it's the mountains that are watching you, not the other way round.'

We rest by the wooded lakeshore, watching mayflies dart across the surface. It's just after first light, and mist still cloaks the skyline, obscuring the mountains behind a silvery shroud. Somewhere in the murk is the summit I've come to conquer: Bobotov Kuk, Montenegro's highest peak.

'At this time of year there is often cloud in the morning,' Slavko reassures me. 'But do not worry. I know the weather in Durmitor. The sky will clear as we approach the top. I am sure of it. And you will see the finest view in the Balkans.'

He grins confidently, sipping from a battered water bottle. Slavko has spent his life exploring Durmitor's mountains, and in the couple of days I've spent in his company, he seems to have had no need for either compass or map. He's led me to forest glades, deserted lakes, and remote mountain huts; we've foraged for wild chanterelles and sipped on pine needle tea, and spent our afternoons spotting peregrine falcons, honey buzzards and golden eagles. We've even followed the footprints of one of Durmitor's most elusive residents – a brown bear. So I'm inclined to trust his forecasting skills, but looking into the thick grey clouds, I can't help but have doubts. We set off up the trail, climbing gradually out of the forest onto the scree-strewn slopes of the Durmitor massif.

Montenegro might not be that well-known as a walking destination, but among the hiking cognoscenti, its mountains

– especially those of Durmitor National Park – are rightly revered. Sprawling over 339 sq km (131 sq miles), Durmitor is Montenegro's largest national park, and one of Europe's last great pockets of wilderness: a Unesco-protected landscape of forests, mountains, meadows and canyons that's changed little since the last ice age. The park provides a refuge for some of Europe's rarest creatures, including the lynx, grey wolf and brown bear, and much of it is still cloaked in old-growth trees; some of Durmitor's virgin black pines are the last remnants of the great forest that once stretched all the way from the Russian steppes to the Atlantic coast.

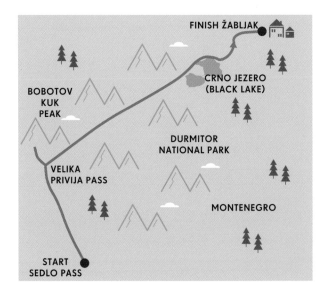

From left: reflections in the inky water of Crno Jezero (Black Lake); making the descent from Boboto Kuk; honey buzzards can be spotted on the trail. Previous page: hiking in Durmitor National Park

But for hikers, it's the mountains that provide the main attraction. The national park is host to 48 mountains over 2000m (6562ft), all far more lightly trodden than their Alpine or Pyrenean cousins – so, for hikers who prefer their trails uncrowded, Durmitor is a dream come true.

At 2523m (8278ft), Bobotov Kuk is the monarch of the Durmitor massif. Despite its stature, the mountain can be climbed in a day, requires no special equipment or expertise, and – famously – provides a panorama that takes in the borders of three neighbouring nations: Montenegro, Bosnia & Hercegovina and Serbia.

There are two common routes to the top: the Sedlo Route, a three-hour climb from the Sedlo Pass, or the more challenging trail from Žabljak via Crno Jezero (Black Lake), which approaches Bobotov Kuk from the northeast. Slavko's decided to combine the two, ascending the Sedlo Route and descending to Žabljak.

Though steep and winding, the Sedlo trail is straightforward – at least to begin with. We climb beyond the treeline onto open meadows, traversing areas of scree as we near the mountains'

flanks. Below us stretches a green mantle of pines; ahead, a chain of karst pinnacles studs the skyline, white and stark as a wolf's jawbone. After a couple of hours climbing, we reach Velika Privija Pass, and I get my first glimpse of the hulking, steep-sided profile of Bobotuv Kuk.

From here, the hiking gets harder – and the drops considerably greater. We scramble onto the mountain's shoulder, and pick carefully along a narrow path strewn with gravel and rubble. As we climb higher, fixed cables provide a handhold at the more exposed sections: I hold on tight and haul myself up the rock face, trying not to contemplate the yawning void beneath my feet. As we near the summit, the clouds break up and golden sunshine lights up the mountaintop. 'You see?' Slavko exclaims, bearded face beaming. 'Just as I told you. The mountain is smiling on us. Come! Now let's enjoy the view.'

We sit down on the summit, looking out over a chain of rumpled peaks that extends out across the border into Bosnia & Hercegovina and Serbia. Rainclouds race across the landscape,

"Below us stretches a green mantle of pines; ahead, a chain of karst pinnacles... [as] white and stark as a wolf's jawbone."

chased by spears of sunlight that illuminate the forests and fields below like search beacons. In the distance, we watch a pair of eagles whirling in the updraft, circling on invisible currents, masters of all they survey.

'This deserves a toast,' Slavko says, pulling out a flask from his backpack. 'My brother's home-made rakija, made from grapes in his own garden!' He pours us each a measure into steel cups, inhaling the boozy, grape-scented fumes. *'Živjeli!'* he says with gusto, clinking my cup before knocking back his rakija in one. I follow his lead, and feel the fiery liquid radiating from my belly into my bones.

We stay on the summit for an hour, picnicking on bread, cheese and fruit. Then, reluctantly, I take a last look at the view before beginning the trek back down the mountain into the wild valley to Crno Jezero. There's a lot more walking to be done yet today – but Slavko knows the way, and we have plenty of rakija to keep us warm on the way home. I can't think of anywhere I'd rather be. **OB**

ORIENTATION

Start // Sedlo Pass
Finish // Žabljak
Distance // 16.5km (10.2 miles)
Duration // Eight to nine hours
Getting there // Durmitor is 125km (78 miles) north of Montenegro's capital, Podgorica. You'll need a car.
When to go // August and September are ideal for hiking in Durmitor. Average temperatures peak at 30°C (86°F) in July and August, 20°C (68°F) in April and October.
What to wear // Light breathable gear, high-ankle boots, base layers and waterproofs.
Where to stay and eat // The ski town of Žabljak has hotels, B&Bs and apartments for rent, as well as a good supply of seasonal cafes and restaurants.
Things to know // *'Zdravo'* is Montenegrin for 'hello', but you'll sound more local if you say *'dobar dan'* (good day).
More info // www.visit-montenegro.com

*Opposite: trekking through the Velebit
Mountains in Croatia*

MORE LIKE THIS
BALKAN TRAILS

PREMUŽIĆ TRAIL, CROATIA

Winding for 57km (35 miles) through the
beautiful Velebit Mountains, the Premužić
Trail was developed in the 1930s by
Ante Premužić, a forestry engineer and
dedicated mountaineer. It's considered
by many hikers to be the most beautiful in
Croatia, allowing access to remote sections
of the Northern Velebit National Park, as
well as two of the country's most impressive
karst ranges, Hajdučki and Rožanski Kukovi
– an alpine fantasy-land of chasms, ridges,
caves, cliffs and obelisks. The customary
start and end-points are Zavižan and Baške
Oštarije. The trail usually takes three to
four days to complete, with accommodation
at mountain huts en route.
Start // Zavižan
Finish // Baške Oštarije
Distance // 57km (35 miles)
More info // www.np-sjeverni-velebit.hr

THE BLUE LAKES, ROMANIA

Romania's location alongside the mighty
Carpathians provides some of the most
impressive mountain scenery in Europe. But
there are other treasures too – including
the celebrated Blue Lakes, found in
Cheile Nerei-Beusnita National Park. Fed
by karst springs deep underground, the
lakes are famous for their clear cerulean-
blue waters, which look almost tropical
in colour. Various hiking routes connect
the main lakes together, and are mostly
easy-going day hikes; for something more
adventurous, there is also a maze of
wild gorges to explore, carved out by the
rushing course of the Nera River. Camping
out in the canyons overnight makes for a
truly wild experience – especially since the
Carpathians are still a refuge for brown
bears, wolves and wild cats.
**Start/Finish // Sasca Română is a good
base for hikes in the park**
Distance // Various
More info // www.uncover-romania.com

TARA NATIONAL PARK, SERBIA

You could hike for a lifetime and still
not cover all the trails criss-crossing
the mountains of Tara National Park,
inaugurated in 1981, and arguably
Serbia's most popular and pristine nature
reserve. Covering more than 250 sq km
(97 sq miles) of gorges, lakes, forests,
caves and sinkholes, it's heavily forested
– and one of the only endemic homes of
the Serbian spruce *(picea omorika)* now
a common sight in gardens and parks all
over Europe (it's also a popular Christmas
tree). One of the park's best bang-for-
buck hikes is the easy trek from the resort
of Mitrovac to the viewpoint of Banjska
Stena, a stunning lookout over the Drina
canyon that feels almost Canadian with
its wraparound vistas of lakes, mountains
and view-framing pines.
Start // Mitrovac
Finish // Banjska Stena
Distance // 14.8km (9.2 miles)
More info // www.explore-serbia.rs

SLOVENIA'S JULIANA TRAIL

Trace a two-week loop around Slovenia's three-headed national peak, Triglav, through dense pinewoods and gorges, past thundering cascades and glittering lakes guarded by medieval castles.

Delve into the dense pine forest beneath jagged Špik peak, following the slippery limestone trail beside the teal-blue Martuljek river, and you'll be rewarded with one hell of a slap.

In Slovenia, that's a good thing – *slap* being the local word for 'waterfall'. And Spodnji Martuljkov slap (Lower Martuljek Falls), tumbling 29m (95ft) over several tiers into the gleaming gorge it's carved below, is a true scene-stealer – particularly in late spring, when I visited, as abundant snowmelt from the mountains above amplifies the torrent.

This magnificent cascade is a short detour from Stage 1 of 17 stages on the Juliana Trail, the recently waymarked 270km (168-mile) hiking circuit around the Julian Alps. This wandering path dips in and out of Triglav National Park, the 840 sq km (324 sq mile) biosphere reserve surrounding 2864m (9396ft) Mt Triglav (Three Heads), Slovenia's heftiest mountain and national symbol, represented on the flag.

It's said that every Slovenian should climb Triglav at least once. Fortunately, there's no need to summit this spectacular peak to enjoy every aspect; despite a few testing ascents, the Juliana Trail never tops 1500m (4921ft) in altitude. It's designed instead to showcase the region's diverse scenic, cultural, culinary and historical attractions, visiting medieval walled towns, castles and relics of two world wars. There are waterfalls aplenty, of course, and fine food: this is truly a land of milk (or, rather, cheese) and honey – cows and beehives are ubiquitous.

Starting Stage 1 in Kranjska Gora, I tramped the southern slopes of the Karavankas Mountains separating Slovenia from Austria to the lookout at Srednji Vrh, where I drank in my first

glimpses of Špik and Triglav, familiar companions over the days that followed. But I soon discovered that the trail's focus is as much on people as landscapes. And beyond Jesenice, an iron town with an industrial heritage that stretches back to the Middle Ages, I was introduced to a succession of characters who, in very different ways, define modern Slovenia.

In Vrba, just off the main route, I encountered France Prešeren, the 19th-century romantic poet whose verse cemented Slovenia's sense of nationhood while still under the yoke of the Austro-Hungarian Empire. After independence, his poem *Zdravljica* (A Toast) provided lyrics for the national anthem.

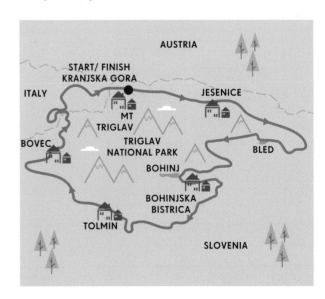

A short stroll alongside fields studded with traditional *kozolci* (hayracks) brought me to Breznica, where I admired the Carniolan beehives of pioneering 18th-century apiarist Anton Janša. Like a miniature medieval-style art gallery, the front of each beehive sports a colourful painting of a folk tale: a hunter's pall borne by wild animals, a fox shaving a man, a tailor being chased by a snail. If there's one thing more Slovenian than bees or Prešeren's verse, it's *žganje* (schnapps) – you're likely to be offered a quick *špička* (shot) at any time of day. That morning it was an octogenarian carpenter, a friend of my local guide, who insisted on a post-breakfast pear schnapps, a shot of fruity liquid fire that warmed the cockles but slowed the legs.

Climbing into a forest, our steps fell in time to the metronomic beat of a nearby woodpecker. Again, it was a scene – and a sound – with which I became familiar: some 60% of Slovenia is wooded, providing shelter from sun and rain alike along the trail. Emerging from the trees, we gazed down at Begunje na Gorenjskem. The village is dominated by the Elan ski factory and Katzenstein Mansion, housing the Museum of Hostages; commandeered by the Gestapo in 1941, its cells still bear the scratched graffiti from some of its 12,000 inmates – a moving memorial to a desperate period of occupation and resistance. Coachloads of Teutonic tourists, though, come to Begunje to pay homage at the home of Slavko Avsenik, the musical genius who spawned the genre of Oberkrainer, blending folk, brass, polka and waltz, and selling more than 30 million records. If you've ever munched wurst at a German Christmas market, chances are the soundtrack was Slavko's 1955 blockbuster 'Na Golici' (Trumpet Echoes), reputedly the most-played instrumental piece in history.

Continuing south to Radovljica's medieval moated heart, I watched *lectarstvo* (gingerbread decorating), a local speciality since 1766, before strolling on to Bled, Slovenia's tourism pin-up. Blessed with a clifftop castle overlooking a sparkling lake, it's undeniably photogenic – and unsurprisingly popular: convoys of wooden *pletna* (traditional canopied gondolas) ferry tourists across to the island church. Here I fuelled up on *kremšnita* (artery-clogging Bled cream cake) for the more-testing alpine sections of the trail.

Plunging northwest into Triglav National Park, I navigated narrow limestone Pokljuka Gorge – hiding place of Slovenian partisans during WWII – and climbed through fairy-tale woods where ostrich ferns swayed like verdant feather boas. On the plateau above, I roamed among wild saffron and gentian, between larch-shingled cabins awaiting the arrival of the transhumance. Then I traversed Barje Goreljek, Europe's highest peat bog, and descended through farming villages to Lake Bohinj. Bigger, wilder and quieter than Bled, and if anything more picturesque – indeed, Bohinj means 'God's Land' in the local dialect. The meadows above are spangled with 300 species of wildflowers; the trails are rockier and more alluring; the food even more tempting, from Bohinj trout to aromatic Mohant cheese,

BEE KIND, REWIND

Behind the church in Breznica, you'll encounter an extraordinary kaleidoscopic apartment block – for bees. This is the hive complex created by Anton Janša (1734–73), 'father of modern beekeeping'. The front of each individual unit of a traditional Carniolan beehive is painted with a scene from folklore or the Bible in a charming style emulated across Slovenia, where honey-makers are revered. Learn more about Janša's endeavours at the Beekeeping Museum in Radovljica.

Clockwise from top: wooden chapel at Vršič Pass; Tolmin Gorge; Anton Janša's memorial apiary. Previous page: looking towards Mt Triglav

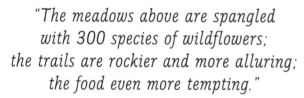

*"The meadows above are spangled
with 300 species of wildflowers;
the trails are rockier and more alluring;
the food even more tempting."*

ORIENTATION

best sampled straight from an artisan's door along
the cheesemakers' trail.

A daunting ridge separates Bohinj from the Soča Valley
which, during WWI, became the infamous Isonzo Front between
Italian and Austro-Hungarian forces; numerous castles, forts,
museums, trenches and bunkers along or near the route add historic
flavour to what's arguably the most dramatic stretch of the Juliana
Trail. At Tolmin I squeezed into the namesake gorge where luminous
blue-green waters surged between narrow rock walls, stepping over
primeval-looking fire salamanders glistening on the trail. And finally,
en route to Bovec, I ended my walk as it had begun, with a slap: the
15m- (49ft)-high Kozjak Falls thundering into a preternaturally round
cavern – a suitably circular denouement to a spectacular circuit. **PB**

Start/Finish // Any town on circuit; Kranjska Gora, Bled,
Bohinjska Bistrica and Tolmin are convenient entry points.
Distance // 270km (168 miles)
Duration // 10 to 14 days
Getting there // Buses from capital Ljubljana serve key
access points; trains reach northern and eastern areas,
usually involving a change at Jesenice.
When to go // March to October; snow can linger on
higher ground into June.
What to wear // Lightweight walking clothes are mostly fine,
though waterproofs and sturdy hiking boots are essential.
Where to eat // Hiša Franko (www.hisafranko.com),
arguably Slovenia's top restaurant, is near Kobarid.
Tours // Hike and Bike (www.hikeandbike.si) offers self-
guided and guided multiday walks covering most of the
Juliana Trail.
More info // www.julian-alps.com

*Opposite: ascending the ashy slopes of
Mt Etna in Sicily*

MORE LIKE THIS
ENCOUNTERS
WITH ICONIC PEAKS

MT OLYMPUS, GREECE

Greece's highest peak – and, according
to legend, abode of ancient gods Zeus,
Hera et al – Mt Olympus (2917m/9570ft)
offers a suitably celestial challenge for
hikers. Though not a technical climb, the
final summit haul involves some vertiginous
scrambling, so be prepared with good
boots, a head for heights and clothing for
all weather – even in high summer, you
might encounter blazing sun, rain, hail and
snow all on the same day. Ascend from the
cheerful coastal town of Litohoro along
the long-distance E4 trail past historic
Agiou Dionysiou Monastery to the tavern
at Prionia that marks the start of a thrilling
circuit. Cross sheer ridges, wildflower-
strewn slopes, and forests of beech, black
and Balkan pine to reach one of the simple
refuges from which you'll make your early
morning attempt on Mytikas, the topmost
summit, to be rewarded with suitably
heavenly views far across the mountains of
northern Greece.
**Start/Finish // Litohoro
Distance // 44.5km (27 miles)
More info // www.trekking.gr offers
information on guided hikes.**

MT KORAB, NORTH MACEDONIA
AND ALBANIA

The highest point in North Macedonia is
also the tallest peak in Albania – the might
of Mt Korab (2764m/9068ft) straddles
the two Balkan nations – though access is
arguably easier from the former Yugoslav
republic. You'll need your own transport
and, ideally, an experienced guide
accustomed to dealing with patches of
late-lying snow and the fierce shepherds'
dogs you may encounter en route. Set out
from the trailhead in Mavrovo National
Park, near the border post at Strezimir
(check whether permits are currently
required), climbing through enchanting
silver birch woods before emerging into
alpine meadows sprinkled with blueberries,
cowslips, violets and wild saffron blooms.
The summit approach follows trails dotted
with purple-veined marble slabs, then a
fanged ridge ending in the main peak of
Korab, a stark pinnacle of fractured rock.
**Start/Finish // Strezimir Watch Tower,
Mavrovo National Park
Distance // 16km (10 miles)
More info // www.intoalbania.com**

MT ETNA, SICILY, ITALY

Europe's tallest active volcano, the vast
black cone dominating eastern Sicily, has
been smoking, rumbling and periodically
spewing columns of ash for the past 2.6
million years – indeed, its name derives
from the Greek meaning 'I burn'. At 3320m
(10,892ft) more or less – depending on
recent geological shenanigans – an ascent
isn't to be taken lightly, and indeed access
to the upper of the four main craters may
be prohibited if activity levels are high. But
the forbidding black lava fields that blanket
its slopes, relics of past eruptions, offer
dramatic hiking amid lunar landscapes and
panoramic vistas to the Mediterranean,
nonetheless. Don tough boots (that jagged,
friable terrain is punishing on footwear)
and join an experienced guide to hike via
belching fumaroles to the summit crater.
**Start/Finish // Rifugio Sapienza,
Nicolosi
Distance // 10–15km (6–9 miles),
depending on highest accessible point
More info // www.visitsicily.info**

ON FOOT THROUGH A LAND OF VANISHING LAKES

With an evocative, ever-changing landscape and a hearty slow-food culture, Jini Reddy discovers a hike through Slovenia's peaceful Karst that feeds every one of the senses.

'm sitting on a mossy stone deep in a lush forest when I hear the crackling of branches. I think nothing of it, until I emerge from the woods and see a sign pointing to where I've just been. On it is the unmistakable silhouette of a bear. There are thought to be around 500 to 700 brown bears in Slovenia and, although close encounters are unlikely, it is only later I'll learn that they like to hang out in forests like these.

The crackling takes on new significance and sends a thrill up my spine. Not a feeling of unease or fear – more a primal satisfaction. I'm hiking through the beating heart of West Slovenia's Karst, taking over a week, and staying at tourist farms and B&Bs along the way. I love walking, but this is the first long-distance hike I've done on my own, and I'm placing a lot of faith in my route notes and compass, one I've only just learned to use.

Why the Karst in a country not short on green landscapes? For starters, it's off the beaten track, pristine, full of forests, woodland, meadows and unspoilt villages, with an ever-present backdrop of mountains. The region is known for its caves and vanishing lakes too. They rise in the autumn, then flow away in the spring, disappearing into sinkholes in caverns – some look like craters left by UFOs.

I begin by striking out on foot from the village of Landol, following a lift from Ljubljana. Charting my course by compass, route notes, spire and hilltop castle, I stride along country lanes dotted with shrines, through sleepy villages and into forests alive with birdsong. The wildflowers dazzle and the greens are kaleidoscopic – pine, hazel, oak, cherry, birch, linden, spruce and many more trees thrive here. I see no one, bar the odd farmer on a tractor.

One of the joys of any day-long hike is the evening meal, and Slovenia is foodie heaven. When I reach the first farmhouse that I'm staying in, a slobbery St Bernard bounds up to greet me and my host waves as he ushers the cows in from the fields.

Dinner is the first of many rustic feasts: *Pršut* (ham) from the farmer's pigs, a beef stew, home-made apple pie and a floral tea conjured from dried flowers and herbs. In the morning a cockerel shocks me into wakefulness, and after beehive honey, bread and cakes, plum preserve, eggs and more ham, I'm sent off with a picnic lunch.

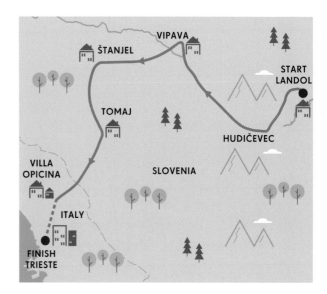

The Škocjan Caves are a Unesco World Heritage site, and a must for any visitor to the region, up there with the likes of the Grand Canyon and the Great Barrier Reef for the 'wow' factor. The extraordinary high-ceilinged caves are like a subterranean cathedral for giants and truly breathtaking. All sound is drowned out by the roar of the Reka River as it cascades through the underground gorge, to resurface miles away in Italy.

From left: inside the cavernous Škocjan Caves; rolling vineyards of the Vipava Valley; cured ham and local wine are highlights of the region. Previous page: built into the karst landscape: Predjama Castle

I have the scenery all to myself which, selfishly, is how I like it, and my confidence grows. Out here, there's virtually no reminder of Slovenia's tumultuous history; until the 20th century it was under foreign rule, mostly the Habsburg monarchy of the Austro-Hungary Empire. After WWI it became part of the soon-to-be Yugoslavia, and was occupied by the Nazis in WWII. In 1991, following the short Ten-Day War, the country gained independence and in 2004 joined the EU.

I wander through the Vipava Valley and beyond the eerie, medieval Predjama Castle and the dark, damp woods south of Strane, before entering Slap. The sun shines as I amble along, and the area feels richly Mediterranean, with terracotta-roofed villages making way for a maze of vineyard terraces – one of which I manage to briefly get lost in. (Getting lost is a great lesson in trust and patience, I learn.)

That evening I treat myself to a meal at Cejkotova Domačija, in the medieval village of Goče. It's a lovingly restored, 450-year-old solid brick home of a renowned wine producer. Here grapes have been grown biodynamically for generations. In a candlelit cellar I sip on a full-bodied Merlot and an extraordinary, aromatic Picolit. Following a six-course feast of local delicacies, I'm offered a nectar called Lady's Liqueur. It's made with prune, cognac, wine, grape juice and a secret ingredient. The thick, honey-coloured drink makes me purr, and that night I sleep like a (karst) stone.

On it goes, one lyrical, sense-drenched moment to the next, each footstep bringing new discoveries. After a glorious, meadow-and-wood-filled hike up to the hilltop fortress village of Štanjel I learn that Wanda Newby, wife of the late travel writer Eric Newby grew up here and wrote a book about it called *Peace and War*. Here I drink schnapps made with 40 herbs by my hostess and eat honey from local hives.

Štanjel is a typical Karst village: the buildings are made from limestone and the winding alleyways are dappled with pine, juniper and fruit trees. Songbirds flit about mulberry trees. At times, I'm told the locals feel the strength of the northeast Burja wind that blows from the top of the Julian

*"One of the joys of any day-long
hike is the evening meal, and
Slovenia is foodie heaven."*

Alps. It's so strong sometimes, up to 200km/h (124mph), that the roads are closed.

The following evening, after a hike through more Karst woods to Tomaj, I reward myself with a glass of strong, iron-rich Teran wine. It's unique to the area and grown on its terra rossa – red soil. Fortified, the next day I head to Lipica village (home to the Lipizzaner, one of the world's most famous breed of horses) and pay a visit to the Škocjan Caves, before returning to Tomaj. Finally, I lace up my boots for the last leg of my hike.

The heavens open, I pull on my waterproofs, criss-cross woodland tracks scattered with limestone formations, hug vineyards, duck through hedges and over railway bridges. I triumphantly hop across the border into Italy – demarcated by a small yellow sign amid scrub. The Karst will morph into the streets of Opicina, a hilltop suburb, and then a bus will deposit me in Trieste. For now though, I break into a grin and take a swig from a hip flask filled with blueberry liqueur. I feel a sense of achievement, but something else: the journey has meant mapping not just the soul of the Karst, but more of my own too. **JR**

ORIENTATION

Start // Landol, Slovenia
Finish // Trieste, Italy
Distance // 73km (45 miles)
Duration // Five days (you can reduce this to a three- or four-day hike by taking lifts to skip sections).
Getting there // Austrian Railjet train (via TGV and Eurostar connections from Europe and London) will take you to Ljubljana. For detailed information on the route, visit the excellent www.seat61.com. Ljubljana Jože Pučnik Airport is Slovenia's international airport.
When to go // The best months are April, May, June, September and October.
Where to stay // There are hotels, inns and farm accommodation in the villages on the route.
Tours // On Foot Holidays (www.onfootholidays.co.uk) offer self-guided tours of the route.
More info // www.visitkras.info

Opposite from top: taking in the views of the Lanaitho Valley on the Great Trail of Supramonte; mountain hut in the heart of Bavaria's Steinernes Meer (Rocky Sea)

MORE LIKE THIS
HIKES IN LIMESTONE

GREAT TRAIL OF SUPRAMONTE, SARDINIA

Blazing a trail through the heart of Sardinia's limestone Supramonte massif, this four-day, moderately challenging hike kicks off at the 1116m (3661ft) saddle of Arcu Correboi before wending its way north to Su Gologone, a jewel-green spring that is the final outflow point for Italy's largest underground river system. Though not as intimidatingly high as other mountain ranges, the Supramonte is nevertheless impressively wild. Here, ragged limestone peaks rise like natural fortifications above ancient forests of holm oak trees. Its karst plateaux are spectacularly riven with gorges and pitted with caves and sinkholes. As you walk, expect to be wowed by the mysterious nuraghi (Bronze Age standing stones), rare wildflowers such as the bright-pink, Gennargentu rose, and peregrine falcons. As there are few discernible trails, enlisting a guide is wise. Nights are spent under canvas or in *pinnetos*, stone-built shepherds' shelters.
Start // Arcu Correboi
Finish // Su Gologone
Distance // 50km (31 miles)
More info // www.climbingsardinia.com

KYRENIA MOUNTAIN TRAIL, CYPRUS

Offering an intense hike of Northern Cyprus' Kyrenia Mountains, this trail reveals a wild, silent side to the island that few get to see. Only by striding along the spine of this limestone massif can you begin to appreciate its raw beauty. The 18-stage hike crosses over crags and along forest paths west to east, from Koruçam Burnu to Zafer Burnu. In so doing, it dips deep into forests fragrant with pine and eucalyptus where cicadas drone, orchids bloom and lizards dart from the undergrowth. On the one side is the glitter of the coast, on the other the sweep of the Mesaoria plain. In between you'll find stuck-in-time villages, churches and monasteries. Moments to remember include the rocky battlements of the Five Finger Mountains, the improbably perched Crusader castle of St Hilarion and the exquisite ruins of Bellapais Abbey.
Start // Koruçam Burnu (Cape Kormakitis)
Finish // Zafer Burnu (Cape Apostolos Andreas)
Distance // 240km (149 miles)
More info // www.northcypruswalk.com

STEINERNES MEER, GERMANY

One of Europe's most wondrous karst plateaux, the Steinernes Meer (Rocky Sea) lives up to its name, with deeply fissured limestone rolling away like breaking waves. This three- to five-day high-level hike is pure drama, properly immersing you in the Alps that pop up on the border between Bavaria in Germany and Salzburgerland in Austria. Standing sentinel on the horizon is the Schönfeldspitze, a real fang of a mountain.

This moderately challenging hut-to-hut walk begins at the fjord-like, bottle-green lake of Königssee, before ascending through alpine pastures to Carl-von-Stahl-Haus, then picking its way up to the 2276m (7467ft) Schneibstein, where you might spot ibex and chamois. From Wasseralm hut it heads on to Funtensee, a gem-coloured lake rimmed by horn-shaped peaks. The trail then leads up and down through sensational karst scenery and meadows to Kärlingerhaus and Ingolstädter Haus huts before descending to the wildly romantic Wimbach Valley.
Start // Königssee
Finish // Wimbachtal (Wimbach Valley)
Distance // 57km (36 miles)
More info // www.berchtesgaden.de

FRONTIERLAND: THE PEAKS OF THE BALKANS TRAIL

Make your way to the remote borders of Montenegro, Albania and Kosovo to set foot in a once-forbidden mountain wilderness where, today, walkers are warmly welcomed.

God took six days to create the earth, the sea and the sky. But, so a local legend goes, the devil took only 24 hours to create the Accursed Mountains. It was a full day's work. He would have scored deep ravines with his pointy tail. He would have sculpted spires of rock with his evil little claws. And, long after he finished the Mountains, the curse remained, for this range has always been synonymous with bandits, blood feuds, avalanches, and miscellaneous misfortunes for anyone foolish enough to visit.

Today, the Accursed Mountains straddle the borders of three nations: Montenegro, Kosovo and Albania. Setting out on a morning stroll in early summer, you suspect the Almighty would be impressed by his rival's handiwork. Because, with devilish deception, it is a place of radiant, intense loveliness.

My walk starts in the village of Vusanje, Montenegro, near a timber minaret carved with crescent moons and petals. Before long, I am far from settlements, walking through wildflower meadows where the ground itself seems to move with the fluttering of thousands of butterflies. There are mighty limestone mountains crumbling into wind-scoured boulder fields, and stone shepherds' huts, their chimney stacks toppled and slumped in mimicry of the peaks above. Most of the time, there are few hikers. It feels like a mini-Yosemite in the Balkans – a real back-of-the-wardrobe secret land that has somehow evaded the attention of the outside world. There are clues as to why. Four hours' walk from Vusanje, I cross the Montenegro–Albania border, where derelict military bunkers watch from above. Beyond them lies the village of Theth, Albania. It is roughly 23km (14 miles) from Vusanje but, until 1991, it might as well have been the far side of the moon.

'If you were caught walking in these mountains in those times, you would have gone to prison,' says Pavlin Polia. 'Or worse.' Pavlin is a mountain guide and guesthouse owner in Theth. When he was a youngster, Theth was part of Communist Albania, a regime unrivalled in Europe for brutal oppression and crippling poverty. Its paranoid dictator, Enver Hoxha, built more than 170,000 of his bunkers across the country, partly to repel enemies – but as much to make sure citizens stayed put.

For decades, the Accursed Mountains served as Hoxha's giant geological Berlin Wall (one that conveniently brewed its own thunderstorms). Its treacherous passes became the ultimate hurdle

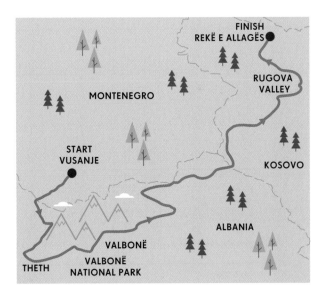

for anyone escaping Albania to reach the relative freedom of Montenegro, then part of Yugoslavia.

Over coffee in his guesthouse in Theth, Pavlin tells me about escape attempts – the 70-strong family who sneaked over the frontier on Hoxha's birthday, when the border guards were partying and looking the other way. And nameless others who tiptoed into the beech forests after nightfall, never to be heard from again.

Communism may be a memory, but only in the past few years have geopolitical developments allowed these mountains to open up to hikers. Pavlin is among the founders of the Peaks of the Balkans trail – a 192km (119-mile) hiking route that passes through three nations in a lap of the Accursed Mountains. The full trail is a two-week-long odyssey of which I was tackling a six-day portion.

After spending a night in Theth, the Albanian leg of the trail leads me towards the Valbonë Valley over a rocky pass. Climbing higher, the view soon expands into widescreen mode: giant citadels of rock, meadows tinged blue in the heat haze, eagles riding thermals from the Adriatic. From the highest point of the pass, you see clearly how the Accursed Mountains are one of the last redoubts of wilderness in the Balkans. Somewhere on the ranges below live wolves and brown bears. And, of course, the critically endangered Balkan lynx, barely a few dozen of which roam the rocky plateaux, their whiskers twitching in the highland wind.

Wherever you walk in the Accursed Mountains, borders are a constant companion. Sometimes a border shimmies along a knife-edge arête. Often it plunges into a frozen lake and climbs out on the other side. Very occasionally it ambushes you with a weatherbeaten sign proclaiming something like 'Welcome to MO TE EGRO'.

As the trail enters Kosovo, the landscape subtly changes character. Vertical peaks lapse into gently contoured hills, and broadleaf forests where wild strawberries and apricots grow by the trail. Splitting the landscape in two is the Rugova Gorge, where little cafes watch over a foaming river, and Kosovars come for picnics at weekends.

It looks like a picture of timeless serenity but, here again, the Accursed Mountains are deceptive. In 1998, during the last chapter of the Balkan Wars, Yugoslav forces rolled in from Montenegro and Serbia to battle the forces of the Kosovo Liberation Army. Amid the genocide of Kosovar Albanians, bloody fighting saw farmhouses torched and artillery fire breaking the hush of the Rugova forests.

Complex though political borders may be in the Accursed Mountains, they overlay an even more complicated map of ethnic and religious boundaries – of which hikers can get a tiny sense in Kosovo. In one part of the Rugova Valley, you might stop inside the Serbian Orthodox monastery in Peja, and squint to see frescoed saints in the shadowy heights. In another, you can hear the call to prayer from the village mosques, whose minarets inch above the treetops. As well as Albanians and Serbs, there are Bosniaks, Macedonians, Roma, Egyptians. The ethnic mix has been combustible in the past. Today, most look to the path ahead.

BUNKER PARTY

The Albanian pillbox is a wonder of architecture largely because there are some 173,350 of them – nearly ten to every square mile. Built between 1967 and 1986 under Enver Hoxha's 'bunkerisation' strategy, they were never actually used to defend the country, but are an omnipresent feature of the Albanian landscape. They've been adapted as pizza ovens, mushroom farms, cafes and the location for many a teenage love tryst.

Clockwise from top: making pancakes in Rekë e Allagës; a church in Theth, nestled in valley; a Hoxha-era bunker overlooking the Albania-Montenegro border. Previous page: the Accursed Mountains

"It feels like a real back-of-the-wardrobe secret land that has somehow evaded the attention of the outside world."

The end of my hike comes in the village of Rekë e Allagës, and the home of Mustafa and Fethiye Nikqi. Mustafa rebuilt his Rugova farmhouse after it was destroyed in the war, and more recently opened it as a guesthouse. Today he welcomes a fraternity of hikers, united in the love of roaming this landscape. In small ways, he says, the Peaks of the Balkans trail encourages understanding across frontiers. Guides from all countries intermingle; guesthouses call lodges over the border to let them know a hiking group is on their way. 'If we had had this path 25 years ago, perhaps there would have been no war,' says Mustafa. 'The Peaks of the Balkans trail is, in some ways, like a stitch in a wound.'

Sunset lingers on the high points of the Accursed Mountains – casting golden beams on Rekë e Allagës while the world below is swallowed in shadows. For now, this is the Balkan landscape as God (or the devil) left it: an immensity of mountain, forest and meadow that is nothing if not European. **OS**

ORIENTATION

Start // Vusanje, Montenegro
Finish // Rekë e Allagës, Kosovo
Distance // 105km (65 miles)
Duration // Six days. The full circuit takes 10 to 13 days and can be commenced from any point on the trail.
Getting there // Vusanje is a five-hour drive from Podgorica.
When to go // May to October.
What to pack // GPS, compass, first-aid kit and phone.
Where to stay // Local guesthouses, mountain huts and lodges are available. Book in advance.
Where to eat // Carry enough food and water with you for each day. Grocery stores and cafes are rare.
Tours // Walking independently is an option. However, a guide is recommended: try Zbulo (www.zbulo.org) in Albania and Butterfly Outdoor (www.butterflyoutdoor.com) in Kosovo.
More info // www.peaksofthebalkans.com. Cicerone's *Peaks of the Balkans* Trail is an essential resource for hikers.

Opposite: hiking past a bank of limestone on the Peaks of the Balkans Trail

MORE LIKE THIS
DAY HIKES ON THE PEAKS OF THE BALKANS TRAIL

VUSANJE TO THETH

Said by some to be the most beautiful stretch of the trail, this easily navigable route follows the Ropojana Valley, with around 1000m (3281ft) of ascent. Bearing south from Vusanje, highlights include an abandoned Yugoslav military barracks, and the steep descent from the Qafa e Pejës pass into Theth. In Theth, be sure to pay a visit to the extraordinary 'lock-in' tower, a legacy of the complex blood feuds of the Accursed Mountains.
Start // **Vusanje, Montenegro**
Finish // **Theth, Albania**
Distance // **21km (13 miles)**
More info // **www.peaksofthebalkans. com**

THETH TO VALBONË

The most well trodden of all the Peaks of the Balkans stages, this hike affords extraordinary views from the top of the Valbonë Pass. Setting out from Theth, hikers ascend steeply through forests before crossing the saddle between the peaks of Maja Alijes and Maja e Boshit. From here, it's a steady descent towards Rragrami, and a walk along a stony river bed to Valbonë. You'll find a couple of small 'cafes' lining the trail, stocking drinks and snacks.
Start // **Theth, Albania**
Finish // **Valbonë, Albania**
Distance // **19km (12 miles)**
More info // **www.peaksofthebalkans. com**

REKË E ALLAGËS TO HAJLA

Rekë e Allagës is the most suitable base for adventures in Kosovo's Rugova Valley. If you're arriving from the east, it's readily accessed on tarmac roads from the town of Peja, home to an Ottoman bazaar and a beautiful Serbian Orthodox monastery. For a bracing day walk from Rekë e Allagës, follow the Peaks of the Balkans trail northwest through forests and meadows to the summit of Hajla – a rocky spine that marks the Kosovo– Montenegro border.
Start // **Rekë e Allagës, Kosovo**
Finish // **Hajla, Kosovo–Montenegro border**
Distance // **12km (7.5 miles)**
More info // **www.peaksofthebalkans. com**

WALKING HISTORY: THE LYCIAN WAY

Linking ruined Mediterranean cities once inhabited by the ancient Lycians, the Lycian Way runs from Turkey's golden beaches and seaside towns to hill villages and mountainous hinterland.

As I wandered out of the fishing village of Üçağız, the locals were just starting to go about their business after their ritual Turkish breakfast. No dallying and just a quick wave to the early birds outside the teahouse, as I was keen to put a few miles of Mediterranean coastline behind me before the freshness of the spring morning melted away. The next village on the Teke Peninsula, the bulge of beaches and holiday towns backed by the olive-grove-dotted foothills of the Western Taurus Mountains, was only accessible by foot or boat. Named after the Byzantine *kale* (castle) overlooking its handful of houses, Kaleköy promised to be well worth the 4km (2.5-mile) walk.

This was a small but typically scenic section of the Lycian Way: the 540km (335-mile), 29-day waymarked footpath that follows the Teke Peninsula between the tourist towns of Fethiye and Antalya, skirting the coast and climbing into the rugged back country en route. Ascending a rocky track through the Mediterranean scrub, I was soon overlooking a cerulean bay broken by the undulating outlines of islands and peninsulas. Reaching a boat-building yard, where wooden gulet yachts were under repair for the coming summer, I climbed a footpath towards the castle and emerged on a ridge studded with towering Lycian tombs, with more emerging from the shallows of the bay below.

Across the bay was the island of Kekova, fringed by the underwater ruins of the Lycian city of Simena, which was submerged by earthquakes around two millennia ago. After enjoying a meze lunch on a pensione terrace, a local fishers ferried me across to take a closer look at the Batık Sehir (Sunken City). The smashed amphorae, building foundations and staircases disappearing into the blue depths exemplified the Lycian Way's appeal of discovering spellbinding ancient history in a wild Mediterranean setting.

The footpath was researched, designed and waymarked by British amateur historian Kate Clow in the late 1990s. Aiming to identify and protect Turkey's ancient byways, and to offer a journey back through the millennia to the Mediterranean in the time of Lycia, Clow entered a competition run by a Turkish bank. Winning the competition and a grant, she spent years exploring this sublimely beautiful part of Turkey and bringing local hill farmers round to her envisioned trail and the benefits of tourism. The path is now one of a dozen walking, cycling and horse-riding routes marked and maintained by the Culture Routes Society, and it remains Turkey's original and most popular long-distance trail.

True to the Lycian Way's spirit of discovering this region rather than rigidly following a set route, the trail offers many possible detours, extensions and variations as it crosses the ancient territory of the mysterious Lycians. First mentioned in Homer's *Iliad*, the Lycians inhabited this part of Anatolia from at least three millennia ago, and were likely descended from the Lukka mentioned in ancient Hittite texts. Their high point was the Lycian League, a loose confederation of some 25 city states, often credited with being history's first proto-democratic union. The trail wends its way past the key remnants of the League, which was formed around 165 BCE and absorbed by the Roman Empire two centuries later. The moss-covered ancient ruins on the route include Letoön, a religious sanctuary dedicated to Zeus' lover Leto, the national deity of Lycia; the Roman theatre and pillar tombs at Xanthos, the grand Lycian capital until Brutus attacked in 42 BCE and the inhabitants committed mass suicide; and Patara, where a meadow strewn with Lycian ruins, including a 5000-seat theatre and a colonnaded street, leads to Turkey's longest beach. The League debated public issues in Patara's *bouleuterion*, or council chamber, which is often cited as the world's first parliament.

As much as for its history, the trail's appeal lies in its mix of romantic ruins and Mediterranean scenery with the comforts of whitewashed harbour towns, such as Kaş and Kalkan, where hikers enjoy well-earned fish and meze feasts. A favourite chill-out spot along the way was Kabak, another village with limited access, reached only by foot or high-clearance vehicle down steep forest tracks. The valley's traditional industries of farming and beekeeping have been joined by a handful of New-Age retreats offering rustic cabins, morning yoga, and terrace restaurants with sea views. It was a wonderful place to relax after braving the rope-assisted path up from the beach at the foot of Butterfly Valley's sheer cliffs.

BURIED TREASURES

The Lycians' distinctive cliff tombs, 'house' tombs, sepulchres and sarcophagi pepper the area's bays, fields and mountainsides, adding further lyricism to the scenery. Good examples include Fethiye's Tomb of Amyntas dating to 350 BCE, with its temple facade carved into the cliffs above town; Kaleköy's 'house' tombs rising mythically from the bay; the 4th-century-BCE King's Tomb, with two lion heads on its lid, in Kaş old town; and Myra's honeycomb of rock tombs, climbing the cliff outside present-day Demre.

Clockwise from top: rocky terrain on the Lycian Way; ancient ruins of Xanthos near Kalkan; contemplating that descent to the beach. Previous page: surveying the coastline en route

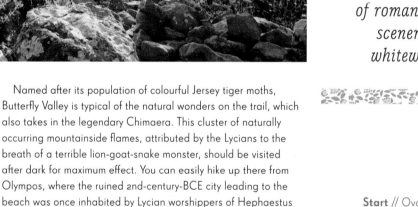

"*The trail's appeal lies in its mix of romantic ruins, Mediterranean scenery and the comforts of whitewashed harbour towns.*"

Named after its population of colourful Jersey tiger moths, Butterfly Valley is typical of the natural wonders on the trail, which also takes in the legendary Chimaera. This cluster of naturally occurring mountainside flames, attributed by the Lycians to the breath of a terrible lion-goat-snake monster, should be visited after dark for maximum effect. You can easily hike up there from Olympos, where the ruined 2nd-century-BCE city leading to the beach was once inhabited by Lycian worshippers of Hephaestus (or Vulcan, god of fire). Today, Olympos is equally famous for its 'tree house' camps, where hikers enjoy hammock time and campfire camaraderie while staying in the misnamed cabins, few of which are above terra firma.

For me, another surprise was Kayaköy, a village marked more by the 20th century than the Lycians, with its ruined 'ghost town' of Levissi created by post-WWI population exchanges between Turkey and Greece. The inspiration for Louis de Bernières' novel *Birds Without Wings*, hillside Levissi was abandoned by its Ottoman Greek inhabitants and never repopulated, leaving eerie streets composed of crumbling stone houses, churches and a castle overlooking modern Kayaköy.

Other walkers I met on the trail enthused about camping in olive groves, sharing their picnic with a Turkish farmer or feasting on a home-cooked meal in a village pensione – just a few of the memorable encounters and surprises that await on Turkey's Mediterranean byways. **JB**

ORIENTATION

Start // Ovacık (between Fethiye and Ölüdeniz)
Finish // Antalya
Distance // 540km (335 miles)
Duration // Approx 30 days
Getting there // Regular buses and local dolmus minibuses ply the coastal D400 highway between Fethiye, 45km (28 miles) east of Dalaman International Airport, and Antalya International Airport.
When to go // Clement temperatures make spring (March to May) and autumn (September to November) the best.
Things to know // Pack light, though helpful guesthouse owners will often drive your bags to your next stop.
More info // Kate Clow's useful *Lycian Way* guidebook is available, along with hiking maps, through Trekking in Turkey (http://trekkinginturkey.com).

MORE LIKE THIS
WALKS THROUGH TIME

IL CAMMINO DI DANTE®
(DANTE'S PATH), ITALY

A meditative meander in the footsteps of Italy's divine poet, Dante's Walk is a slow travel delight. Running from Ravenna in the fertile Po Valley and over the Apennine Mountains to Florence and back, this 20-stage trail is a love letter to Italy's most-feted literary legend. Retracing the poet's route through Emilia-Romagna and Tuscany, it is bookended by cities that are cultural feasts: the Byzantine mosaic-encrusted marvel that is Ravenna, where Dante came in exile, completed his epic poem, and where his tomb now stands. And the Renaissance dream that is Florence, where the Museo Casa di Dante keeps the memory of the divine poet alive at the site of his birthplace. En route, lyrical landscapes unravel: the medieval village of Brisighella with its eyrie-like fortress, say, or the waterfalls of Acquacheta, which Dante described as 'a single leap fed perhaps by a thousand torrents'.

Start // Ravenna
Finish // Florence
Distance // 395km (245 miles)
More info // www.camminodante.com

HADRIAN'S WALL COAST TO COAST,
ENGLAND

What have the Romans ever done for Britain? Built Hadrian's Wall as the northern frontier of their British territory, that's what. Snaking for 135km (84 miles) across Northumberland and Cumbria, this National Trail is a spectacular week-long romp, with 2000 years of history, urban culture, post-industrial heritage and lush landscapes all in the mix. Hike it from east to west – as the wall was built back in 122 CE – and you'll begin at Wallsend, 8km (5 miles) east of Newcastle, and end at Bowness-on-Solway on the Solway Firth estuary, just west of Carlisle. The wall traces a dramatic line across rolling hills, bare moors and fields, with the march along it taking in some of the country's most poetic landscapes, not to mention remarkable Roman sites, such as Housesteads Fort and Brocolitia Temple. Gradients are mostly gentle, with the higher, wilder section between Chollerford and Birdoswald presenting more of a challenge.

Start // Wallsend
Finish // Bowness-on-Solway
Distance // 135km (84 miles)
More info // www.nationaltrail.co.uk

CORYCEAN GROTTO TO DELPHI,
GREECE

Delphi was the navel (*omphalós*) of the world to Ancient Greeks. This unforgettable day hike takes you via the slow-but-spectacular way to Delphi, following the Archaio Monopati, one of the oldest still-used footpaths on the planet. Beginning at the stalactite-encrusted Corycean Grotto, once used for Pan worship and wild, wine-fuelled orgies celebrating Dionysus, the well-marked trail leads gently down the slopes of 2457m (8061ft) Mt Parnassos to link up with the E4 long-distance path. The route delves into the forested wilds of the Parnassos National Park, passing sun-dappled glades and springs. The views are nothing short of extraordinary, with mountains rippling above Delphi and the Gulf of Corinth shimmering in the distance. The final stretch zigzags down to Delphi, perched throne-like on a mountainside, with the Doric columns of its Temple of Apollo and amphitheatre held high to the heavens.

Start // Corycean Grotto
Finish // Delphi
Distance // 13.7km (8.5 miles)
More info // www.visitgreece.gr

*Clockwise from top: Hadrian's Wall
through the mist from Housesteads
Crag; a Byzantine-era mosaic in
Ravenna; sanctuary of Athena, Delphi*

SARAJEVO'S MT TREBEVIĆ TRAIL

A trek to the peak above the capital of Bosnia & Hercegovina mixes culture, history, panoramas, and a fresh new perspective on an incredible city.

After receiving a text from a friend and regular hiking companion to meet for a trek to the peak of Mt Trebević, I instinctively fall into a typical rhythm. Like a migratory bird, without thinking, I head to Sarajevo's Ottoman-era bazaar in the city's heart. That moment can then be broken down to its most elemental sensation: smell – or more accurately, a combination of smells. Sitting in a cafe in Bosnia & Hercegovina's capital, which is cradled in a valley and straddles the Miljacka River, the mountain we will soon summit looks down from above into the ancient market streets, and the aroma of history and culture finds me.

On this day, as with most, there is a dominant note of traditional coffee, which is thick and strong and cooked on a stove until it froths in a copper pot called a *džezva*, as it has for centuries. From some doorways leading onto the labyrinth of flagstone, pedestrian-only alleyways, the bouquet of fresh bread and *burek* – filled filo pastries – scent the air. From others, hookah smoke wafts. The mixture sets off a Pavlovian reaction. I subconsciously doublecheck my gear for water, a hat, sunscreen, a raincoat, walking sticks, and an extra layer for warmth at the top of the 1629m (5344ft) Mt Trebević.

When I receive the second text, I leave coins on the table for my cup, throw my pack over my shoulders, and start for the trailhead near the Hadžijska Mosque on the riverbank in the Old Town. My friend, Thierry Joubert, is waiting. For nearly 15 years, Thierry and I have left from Sarajevo's cobblestones to make this trek, which climbs 1000m (3281ft) and is guided by 400 markings and signposts along the way. The route – just over three hours and 10km (6.2 miles) of easy-to-medium difficulty with moments of steep exertion – is the same. The journey is always different.

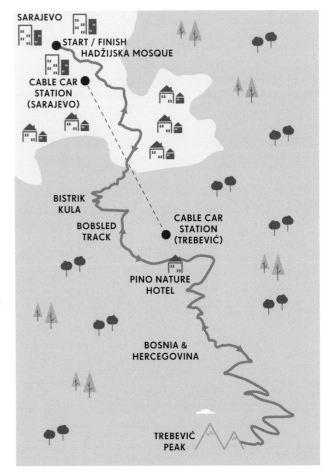

CABLE CAR

Sarajevo's newly rebuilt cable car is the right choice for responsible-minded adventurers who want a different perspective on Mt Trebević. The original system, built when Bosnia & Hercegovina was still part of Yugoslavia, ceased operations for more than a quarter of a century. The new gondolas began shuttling passengers again in 2018. The line starts from the Bistrik neighbourhood of the city and drops mountain-goers off near the bobsled track below the peak.

Clockwise from top left: homemade burek; red-tiled roofs of Sarajevo; the 1984 Olympic bobsled run snaking through the forest; fortifying Bosnian coffee; Previous page: cable car to Mt Trebević

First, we pass through *mahalas* (neighbourhoods) clinging to the foothills. Apple and cherry trees surround the clusters of homes. Then, following trail markers, we pass under the cable-car line, renovated and reopened in 2018 after decades of inactivity, which leaves from just southeast of the city centre and ends midway up the path. We begin our ascent up secluded slopes and into forests of spruce, beech, and fir trees, that grow denser as we leave the noise and commotion of the city.

'People call Trebević the lungs of Sarajevo,' Thierry says as we walk and talk about the value of having a mountain inside the city limits. Thierry is the director of Green Visions, a local adventure operator that leads tours to this peak and throughout the Western Balkans region. 'This is like our playground, our escape, and our place to just leave the worries behind. We hike here, cycle here, go snowshoeing...it is good for whatever ails you and there is a history lesson around nearly every switchback along the trail. Every place should be lucky enough to have such a getaway in their backyard.'

As we continue into the forest, about an hour along the trek, we make a stop at the shell of Bistrik Kula, a military tower built during the Austro-Hungarian occupation of the country in the late 19th and early 20th centuries. Views of the capital open up behind, reminding us of how far we've already hiked. We're also reminded how complex the history is here. In the 1960s, when Bosnia & Hercegovina was one of six Yugoslav republics, the site was repurposed as an astrological observatory: a place to look into the heavens from a spot where the cultures of people, religions, and empires met and melded here on Earth.

Our path suddenly feels like a trek between museum exhibitions dedicated to adventure as we reach the next stop: the husk of the bobsled and luge track, built, and used, for the 1984 Winter Olympics. One of the genuine highlights of a visit to Sarajevo, the concrete shell, which spans 1300m (4265ft) and is enjoyed today by skateboarders and mountain bikers, is largely intact despite damage inflicted during the conflict of the 1990s.

> *"This is like our playground, our escape, and our place to just leave the worries behind."*

Seeing the oft-photographed bobsled, dense with graffiti, is surreal and familiar – like seeing a retired sports hero buying stamps at the post office. The swirl of emotions is thick here. The structure represented a high point for the country of Yugoslavia, yet also serves as a reminder of challenging times. Most importantly, this hulking track, which sits peacefully in the forest, also seems to have become a repurposed cultural emblem of the city today: joyful, bright, colourful, a canvas for creativity, and frozen in time.

As we pass the Pino Nature Hotel, the base of the peak begins to turn up in earnest. Reaching the summit, the air thins. The valley and city of Sarajevo – where Ottoman, Austro-Hungarian, and modern European architecture, art, food, and urban rhythms mix – spreads out below. From here, the city and its surrounding natural landscape now seem so connected, in more than a geographical sense.

'Everyone has an opinion about Sarajevo, its history, and what it represents,' Thierry tells me as we pull out a thermos of tea and some chocolate. 'But, Trebević doesn't care. It's just here to give us perspective, a workout, a place to meditate, or all of the above. This is more than a hike. This peak both defines and forgives the city and provides inspiration in the clouds.' I'll drink to that. **AC**

ORIENTATION

Start/Finish // Hadžijska Mosque
Distance // 20.2km (12.5 miles)
Duration // The hike is around six hours as a round trip, but allow for the entire day to visit and photograph the Bistrik Kula and Olympic bobsled. You can also shorten the return journey by taking the cable car back down the mountain.
When to go // Though hiking is possible all year, including snowshoeing in the winter, the best time to trek is late spring (May) and early autumn (September).
What to pack // As always, take rain gear, water, sunscreen, and a hat. In the shoulder months, bring an extra layer for the brisker breezes at the summit.
Tours // Green Visions run both regular hiking and snowshoeing to the peak of Mt Trebević (www.greenvisions.ba).
More info // www.visitsarajevo.ba

MORE LIKE THIS
CITY PEAKS

MT DAJTI, TIRANA, ALBANIA

One of the most convenient aspects about cities in the Western Balkans is that most are within a short distance of great hiking. Mt Dajti, which guards Albania's capital, Tirana, is a splendid example. Hikers can walk to the trek's base from the city centre. Also on offer, however, is the Dajti Ekspres cable car, which takes visitors to the heart of the 294-sq-km (114-sq-mile) Mt Dajti National Park in about 15 minutes, providing exceptional vistas and photo opportunities along the way. From there, a three-hour, 500m (1640ft) in ascent hike climbs to the mountain's south peak, the 1580m (5184ft) Tujani Peak, not quite the top, but the furthest one can walk. After passing the Cherry Pass, secluded forests of oaks and beech trees await the hearty, who are rewarded at the summit with exquisite panoramas and a bird's-eye view of Lake Bovilla cradled in the mountains.

Start // Dajti Ekspres station
Finish // Tujani Peak
Distance // 12km (7.5 miles)
More info // www.www.outdoor albania.com

MT VODNO AND MATKA CANYON, SKOPJE, NORTH MACEDONIA

For the complete spectrum of views, trekking challenge, history, different landscapes, and culture, you would be hard-pressed to top this hike that begins right in Skopje's backyard. From the southwestern edge of North Macedonia's capital's city centre, walk or take the cable car to the Millennial Cross, which marks the peak of Mt Vodno (1066m/3497ft). From here, soak in a panorama that includes the entire city. Then take the rolling trail west along the ridge to Matka Canyon. For most of the route, which stays within a skip and jump of the Treska River and Treska Lake, you are alone – though just minutes from the city – with only the surrounding peaks and wildflowers. You'll pass artificial structures such as the Sveti Nikola Šiševski monastery and its peaceful garden, before you come to Matka Canyon. Flag down a boat to get to the other side and a much-deserved lunch of fresh trout.

Start // Central Skopje
Finish // Matka Canyon
Distance // 17km (10.6 miles)

PUNTIJARKA TRAIL, ZAGREB, CROATIA

Although the path itself may not overwhelm with its length, this trek in Medvednica Nature Park, just above Zagreb, the Croatian capital, is a perfect escape-the-city hike. There are more than 70 routes on Mt Medvednica, which is a part of the Dinaric Alps. To get to the Puntijarka Trail from the city centre, take the number 14 tram to the base of the mountain and then the number 15 tram to the Sljeme Tunnel near the beginning of the hike. Don't worry, in both cases you're taking the tram to the end of the line and following other mountaineers off. The walk is easy-to-moderate difficulty and takes about two hours to complete its near 6km (3.7 miles). After climbing through the forest, take a break at the Puntijarka Mountain Lodge for traditional beans and sausage, excellent strudel, and a cold beer at an outdoor table.

Start // Sljeme Tunnel
Finish // Puntijarka Mountain Lodge
Distance // 5.9km (3.7 miles)

Clockwise from top: the Matka
Canyon, a day hike from Skopje; the
forest path to Mt Dajti outside Tirana;
taking a break from the trail

ACROSS THE BALKANS ON THE VIA DINARICA TRAIL

The Via Dinarica Trail stretches across the Western Balkans, giving hikers access to ancient paths, soaring mountaintops and some of Europe's last Old-World communities.

I t was still dark when the smell of coffee filled our log-cabin mountain hut on the Via Dinarica Trail, a hiking route that traverses the western half of the Balkan Peninsula in southeastern Europe. We were in Bosnia & Hercegovina's Sutjeska National Park, two days into a week-long, cross-border trek. The country's tallest peak, the 2386m (7828ft) Mt Maglić, and dense forests separated us from Montenegro. As the aroma of the roasted beans reached our bunks, the world here – the valleys, rivers, chamois, goats, villages, sheep, atonal cowbells, farms, vineyards, roosters, olive groves and kaleidoscopic wildflower meadows crowding the landscape – also seemed to spring to life like a Balkans-wide alarm clock clanging on a bedside table.

Morning coffee on the trail is sacred everywhere, but nowhere so much as the Balkans and the Via Dinarica, which links the summits and the most isolated pockets of Slovenia, Croatia, Bosnia & Hercegovina, Montenegro, Albania, Kosovo and North Macedonia. Regardless of where you trek along this nearly 1931km (1200-mile)

route, which crosses the Dinaric Alps and Šar Mountain Range, the thick, stove-cooked, liquid blackness is more than an addictive wake-up remedy; its consumption here, where the East meets the West, is a metaphor for life. Your dented metal camping mug holds history. It holds the dawn. It holds promise. It holds centuries of gossip and compromise. It is a cup full of empires: Greek, Roman, Byzantine, Ottoman, Austro-Hungarian. It brims with drawn-out tales, secret strategy sessions and comrades sitting around a rough-sawn table. *Kafa* (coffee) is to be enjoyed with a hand-rolled cigarette and tumbler of local schnapps. In the Balkans, it is a hard-working and multipurpose ritual as well as a caffeinated elixir.

Hard-working and multipurpose are also apt descriptors for the Via Dinarica Trail, which offers both easy-to-moderate walking stages and sections that demand technical prowess. It links seven countries, dozens of national parks and Unesco sites, and many of the region's highest mountaintops. Trekkers can tackle it with hardcore adrenaline. But the trail is more than that: it is a cultural corridor to be embraced by time travellers and history buffs for three months or three days. The path is a lens on to some of the last remaining Old-World, authentic communities in Europe. Mornings here mean trekkers rustle out of sleeping bags, affix headlamps, pull on trousers and lace up boots – to be sure. Sunrise also means it's time for village farmers to coax and stoke embers in iron woodstoves. When light cracks the horizon, herders step out of dirt-floor lean-tos in nomadic camps and survey their flocks amid dew-covered rolling hills, as they have done since time immemorial.

The Via Dinarica is just over a decade old. However, the route's building blocks date back centuries and, in some cases, are prehistoric. The concept, which stitches together shepherds' transversals, ancient trading roads, military trails and mountaineering paths, became official in 2010. In 2013, a project tracked and recorded much of the trek's length. Since, the Via

> "The recent trend in tourism is 'real experiences'. Well, we have hundreds of years of real experiences to be discovered."

Dinarica has become a cross-border, collaborative chorus for the countries of former Yugoslavia and Albania – a unified way to promote this previously unheralded adventure-travel playground.

'One powerful aspect of the Via Dinarica is its value as an adventure tourism tool to bring travellers to places most people don't know exist', says Aleksandar Donev, the Director of the Agency for Promotion and Support of Tourism in Macedonia. 'But another great aspect is the trail's ability to give locals – from Slovenia to North Macedonia – a way to share traditions they've been perfecting for generations. The recent trend in tourism is "real experiences". Well, we have hundreds and hundreds of years of real experiences to be discovered here.'

GOURMET DELIGHTS

You'll enjoy the coffee, but that's not the only gourmet pleasure on the Via Dinarica. Stopping in villages along the route is like a progressive meal, with fresh meats and vegetables from beginning to end. Each country is proud of its gastronomy, which was a Slow Food concept long before the term existed. Try to buy any of the farm-fresh and homemade bread, cheeses, greens, honey and liqueurs you can get your hands on along the path.

Clockwise from top: Church of St John at Kaneo, North Macedonia; a shepherd boy and his charge; on the approach to Mt Sneznik in Slovenia Previous page: hiking in the Maglić massive, Bosnia & Hercegovina

After coffee and reorganising gear into backpacks – carefully jiggering wedges of cheese, sausages and packets of peanuts among wet-weather gear and layers – we set out from the hut for the craggy climb up Mt Maglić, the top of Bosnia & Hercegovina. It was slow going, a vertical crawl: handholds and careful foot placements. When we reached the summit, I caught up with a regular hiking companion, a Bosnia & Hercegovina native who has trekked nearly every section of the Via Dinarica with me over three years of piecing together stages when our schedules allowed.

'There are wonderful similarities across the Via Dinarica, but it's always different because there are so many interpretations of landscape, culture and history', he said. 'When you walk through Croatia, you parallel the Adriatic Sea. In Albania, you are under soaring peaks. In North Macedonia, you straddle a ridgeline border with Kosovo. This trail gives hikers a route to untouched mountaintops. It gives hikers a way to see villages and shepherd communities that may not be here in 10 years.'

We descended the other side of the mountain into Montenegro and stood on a ridge, resting on our hiking sticks, looking down at the heart-shaped, glacial Trnovačko Lake – a calling-card photo-op along this section of the trail. After several minutes, we started again. The border crossing and a new country seemed to give us an extra pep to our step. When my friend was several yards ahead of me he looked back over his shoulder. 'At this next clearing, let's take a break', he said. 'I'll pull out the stove and we can make some coffee.' **AC**

ORIENTATION

Start // Postojna, Slovenia
Finish // Ohrid, North Macedonia
Distance // 1930km (1199 miles)
Duration // Three to four months for total route
Getting there // Fly into Ljubljana, Slovenia, an hour's bus ride from the trailhead. Depart from Skopje, North Macedonia, about 2½ hours by car from Lake Ohrid.
When to go // The best Balkans hiking is in late spring (May and June) and autumn (September and October).
Where to stay // Staffed mountain huts, unstaffed shelters and homestays abound. Packing a tent widens options.
What to take // A sleeping bag, wet-weather gear, layers and sunscreen should be in your backpack. Broken-in, high-quality hiking boots are a must.
More info // For guided information, contact the Via Dinarica Alliance (www.via-dinarica.org): a cooperative of adventure operators. For accommodation, route and conditions, check out the Via Dinarica site (https://trail.viadinarica.com).

Opposite: on the Via Alpina through the Wetterstein range in Germany

MORE LIKE THIS
CROSS-BORDER EUROPE

VIA EGNATIA

Paved between 146 and 120 BCE, the Via Egnatia (VE) connected Rome to Istanbul (then Byzantium), and thus the Western Roman and Eastern Roman Empires. 'In its long history, VE has been used intensely, decayed, was restored several times and decayed again', states *Via Egnatia on Foot*, a guidebook published by the Via Egnatia Foundation. After centuries of relative dormancy, the trail – running through Albania, North Macedonia and Greece – has been resurrected with 485km (301 miles) of the original 1100km (684 miles; to Turkey) described and marked with GPS tracks. Once used for travel, trade and military movements, today the route combines cities, ancient ruins, mountain views and rural expanses. If you prefer to go guided, the Albania-based Our Own Expeditions takes walkers from Durrës, Albania, to Thessaloniki, Greece.
Start // Durrës, Albania
Finish // Thessaloniki, Greece
Distance // 485km (301 miles)
More info // www.viaegnatiafoundation. eu; ourownexpeditions.com

NORDKALOTTLEDEN TRAIL

Also known as the Arctic Trail, the Nordkalottleden Trail runs 800km (497 miles) and crosses borders 15 times as it snakes through Norway, Sweden and Finland. Described as the most northerly long-distance hike in Europe, the entirety of the route sits within the Arctic Circle. This is, not surprisingly, not a path for the winter months. Trekking should be done from July to September, which will allow expeditions sufficient time – around 45 days of moderate backpack walking – to complete. The well-marked track, which also features a solid hut system from end to end, was proposed in 1977 and supported by all three countries. The Nordkalottleden was realised in 1993 and takes adventurers through wide-open expanses and giant skies, and along lakes, glaciers and gorges.
Start/Finish // There are three starting and ending points: Kautokeino, Norway (north); Sulitjelma, Norway (south); Kvikkjokk, Sweden
Distance // 800km (497 miles)
More info // www.nationalparks.fi; www.traildino.com

VIA ALPINA

In 2005, the Alpine Convention completed the markings and signage creating, officially, the first trans-Alps trail: the Via Alpina. There are five routes that make up this system of tracks, which connects the countries and already well-established paths of the Western Alps. However, the spine of this network is the Red Trail, which runs from Trieste, Italy, to Monaco, and links eight nations: Italy, Slovenia, Austria, Germany, Liechtenstein, Switzerland, France and Monaco. This hike covers approximately 2414km (1500 miles) over 161 stages, and crosses country borders a whopping 44 times. Along the way, mountaineers walk within a stone's throw of the continent's highest peaks, trek through hidden villages, stay in huts and learn more about honest European life and gastronomy than they would ever imagine.
Start // Trieste, Italy
Finish // Monaco
Distance // Approximately 2414km (1500 miles)
More info // www.via-alpina.org

STAIRWAY TO THE VIKOS GORGE

High geologic drama and wonders both natural and human-made distinguish this looped hike into Greece's deepest canyon.

The excursion started as an afterthought — and perhaps that's why it turned out the way it did. My husband and I had already been hiking on the island of Corfu, and the mainland's mountainous Zagori region, where the Vikos Gorge extends 20km (12 miles) and nearly 1km (0.6 miles) deep, was not far by ferry and bus. After the sunny island, the gorge looked like a solid day-hike and a nice change of scenery.

That scenery is in the canyon itself and the rugged Tymfi Massif. But it's also in the more than 40 villages tucked into the folds of the mountains, all built out of the local grey limestone and pale sandstone, from doorsills to roof peaks. It makes a kind of accidental camouflage, so the villages are nearly impossible to spot from a distance. The houses pop into focus only when you're close.

The day before we hiked, we admired the gorge from above, at the Oxia Viewpoint on the south rim. Nearby is the so-called Stone Forest, where the limestone forms natural stacked towers, easily felled for building. At the viewpoint, we were high enough to look down on golden eagles. Somewhere far below, hidden in dark-green shadow, was the trail we'd hike.

The typical route through the gorge is about 12km (7.5 miles), between two villages on the south rim. We decided to go southeast to northwest, rewarding ourselves with the cold spring of the Voïdomatis River, below the village of Vikos. But after more reading, we decided to start not in the usual village of Monodendri but further southeast, in a village called Vitsa, to enjoy another regional feature: a stone staircase.

To facilitate trade in the 18th and 19th centuries, local craftsmen built a network of stone-paved paths, elegant arched bridges and,

on the most-travelled slopes, staircases. You could tell a Zagori resident, people used to say, because their boots were never muddy. We liked the idea of sauntering into the gorge via the Vitsa Steps, a stone path that had been trod for centuries. Eyeballing the map, we thought it added only a few kilometres to the full hike.

We got a slow start. Our stone inn on the square in Vitsa was cosy, and breakfast bountiful, with fresh fruit and squares of *alevropita*, the region's special crispy feta-topped pie. The owners, familiar with hikers' needs, packed us more for lunch. There was still a little mist over the gorge as we descended the first of the stairs' long switchbacks; we stopped to watch it lift off. Then we

VRADETO STEPS

In the next ravine northeast of Vikos Gorge is the area's most impressive stone staircase, starting near Kapesovo and zigzagging up a nearly sheer cliff to Vradeto. It was the only way to reach the upper village until a road was cut in the 1970s. From Vradeto another trail (fortunately level) leads in about 1km (0.6 miles) to the Beloi Viewpoint on the north rim of the Vikos Gorge, across from Oxia and a bit higher.

stopped to watch what we thought was a baby snake (it was mid-May, just the season) but turned out to be a slow-worm, a kind of legless lizard that lives in a few spots in Greece.

When we reached the canyon floor, we found another scenic distraction, the Missios Bridge, arcing high over the dry bed of the Voïdomatis. These beautiful bridges, of which there are more than 90 throughout the area, look unnervingly thin from the ground, but they're sturdy and wide enough for carts to cross.

By the time we were done with photos of the bridge, the sun was noticeably hotter. Ahead of us stretched the riverbed, a jumble of stones both jagged and water-smoothed, big as boulders and small as rubble.

The Voïdomatis River runs for only for a short while each year here; after the spring ebbs, the gorge is dry enough for hiking. Among the rocks stood isolated pools of water, each a tiny world. At one, we passed many minutes simply watching tadpoles wriggle through the clear water, casting dark shadows on the rocks below. Another pool stretched crystalline green almost the full width of the riverbed, so we took our boots off and waded straight through – a treat under the high sun.

The Vitsa Steps had descended a gradual slope, but soon we were truly in the canyon. The walls began in dense greenery, but soared up to sheer patches of grey and pale-orange stone. The gorge winds a bit, so it was hard to evaluate our progress, and we

> "You could tell a Zagori resident, people used to say, because their boots were never muddy."

walked for a while thinking we'd missed the turn to Monodendri – the point where our extra leg joined the usual route.

Around 3pm, we were surprised by perfectly clear signs for the trail to Monodendri. Far ahead was another bend, and beyond that, the cold river spring – refreshment we'd looked forward to. But we weren't looking forward to the long, shadeless ascent to Vikos village at the end.

Forge on, faster, for the satisfaction of completing the canyon? Or take it easy, and head uphill to Monodendri? We had plenty of daylight, but we were low on water, and we'd already eaten

From far left: wading in the fresh water of Voidomatis River in Vikos Gorge; snapping the surrounds from an Ottoman-era stone bridge; spanakopita, filo pastry filled with spinach and feta cheese. Previous page: Vikos Gorge

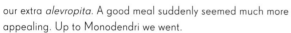

ORIENTATION

our extra *alevropita*. A good meal suddenly seemed much more appealing. Up to Monodendri we went.

There were no stone stairs, just a well-trodden path, fortunately shaded by dense oaks and beech. An hour or so later, we arrived at Monodendri's lower square, all grey stone and green moss, where we ate rustic, buttery filo pies and hearty salads. Then we were energised for a spur hike, down a 1km (0.6-mile) stone-paved road to Moni Agia Paraskevi, a monastery built on the edge of the gorge in 1413. From here, the grey-white riverbed where we'd walked was fingernail-thin.

Thanks to the curve of the gorge, Monodendri is close to Vitsa, where we'd started. So we simply walked back to our hotel, partly on the main road, then on old stone-paved shortcuts, via the village of Kokkini. We were back in Vitsa just as the swallows swooped in for their twilight feed.

Looking on a map, we were embarrassed to see how little of the gorge we'd covered – but we'd seen so much in that short distance. Someday we'll hike the full route. In the meantime, I'm satisfied that by completing our loop on foot, we traveled much as old-time Zagorians had. And it was true: our boots were never muddy. **ZO**

Start/Finish // Vitsa
Distance // 6.5km (4 miles)
Duration // Four to five hours
Getting there // Taxi or rental car from Ioannina.
When to go // May to October are the best months.
What to pack // Carry adequate water; there is only one spring on the route. You'll need boots with ankle support.
Where to stay and eat // There are guesthouses in Monodendri and Vitsa. En Chora Vezitsa (www.vezitsa-zagori. com) in Vitsa is a good option. In Monodendri, both Pita tis Kikitsas and Frossas make excellent *pita* (vegetable pie).
Tours // On Foot Holidays (www.onfootholidays.co.uk) offers a self-guided multiday trip that also climbs Tymfi.
Things to know // To hike the full length of the Vikos Gorge, keep going past the turn-off to Monodendri. From Vitsa, the route is 14km (8.7 miles), approximately eight hours.
More info // www.pindosnationalpark.gr

MORE LIKE THIS
GORGE HIKES

SAMARIA GORGE, GREECE

Rugged Crete is cut through with one of
Europe's longest canyons, and the hike
across it takes one leisurely day. The route
starts with a steep descent of about 600m
(approx. 2000ft) into the canyon, and the
scenery really kicks in after about 6km (3.7
miles), when you reach the abandoned
village of Samaria and the canyon starts to
narrow. At one point, you pass through the
Sideroportes (Iron Gates), stone walls that
are only about 3.5m (11.5ft) apart. Near
the end, the gorge opens onto the broad
pebble beach at Agia Roumeli, and you
can cool off in the Libyan Sea and then
fortify yourself at a waterside taverna. From
there, ferries can take you back to bigger
towns and onward buses.
Start // Xyloskalo, near Omalos
Finish // Agia Roumeli
Distance // 16km (10 miles)
More info // Gorge admission is €5;
most hotels can arrange transport and
tours, if you don't want to go by bus
and ferry. See www.samaria.gr

MRTVICA CANYON, MONTENEGRO

In comparison to Montenegro's
dramatically deep Tara Canyon, Mrtvica
is a tiny crack in the earth. But the Mrtvica
hike allows you to go down into the canyon,
as well as cross a historic bridge, take a
dip in frigid waterfalls, make a wish at a
fairy-blessed natural stone gate, and trek
through a tunnel blasted by the Yugoslav
military. And you'll likely have the walk
almost entirely to yourself. The route starts
at the roadside about 40km (25 miles)
north of Podgorica and leads almost
immediately to the 19th-century Danilov
Most, a bridge suspended over a clear,
trout-rich stream. About 5km (3 miles) in
is the tunnel, Mrtvičke Grede, a long slice
in the cliff, open on the side – it's shady
and makes a good spot for a picnic. Many
hikers turn around here, but it's possible
to continue as far as the tiny settlement of
Velje Duboko.
Start/Finish // Međuriječje
Distance // 15km (9.3 miles)
More info // www.maps.me shows the
route. Locals ask €3 to €5 for parking

SLÅTTDALSSKREVAN, SWEDEN

More a ravine than a gorge,
Slåttdalsskrevan may be only 40m (131ft)
deep, but it's a crack only 7m (23ft) wide in
solid granite bedrock, a mountain broken
clean in half. Hiking here makes you feel like
you're sneaking into another world. The hike
to the ravine requires a substantial climb
up, but the trail is well maintained, with
boardwalks in some spots. The route is part
of the longer High Coast Trail, a trek along
the dramatic fjords that make this a Unesco
World Heritage region. For a day hike with
the best scenery, start on the south side and
after going through the ravine, climb up to
the peak of Slåttdalsberget and return via a
higher trail.
Start/Finish // Skuleskogen National
Park south entrance
Distance // 7.7km (4.8 miles)
More info // www.sveriges
nationalparker.se; www.
hogakusten.com

Clockwise from top: hikers descending
a staircase in Samaria Gorge; Gate of
the Wishes, Mrtvica Canyon; fjords
near the Slåttdalsskrevan gorge

EASTERN EUROPE

BEST OF THE HIGH TATRAS: TATRANSKÁ MAGISTRALA

The High Tatras in northern Slovakia harbour 2500m (8202ft) fang-like summits, mythical tarns, dense forests, blockbuster wildlife – and this rocky trail forging across the entire range.

Goulash followed by lots of *Tatranský čaj*, the legendary 'Tatras tea' that is more skull-splitting spirit than sedate beverage, do not mix well, I think. Not at 7am the morning after, and when you have a mountain range to climb. The High Tatras, the jagged frontier between Slovakia and Poland, is one of the world's smallest mountain ranges of such lofty altitude, with 25 peaks over 2500m (8202ft) in just 260 sq km (100 sq miles) on the Slovak side.

Impressive stuff. However, this also means my hiking companion and I have over 1000m (3281ft) of ascent to climb just to reach the official start of the Tatranská Magistrala, the rugged three-day, 42km (26-mile) east–west traverse of these mountains. And only three days from this rather queasy start before we need to be back in Bratislava. Basic calculations tell me there must be serious physical tests ahead. We had arrived late in Ždiar, the eastern trailhead, and stayed out much later at the raucous *krčma* (pub), getting into the state we now find ourselves in. I hope the mountains will go easy on us – at least to begin with.

The northeast of this massif is dubbed the Belianske Tatry (White Tatras), and is the least accessible, most protected part. This is possibly why the Gorals, an originally shepherding people with distinctive fast-paced music, colourful folk costumes and no-less-characterful log homes, have preserved a traditional lifestyle here. The Goral life was a life apart, and a sense of that isolation hits home as we climb out of the valley. Beech and pine forest carpet the lower slopes until the 1500m (4921ft) mark, the trees then give way to feathery *kosodreviny*, or dwarf-pine forest, and at around 1700m (5577ft) the barren, boulder-strewn open ground the Slovaks call *Tatry* begins, erupting with increasing frequency

into very pointy peaks. We have only been walking for two hours, yet have already experienced three out of four of the topographic zones of the High Tatras: passing from almost primordial arboreal gloom through a flower-splashed band of colour at the treeline into a chilly world of pale lichen-bedaubed rock, impromptu swaddles of mist and vertiginous drops.

It is June, yet snow still coats most slopes around us, making the going slower. We see no other hikers. It is silent enough for us to surprise several *kamzíky*, or chamois, the wilderness-loving goat-antelopes for which these mountains are famous. Their scrabbling hoof-falls fade on the scree. The silence redoubles. We haul ourselves

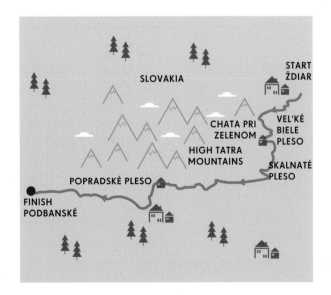

up over Kopské sedlo, a barren saddle, and collapse, calves burning after 1050m (3445ft) of relentless steep incline, beside the pewter-hued tarn of Vel'ké Biele pleso. Five lung-busting hours, and we are at the start of the Tatranská Magistrala. And exhausted.

It was not cruelty that motivated trail planners to start the hike here, many hours' trek from the closest road access, but that this lake announces the divide between the Belianske Tatras and High Tatras ranges. You see it in the rock: lighter limestone makes up the former, darker granite the latter. Still, the toll on the body of the uninitiated hiker can be cruel indeed, and we decide to curtail day one of the walk about an hour further along, at the idyllically situated lakeside Chata pri Zelenom plese, first of the path's mountain huts.

A mound of dumplings and non-alcoholic refreshment later, and we can better appreciate our surroundings: perpendicular ramparts of rock that soar up from the turquoise-hued Zelené pleso lake, then out of sight through cloud to the highest peaks of the High Tatras. We are relieved to remember the Tatranská Magistrala sticks to the slopes below these peaks, not getting close to the 2500m+ (8202ft+) mountaintops. Or so we think. A saunter around Zelené pleso lakeshore the next morning and we spy a trail sign that must be a mistake: it does not point along the lovely level lake path – oh, why not? – but up a ludicrously steep, snow-covered slope of boulders. Nope. No mistake.

Just when we think the trail has become impossibly steep, we spot a rusty old chain hammered into the mountainside, presumably to help flailing hikers haul themselves up. How thoughtful. We test the chain's weight. Some creaks. We exchange glances, the wry sort people exchange when they entrust their lives to the strength of a rusty old chain. And we commence ascent. Aside from one heart-in-mouth moment where, path obscured in snow, we balance on a ledge barely wide enough for both of us, able to see only the giddying drop far below and not the path with firm ground in front of us, things go ok. We top out at 2000m (6562ft) elevation and reach the cable car terminus at Skalnaté pleso having completed the hike's toughest clambers.

From here we drop down into forest and lunch heartily at Hansel-and-Gretel-esque Zamkovského Chata. We descend again to

WALK ON THE WILD SIDE

Being the world's tiniest mountain range of such elevation gives the High Tatras another boast: drastic topographical changes in close proximity. Which, in turn, renders it a wildlife haven. Stars of the show are the brown bear, Eurasian lynx and wolf, rare but very much there. If you miss those, then look for the easier-to-spot *kamzík* (chamois) and the comical marmot: a large ground squirrel with a piercing scream.

Clockwise from top: a mountain cottage; tackling the rocky path; a brown bear. Previous page: a High Tatras chamois

"The barren, boulder-strewn open ground the Slovaks call Tatry begins, erupting with increasing frequency into very pointy peaks."

reach Hrebienok. There is another cable car station, and at this point the doubting demons kick in. The path seems to be tempting us with easy returns to civilisation, warmth and sustenance; it takes tremendous resolve to continue on the arduous climb past Slieszky Dom, Slovakia's highest-altitude mountain, to the exposed summit of Ostrva, again at almost 2000m (6562ft). The subsequent spectacular slalom-like descent to glassy Popradské pleso lake and our accommodation, though, is perfect payback: twisting enough, and so steep our view could almost be from a parachute. Popradské pleso is perhaps the prettiest and most poignant lake on the trail, with its chapel memorial to the lives lost in these mountains. From here there is a relatively straightforward descent off the High Tatras to journey's end at Podbanské. But nowhere on the Tatranská Magistrala does the panorama better highlight how savage High Tatras' topography can be. From Popradské pleso's hotel, at the water's edge looking back up at the rockface we just scrambled down, I get the humbling sense this precipitous mountainside has made a mockery of attempts to tame it; that settlement here has gone as far as it can go. **LW**

ORIENTATION

Start // Ždiar. Note: the official starting point of the Tatranská Magistrala is Vel'ké Biele pleso
Finish // Podbanské
Distance // 53km (33 miles), including hike to Vel'ké Biele pleso
Duration // Three to four days
Getting there // Bus from Poprad to Ždiar.
When to go // Mid-June to September: outside of these months, snow blocks the trails.
Where to stay // *Chaty* (mountain cottages) offer accommodation in dormitories and private rooms, along with dinner and breakfast: Chata pri Zelenom plese, Skalnatá Chata, Zamkovského Chata, Bilíkova Chata and Horský Hotel Popradské pleso.
Tours // Adventoura (www.adventoura.eu) offers day hikes and multiday hikes in the High Tatras.
More info // www.slovakia.travel

*Opposite from top: the Danube
Bend viewed from Visegrád castle in
Hungary; the Cape Emine lighthouse
at the end of the Kom-Emine trail*

MORE LIKE THIS
EASTERN EPICS

ORSZÁGOS KÉKTÚRA (NATIONAL BLUE TRAIL), HUNGARY

Europe's original long-distance trail, and still one of the longest within a single country, the Országos Kéktúra (OKT), or National Blue Trail, is Hungary's greatest hits distilled into one formidable footslog. Taking its name from the colour of its trail signs, the OKT wends from the Austria–Hungary border at the peak of Írott-kő to the nation's frontier with Slovakia at Hollóháza, passing Lake Balaton, capital Budapest, the Danube Bend, Visegrád (where the river views reach their zenith), the plains for which Hungary is renowned, a dozen or more castles and three Unesco World Heritage sites.
Start // Írott-kő (Geschriebenstein)
Finish // Hollóháza
Distance // 1168km (726 miles)
More info // www.kektura.click.hu

KOM-EMINE, BULGARIA

This vast west–east traverse of ridge-rich Bulgaria steps along the Stara Planina, or Balkan Mountains. Bet your last lev on the fact that, if there is a high point to weave around here, the Kom-Emine will find a way, and there is nowhere in Europe you can trek for so long in continuous uplands at this elevation. The trail crosses 29 peaks of 2000m+ (6562ft+), and along the way there's a host of high-altitude mountain huts for memorable stopovers, and so many diversions and alternative routes that the final length of the journey varies by as much as 100km (62 miles). More so in the east, as the path is often poorly signposted, so you'll invariably get a little lost. Still, to conquer the Stara Planina's onslaught of summits and saddles to arrive at Cape Emine's lonely lighthouse, overlooking the Black Sea, is among the most complete hiking experiences on the continent.
Start // Kom Peak
Finish // Cape Emine
Distance // 600–700km (373–435 miles)
More info // www.kom-emine.com

MAIN BESKID TRAIL, POLAND

Poland's lengthiest long-distance path strides along the spine of the Beskid Mountains in the nation's far south, acquainting walkers with this rugged range's multifarious divisions and dynamics. It is a break, too, with the crowds of Poland's most popular massif, the Tatras. The trail kicks off at a sedate spa town, Ustroń, in the Silesian Beskids; crosses the Żywiec Beskids, which feature the highest peak on the route, Babia Góra; and then visits the beguilingly green Gorce Mountains; the Beskid Sądecki; the Low Beskids; and Bieszczady Mountains to wind up in Wołosate, the most southerly inhabited village in Poland.
Start // Ustroń
Finish // Wołosate
Distance // 496km (308 miles)
More info // www.poland.travel

GUIDING STARS: TRANSCAUCASIAN TRAIL

This multiday mixture of high passes and magical river-valley trails links some of Georgia's most photogenic tower-house villages – and in the company of local guides it offers even more.

Sometimes laziness pays. Hiking the Omalo–Shatili and Roshka–Juta sections of Georgia's magnificent Transcaucasian Trail is quite feasible alone. But Jane and I don't like carrying bags. Engaging a guide on horseback for each section seems well worth the remarkably modest expense. And we get much more than we bargained for from two remarkable if utterly different characters.

For the first three days our companion is charming, soft-spoken Tedo, who talks to his horses as to close friends. He can talk to dogs too, an essential skill... as we later discover. Clear rolling paths lead us out of Omalo, the tiny summer-only capital of Tusheti,

crowned by a film-set perfect cluster of *koshkebi* (tower houses). Wide forest vistas reveal an infinity of green mountaintops. In the Tolkienesque hamlet of Dartlo, Tedo has arranged an atmospheric coffee stop at an unmarked local stone house; from here idyllic streamside tracks lead on to Girevi, where our simple homestay is magically illuminated in sunset rays. Day two's narrow, wandering path follows a dancing river, and climbs a flower-filled valley dotted with shattered stone ruins, including ghost villages Hegho and Chontio. On a beautiful grassy meadow Tedo gets exuberant, standing upright on his horse's back to whoop with delight at the display nature has arranged for us.

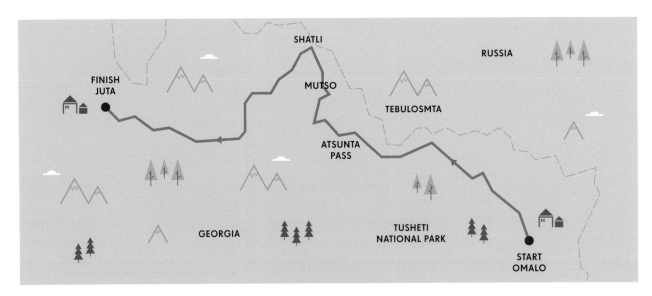

Tonight we're camping on a grassy ledge above a sheep-filled corral. Shepherd Irakli invites us for tea in his rock-walled hovel. Getting there means passing a dangerous canine frenzy of guarding sheepdogs, but at Tedo's firm grunted commands, the dogs fall silent, as though hypnotised. Irakli boils an ash-blackened kettle on smouldering twigs, his poetically wind-sculpted face partially illuminated in the smoky glow. It's a movingly timeless scene and the next morning we return for breakfast. Irakli has slept outside in his thick felt shepherd-gown, a garment so solid and heavy that he can walk out of it and leave it standing. 'The hovel's just for cooking,' he explains. 'If I stayed inside I wouldn't hear the wolves.'

The third day's hike starts with an unbridged river crossing. Most trekkers wade through but we've heard how peak flowing waters drowned a lone Israeli trekker here back in June. For us it's easy – Tedo's horses ferry us across. Dry boots prove a big plus as we zigzag through piles of broken slates to the bleak 3431m (11,257ft) Atsunta Pass. An impression of desolate moonscape is accentuated by the swirling low clouds. Yet suddenly, out of the mists appears an unlikely sight that our brains struggle to compute: a dozen extreme cyclists carrying bicycles over their shoulders. We laugh, wave and wish them well.

There's a joyous feeling of openness as we cross the Khidotani ridge, despite drizzling rain that obscures views of 4493m (14,741ft) Tebulosmta. Occasional shafts of sunlight still pierce the clouds and an absurd arc of rainbow bridges a side valley beneath us.

> ## "At Tedo's firm grunted commands, the dogs fall silent, as though hypnotised."

Bedraggled, we reach a lonely border lookout post where kindly soldiers hand us mugs of coffee. Then, slithering on sodden grass between towering heads of giant hogweed, we descend through the half-abandoned farmsteads of Bakhao, making four stream crossings, one balanced on a narrow metal beam. Finally a semblance of track leads us to the one-family hamlet of Ardoti, where a small, totally unsigned hostel–homestay lies behind thick stone walls incorporating runic petroglyphs.

We're now in Khevsureti, a fabled region whose archaic language is to Georgian what Chaucerian English might sound like to Anglophones. The uninhabited fortified village of Mutso rises in shattered layers above us. Some curious erosion chimneys are followed by thickening woodlands and the spooky 'bone houses' of Anatori, then suddenly civilisation in the form of mystical Shatili. Waving goodbye to Tedo, we explore Shatili's citadel, a *Game of Thrones*-like cluster of dark stone towers and shadowy gateways. Then we track down the village's only taxi: a popular 'cheat' that shaves a long day's walk off the Omalo–Juta trail via an undulating three-hour drive to Roshka.

KOSHKEBI TOWER HOUSES

Many Tushetian villages feature *koshkebi*, spindly stone towers up to five storeys tall. Unlike the better-known *svaneti* towers (also in Georgia), many have pointed roof-caps, but both types are so ancient that even Unesco seems unable to guess exact dates for their construction. It is said that no outsiders ever conquered isolated Tusheti – it simply wasn't worth besieging the hardy populace once they had retreated into their towers. So potential invaders just passed by.

Clockwise from top: the Caucasus; an abandoned village; herded goats. Previous page: mountains of Georgia

Next morning our Roshka homestay has found us a big, brash and boisterous guide who locals nickname 'The Beast'. The morning is freshly fragrant. Patches of blue sky emerge between huge fluffy clouds. Soaring mountains add occasional cameo appearances. While resting at a lovely viewpoint knoll, The Beast pulls out a hip flask. He creates cups by knifing 7-Up bottles in half. Then it's time to drink. In Georgia it's unthinkable to refuse a round of toasts, even at 10am. Cheers to Georgia. To friendship. To women. To peace. And so on. The copious *chacha* (Georgian grappa) seems to propel us up the steep Chaukhi Pass (3431m/11,256ft).

On top, The Beast declares 'We must toast to the pass'. He raids a shepherd's 'bad weather' booze stash and we drink yet more. To passes. To shepherds. To life.

Filled with Dutch courage, we forget our near-total lack of equestrian abilities and any sense of peril and mount the packhorses, cantering down from the pass in a giddy blur. By early afternoon we're trotting into Juta. Chaukhi mountain rises behind us like a gigantic rocky eagle at 3842m (11,424ft), and in the distant valley ahead are hints that the gigantic 5033m (16,512ft) snow cone of Mt Kazbek might be about to materialise. A jolly homestay hostess welcomes us in. 'Before he leaves,' she suggests, 'how about a small vodka for you and your guide? Just one bottle.' And so it continues. **ME**

ORIENTATION

Start // Omalo (Tusheti)
Finish // Shatili (Khevsureti) or Juta (Kazbegi)
Distance // 75km (47 miles) from Omalo to Shatili; 18km (11 miles) Roshka to Juta
Duration // Five days
Getting there // Omalo is a five-hour jeep-ride from Alvani in Kakheti, or a day's travel from Tbilisi: change vehicles in Telavi.
When to go // Best in August or early September.
Where to stay // There are good guesthouses in Omalo, a hotel in Juta, and homestays in several villages including Dartlo, Girevi, Ardoti (only one), Shatili, Roshka and Juta.
What to take // Tent for the night between Girevi and Ardoti, water bottles, snacks (food is available at homestays).
More info // Caucasus Trekking (www.caucasus-trekking.com).

Opposite: the Unesco-listed village of Ushguli has as its backdrop Mt Shkhara, Georgia's highest point

MORE LIKE THIS
CAUCASIAN CLASSICS

SVANETI TRAIL, GEORGIA

Yes. Those hills really are alive... Svaneti is true *Sound of Music* country, with blissful meadowlands and soaring Alpine peaks. Yet with its distinctive *koshkebi* tower houses, it trumps Swiss landscapes, offering two particular tower concentrations in the rapidly developing capital of Mestia, and the Unesco-listed gem village of Ushguli. The whole area was virtually inaccessible in the 1990s, but over the last 15 years new roads have turned Svaneti into one of Georgia's prime visitor attractions. Most tourists zip along the Mestia–Ushguli road as a day trip, but walking is far more interesting. A well-trodden four-day trail allows you to sleep each night en route in a village homestay, though consider pre-booking during the peak July–August period especially for Iprali (on the third night). Also consider leaving spare days to wait it out in case of rain: you won't want to miss those glorious vistas.

Start // Mestia
Finish // Ushguli
Distance // 58km (36 miles)
More info // www.caucasus-trekking. comi; svanetitrekking.ge

BABADAĞ PILGRIM TRAIL, AZERBAIJAN

Although it sits at an impressive 3629m (11,906ft) commanding 360-degree views, summiting Azerbaijan's 'holy mountain' is more of a long, steep stroll than a climb – so long as you go on a fine summer's day. It's a thoroughly rewarding experience, not just for the views but for the fellow hikers you'll encounter after mid-July. Most will be pilgrims who believe that a medieval Muslim hermit 'disappeared' on these slopes in a kind of mystical ascension that has blessed the peak, making seven pilgrimages here the equivalent in spiritual merit to a full hajj to Mecca. Around halfway, at one of the most breathtaking ridge edges, it's a particularly intriguing sight to witness the ceremonial 'stoning of the devil'. The trail is generally walked up and back in a long day (six hours up, four back), starting well before dawn from Gurbangah, a seasonal camp that's a gruelling two-hour 4WD ride from the charming coppersmiths' village of Lahıc.

Start/Finish // Gurbangah
Distance // 17km (11 miles), with a vertical climb of 1420m (4660ft)

JANAPAR TRAIL, ARMENIA

The Caucasus' longest single hiking trail notionally stretches 500km (310 miles), winding from Vardenis on Armenia's Lake Sevan to Hadrut in the self-declared republic of Nagorno-Karabakh. However, only the main Hadrut–Kolatak section is waymarked with the easy-to-spot yellow-on-blue footprint signs. Handily broken up into village-to-village sections of around five hours' daily walking, this is a hike through remote foothill landscapes where you're highly unlikely to meet any other foreign walkers. Nonetheless, using map-guides on the ViewRanger phone app, it should be reasonably easy to find your way to such delights as the Karkar Canyon, the Zontik waterfall, Dadivank and Gtichavank monasteries and the Azokh (Azıx) cave, where archaeologists found the oldest humanoid remains in Eurasia. Beware: although visiting Nagorno-Karabakh is straightforward from Armenia, legally speaking the region is an occupied region of Azerbaijan and entering is considered an offence under Azerbaijani law.

Start // Hadrut
Finish // Kolatak
Distance // 134km (83 miles)
More info // www.janapartrail.org

POLAND TO BELARUS ALONG THE AUGUSTÓW CANAL

Have you ever undertaken a multiday hike between two countries, with just a few hours'
notice? That's what Ash Bhardwaj found himself doing on this cross-border adventure.

I was in a travel office in Białystok, Poland, booking a train
to the capital of Belarus, Minsk, when I spotted something
in a leaflet: a route from Augustów, in Poland, to the city of
Grodno, in Belarus.

I was under the impression that tourists could only enter Belarus
via Minsk, but the travel agent told me about a recently signed
agreement: guided kayak and bike groups could enter Belarus via
the Augustów Canal and stay, visa-free, for up to five days.

However, because I had already acquired a 30-day Belarusian
tourist visa, I could cross the border alone and on foot, and then
continue into the country as normal.

Not quite believing my luck, I cancelled the train to Minsk, and
booked one to Augustów for the following morning. I picked up
some maps at Augustów's tourist office, bought two days' supply
of food from the supermarket, and started my walk from the canal
museum in town.

The path took me through forest to a lake, where locals splashed
around in the early summer heat. Families had set up vast picnics,
including, in one instance, an entire pig roasting on a spit. The
family invited me to sit down for lunch and, when I gently refused,
insisted that I take one of their beers with me.

After that, the path headed deeper into the woods, away from

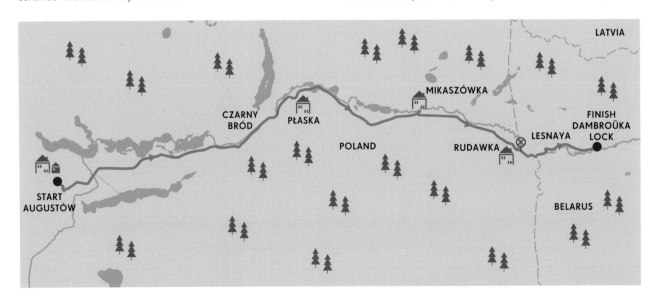

the lake and back towards the canal. Inside the forest I was shaded from the sun, but the air was still: if I stopped for even a moment, I was mobbed by midges, so I rolled down my sleeves for protection, despite the heat.

Other than the odd cyclist, I had the trail to myself, which continued through the forest to Czarny Bród. There it gave way to open countryside, and my first view of the canal since Augustów. Birds flitted around in the sunlight, catching insects in the open space above the water, and I sat on a wooden bridge, eating an apple as I watched them.

When I reached the village of Plaska, the youth hostel was closed and, with no-one around, I resigned myself to sleeping in the woods.

At that moment, two men walked past with a pack of beer, and I pulled out my translating app to explain the situation. They waited until I had finished butchering the Polish language, then one of them spoke up with an English West Country lilt.

'Don't worry mate,' he said, 'This place is only open for school groups. But there's a guesthouse on the farm over there. I'll call the owner and tell him you're coming.'

He laughed at my look of confusion, then handed me a beer as we chatted about Bristol, where he had worked for 15 years as a builder.

Kasia, the farmer's daughter, greeted me at the guesthouse. She showed me to a charming first-floor room with a balcony, and told me that dinner would be ready in a few hours. Then she headed off to help her dad with the farm work. In the meantime, I went for a swim in the lake at the bottom of the garden.

Dinner was soup, sausages and potatoes, and the next morning I was packed off with a hearty breakfast, sandwiches made from leftovers, and warm wishes from Kasia and her parents.

It took me two hours to get to Mikaszówka, where I bumped into some cyclists who had also been staying at the farm. I was about to press on, but they insisted that I first checked out the church near the canal.

I'm glad that they did. The twin-towered church was completely wooden, inside and out, with a curved, hand-painted ceiling, which supported chandeliers. It was full of light, with antlers and photographs on the walls, making it feel more like a hunting lodge than a church.

It was just after lunchtime that I reached Rudawka, the last village in Poland. The Polish checkpoint was a square white tent at the end of a cobbled road and, as the guards scanned my passport, they told me that I was the first solo hiker that they'd seen. They also told me that the Belarusian people were incredibly friendly and helpful.

The canal defined the border here, with the red-and-white post of Poland on the west side, and the green-and-red of Belarus on the east. I crossed the lock bridge, slightly nervous to enter a country renowned for its border sensitivity, and found... no-one.

CANAL HISTORY

The 104km (65-mile) Augustów Canal was constructed in the 19th century, to link the Vistula and Neman Rivers. Part of it passes through Belarus, a territory that at the time of construction was inside the Kingdom of Poland. The canal's basic function was to bypass Prussia, which imposed heavy taxes on goods moving through its territory. Within 30 years of its completion, the canal had become redundant, as railways came to dominate transportation.

Clockwise from top: the meandering Augustów Canal; servicing the lock; Żywiec beer. Previous page: kayakers rising in the sluice

"I crossed the lock bridge, slightly nervous to enter a country renowned for its border sensitivity, and found... no-one."

I wandered into the shiny new border-control building, and called out. A few seconds later, a guard in a smart green uniform appeared, with a tea cup in hand and a bemused look on his face. He welcomed me to Belarus, then returned to his office to fetch me my own cup of tea.

Through a translating app, I explained my intentions, and he enthusiastically nodded along, before giving me the Grodno bus times from the nearby village.

At Lesnaya, I watched a hand-operated ferry cross the canal, and asked the ferryman how to get to the bus stop, wrongly thinking that it was on the other side. By the time I'd understood what he'd said, I'd actually missed the bus, so he called an English-speaking friend, who arranged for a taxi to meet me at the next village. These Belarusians were living up to their friendly reputation.

The taxi was waiting for me when I reached Dambroŭka. As we headed towards Grodno, the driver and I took it in turns to play our music through the stereo. The road climbed up to a rolling plain, and I spotted the city in the distance, on a hill above a glinting river.

'Grodno,' said the driver, with a thumbs up, 'Good!'

'Very good,' I replied. **AB**

ORIENTATION

Start // Augustów, Poland
Finish // Dambroŭka Lock, Belarus
Distance // 47km (29 miles)
Duration // Two days
Getting there // Train to Augustów from Warsaw. Buses to Grodno run from Sapotskin, 4km (2.5 miles) from the Dambroŭka Lock.
When to go // May to September.
Where to stay // Romuald and Danuta Jadeszko offer B&B at their farmhouse near Plaska (www.wsercupuszczy.eu).
Where to eat // You can pick up supplies and basic meals in the villages along the route.
Tours // The Białystok and Augustów tourist offices can help you find a guide and arrange accommodation.
Things to know // Be sure to check the latest visa requirements for entering Belarus with your government.
More info // www.augustow.pl; www.poland.travel

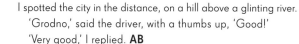

MORE LIKE THIS
BORDERLAND HIKES

BIAŁOWIEŻA FOREST, POLAND–BELARUS

Poland and Belarus also share Europe's last stand of primordial woodland, with a greater mix of tree species than you would find in a more managed forest. The reduced management means more deadwood on the forest floor, which supports lichen, mosses, insects and fungi. The forest is also home to 800 European bison, the continent's heaviest land mammal.

In the early 20th century, railway tracks were laid through the forest for logging. While most of the tracks are long gone, their paths form the basis of walking routes and cycle paths. Currently, some nationals can cross the border visa-free for up to 72 hours, provided an online form is completed. You must stay within the park, and then return via the same crossing. The Belarusian part of the forest is home to Viskuli dacha, where the leaders of Russia, Ukraine and Belarus met in 1991 to sign the Belavezha Accords, which dissolved the Soviet Union.

Start/Finish // Białowieża
Distance // Varies
More info // www.pttk.bialowieza.pl

OFFA'S DYKE PATH, ENGLAND–WALES

If you get your kicks from crossing borders, then there are few better hikes than the Offa's Dyke Path. Offa's Dyke is an earthwork and ditch, supposedly constructed on the orders of the eponymous King Offa in the 8th century to protect his kingdom of Mercia (in modern-day England) from invasions from Powys (modern-day Wales).

The path follows the dyke for 285km (177 miles) from Liverpool Bay in the north to Swansea Estuary in the south. It follows the current English–Welsh border, crossing it dozens of times along its length. It takes most walkers 12 days to complete the whole thing. The route is lined with historic towns in both nations, the ruins of castles and abbeys, and some of Britain's loveliest countryside.

Start // Prestatyn, Wales
Finish // Sedbury Cliffs, England
Distance // 285km (177 miles)
More info // www.nationaltrail.co.uk

GRANDE TRAVERSÉE DES ALPES, FRANCE–SWITZERLAND–ITALY

A spectacular long-distance route across Europe's greatest borderland – the Alps – the Grande Traversée is a month-long odyssey from Lake Geneva to the sparkling Mediterranean. On the way, walk through a changing landscape, from classic Alpine slopes and flower-filled pastures, through snow-covered peaks and some barren high ground, before a descent to the subtropical climate of the Mediterranean. While located almost entirely in France, the route snakes alongside the French–Swiss and French–Italian borders (and over, on occasion). Indeed, there is an imitation Italian version of the trail – Il Grande Traversata delle Alpi – on the other side.

The length of the route, its approximate ascents and 40 mountain passes make it a serious undertaking, but it is not a technical hike and anyone with a reasonable level of fitness should be able to complete it.

Start // Saint-Gingolph, France
Finish // Nice, France
Distance // 508km (316 miles)
More info // www.grande-traversee-alpes.com

Clockwise from top: views of the Mont
Blanc glacier; bison in Białowieza
National Park; ruins of Llanthony
Priory, along the English–Welsh border

RILA MOUNTAINS TRAVERSE

Scramble up lofty peaks and supplicate yourself at ancient monasteries on a testing hike through the lake-studded summits of southwest Bulgaria.

Peering down from an airy ridge, my gaze swept along a chain of azure blotches in the landscape, as if torn from a cloudless northern sky. Cradled in rocky corries, the pools of diverse hues and shapes lay scattered across verdant slopes far to west and east. It was enough to bring a tear to the eye – and not just because of the dramatic views: credit the poetic geographers of old who named Salzata Ezero (Tear Lake) and Okoto Ezero (Eye Lake).

You're never far from pools and streams in Rila National Park, Bulgaria's largest, an 810 sq km (313 sq mile) swathe of peaks, forests and high pastures. Indeed, 'Rila' – possibly from ancient Thracian – means Mountains of Water, probably a nod to its dozens of turquoise and tourmaline glacial lakes.

The cluster of tarns known as the Seven Rila Lakes, including Tear and Eye, is the park's prime honeypot; in summer it teems with walkers and day-trippers. It's an undeniably magical place, but for truly wild expanses you need only climb a little higher into

the mountains. My perch on the crags above lay on a route less trodden: a two-day traverse taking in one of the highest summits and ending with a spiritual and artistic flourish.

The meadows alongside the Malyovitsa Central Mountain School were still spangled with frost when our hiking posse set out into the park early that morning. Through a patch of forest we strolled, watching crossbills snaffling seeds from pine cones to a discordant soundtrack – the buzzbuzzbuzz car-alarm call of spotted nutcrackers. Soon, though, we emerged onto a rocky track tracing a valley floor through scrubby heath, climbing toward a forbidding rock wall above which alpine choughs and buzzards wheeled. There are wild cats and capercaillie, here too, as well as bears and wolves, though you'll be fortunate indeed to spy one.

At the head of the valley, we paid our respects at a memorial cairn bearing plaques and climbing equipment, commemorating Bulgarian climbers who lost their lives in these mountains. The trail steepened rapidly, and we clambered across boulders livid green with lichen, ferns poking between rocks, on the ascent to Elenini Ezero (Deer Lake). Here I scanned the skyline for the agile mammals after which the lake is named; sadly, there was no sign, nor even the shrill alarm whistle of male chamois echoing among the high crags.

Beyond the lake, the trail rose again to the grey ridge ending at Malyovitsa Peak. Not quite the country's roof – that accolade goes to nearby 2925m (9596ft) Musala, tallest in the entire Balkans – Malyovitsa nonetheless reaches a respectable 2729m (8953ft), and attracts a handful of peak-baggers. We joined them briefly, picnicking just below the summit on cheese, salami, tomatoes and cucumbers – ubiquitous on Bulgarian menus – and gazed south along a heavily wooded valley to Rila Monastery, our ultimate destination.

Today, though, our route lay west, winding across a saddle and into granite-flecked hills. To our left, the land undulated softly, embroidered with lakes threading through emerald moorland. To the right, the land fell away more steeply, with outcrops and occasional waterfalls feeding those poetically named lakes.

Sheep and semi-wild horses grazed beneath round-shouldered hills, and isolated huts dotted the lakesides, while the ringing of livestock bells drifted faintly across from high pastures, a softer harmony to the thrip of alpine accentors. Grass, moss and stunted juniper shrubs created an emerald blanket, studded with yellow and violet blooms like a jewels in a regal cape.

A yellow signpost indicated that we were briefly following the E4, the vast trail stretching over 10,000km (6213 miles) from Portugal to Greece. It's a reminder that Bulgaria was for centuries an important junction on trade routes, occupied over the eras by Macedonians, Romans, Bulgars and, latterly, the Ottoman Empire that held sway here for five centuries.

Our destination that day, though, lay within sight. As we descended across moss-springy turf, the sun chiseled crepuscular beams through clouds gathered around crags above Ivan Vazov Refuge, cupped in a smooth-sided gully. Blankets spread over

HERMIT HOME

Saint Ivan of Rila, a shepherd-turned-hermit born in the 9th century, founded the eponymous monastic colony in 927 CE. It moved to its current site in 1335 and, restored following 15th-century Ottoman raids, for centuries acted as a repository preserving Bulgarian culture. The current structure was built after a devastating fire in 1833, though its striking murals are thrillingly medieval. Ivan himself lived apart from the monastery in a cave, where he died in 946 CE.

Clockwise from top: wild horses in the Rila Mountains; high on the ridge of Malyovitsa Peak; the dazzling exterior of Rila Monastery. Previous page: the Seven Rila Lakes

"A two-day traverse taking in one of the highest summits and ending with a spiritual and artistic flourish."

bunks, we huddled around the communal dining table and, by the light of candles and the wood-burning stove, joined in folk songs to which the alien words felt somehow familiar.

Next day we crossed the high moorland again, veering south along the side of a steep ridge and on to the shoulder of a hill, descending to a rudimentary wooden corral on the saddle below. During the Ottoman occupation, this area, known as Pazadere (bazaar), attracted herders bringing animals to graze, breed and sell, away from the attention of the Turkish overlords. We passed tumbledown rectangles of stone, skeletons of abandoned sheepfolds, and chatted (via our Bulgarian guide) with a shepherd who recalled days when these meadows bustled with livestock – today, few flocks and herds roam the area.

The final descent to Rila Monastery led through summery meadows thrumming with crickets, then among silver birches and into a dark forest where mushrooms glistened in the gloaming: huge scarlet agarics, earlike bracket fungi, gelatinous white umbrellas lined our path until we emerged in a busy car park.

After two days of mountain wilderness the colours and patterns of the monastery were almost shockingly bold. So were the crowds: as black-robed and luxuriantly bearded Orthodox monks patrolled a cobbled courtyard, throngs of tourists snapped selfies at the candy-striped Church of the Nativity. Yet stepping into the cool of the cloisters, absorbing the vivid, almost cartoon-like murals depicting infernal torment and divine redemption, I found myself transfixed. It's the perfect end point for a walk that enriches eye and soul alike. **PB**

ORIENTATION

Start // Malyovitsa Central Mountain School
Finish // Rila Monastery
Distance // 36km (22 miles)
Duration // Two days
Getting there // Buses from Sofia to Samokov run hourly and take about 75 minutes; from Samokov, occasional buses run to Govedartsi and Malyovitsa Central Mountain School.
When to go // June to October is best for snow-free paths; winter walking, including mountain ascents, is also popular.
What to wear // Waterproofs, warm layers and sturdy hiking boots are essential.
What to pack // Bring a sleeping bag or liner to Ivan Vazov Refuge for the dormitory; blankets are available.
Where to stay // Krusharskata House (www. hotelkrusharskatakashta.com) is a simple hotel in Govedartsi. Hotel Pchelina (www.pchelina.com) is a comfortable place near Rila Monastery.

Opposite: sunrise from Mt Schober on the Four Mountains, Three Lakes trek

MORE LIKE THIS
LAKELAND LEG-STRETCHERS

FAULHORNWEG, SWITZERLAND

The trail often – and with good reason – dubbed Europe's finest one-day hike is a lofty switchback above Interlaken that rewards with astounding views from the get-go. The adventure starts before you even set foot on the path, with the ride up to Schynige Platte on a cog railway that's been hauling panorama-seekers since 1893. Here you'll admire a southern skyline dominated by three larger-than-life local characters: the snow-capped peaks dubbed the Ogre (Eiger), the Monk (Mönch) and the Young Maiden (Jungfrau). More summits appear as you head northeast across rolling pastures. Crossing the lumpy pass at Egg, continue through wild valleys, around scree slopes and past karst slabs for the ascent to the Faulhorn (2681m/8796ft) and its historic mountain hotel. Refresh yourself with a cool Radler (shandy) – and the spectacular views across Lakes Thun and Brienz, one deep blue, the other a vivid turquoise.

Start // Schynige Platte
Finish // First
Distance // 15.5km (9.5 miles)
More info // www.jungfrau.ch

FOUR MOUNTAINS, THREE LAKES TREK, AUSTRIA

Even in a country famed for its gorgeous glacial lakes, the Salzkammergut region claims an unfair share – and this long-distance trail links three of the finest, capping each of its four stages with a peak affording views across glittering blue. From the shores of the Fuschlsee, climb the 1522m (4993ft) Zwölferhorn before descending to Sankt Gilgen, famed as the home of Mozart's sister Nannerl. From here, skirt serene Wolfgangsee and follow the pilgrim's path to the foot of the Schafberg, conquering its 1782m (5846ft) summit to admire more panoramic vistas, and bed down in its simple mountaintop hotel. Continuing to the Mondsee via the Almkogel, the final stage passes the dramatic ruins of Wartenfels Castle and scales the Schober (1328m/4357ft) before completing the circuit at the Fuschlsee.

Start/Finish // Fuschl am See
Distance // 65km (40 miles)
More info // https://fuschlsee. salzkammergut.at

PILGRIM PATH, SWEDEN

The Dalsland region of southwest Sweden is an aquatic adventure playground, laced with trails and studded with more than 1000 lakes, ranging from blink-and-you'll-miss-'em meres to Vänern, largest in the European Union. Following a route once trodden by the devout en route to St Olav's shrine in Nidaros (now Trondheim, Norway), the Pilgrim Path snaking north from Vänersborg skirts numerous lakes, as well as bird-bustling nature reserves, fairy-tale pine forests and fascinating medieval churches. Starting with gentle gradients in the south, and dotted with simple sleeping shelters and campsites, the terrain becomes wilder and more mountainous as you head north, offering dramatic views across the glittering lakes before completing the pilgrimage at the ruined church and holy spring of St Nikolai in Edsleskog.

Start // Vänersborg
Finish // Edsleskog
Distance // 100km (62 miles)
More info // www.vastsverige.com

ROCK STARS OF CZECH SWITZERLAND

This vista-rich hike takes walkers over, under and around some of the Czech Republic's most dramatic rock formations, including Europe's largest natural rock arch.

Spanning almost 80 sq km (31 sq miles), the dramatic Saxon Switzerland National Park straddles the border between Saxony and Bohemia in the Czech Republic's far north. It's a remote region of rock towers and arches, deep-cut gorges and pretty, half-timbered villages, but is easily accessible from Prague. Our 20km (12.4-mile) hike takes in the best the park has to offer.

We were starting out at a place called Tři prameny (Three Springs) where a red-marked trail left the road heading east from Hřensko. We climbed through thick pine forests, gaining altitude, until we reached what I was here to see. The Pravčická

brána (Pravčická Gate) is an impressively proportioned, naturally formed sandstone arch that rises high above a traditional timber mountain chalet. In fact, at 26m (84ft) wide and 16m (52ft) tall, it's Europe's largest natural rock arch and one of the most symbolic sights in the Czech Republic. Sadly for me, but happily for the arch, visitors have long been banned from clambering across the top. Anyhow, the best views (and selfies) of the arch are from below. I've heard geologists estimate it won't come crashing down for another 100,000 years, so I take my time striking a pose with my new favourite rock star.

The number of fellow hikers unsurprisingly thins out past the

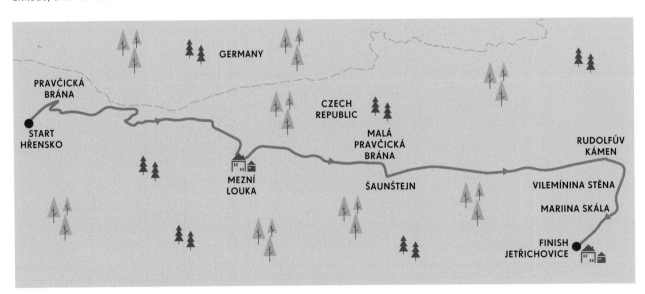

Pravčická brána, as we tackle the main body of the hike. The next 3km (1.9 miles) must be one of the best stretches of walking in the Czech Republic, a pageant of absurd rock pinnacles, towering sandstone cones, pillars and needles, overhanging cliffs ready to topple, bulbous boulders and warrens of stone; the high-strung path ducking and weaving between them. Each weird-and-wonderful formation bears its own descriptive name – the Fortress, the Great Wall of China, the Huntsman's Horn – and each turn reveals ever more unlikely shapes in grey sandstone.

Things calm down a bit as we descend into the only place of human habitation on the route, the tiny village of Mezní Louka, just a huddle of campsite, a hotel and a couple of handy restaurants.

Beyond Mezní Louka, the red trail rises back into the forests that cling to the rock, tree roots wedged into cracks and spreading across the stone. Another 3km (1.9 miles) of easy walking brings us to another rock arch, the aptly named Malá Pravčická brána (Small Pravčická Gate), a miniature version of its more famous friend, but with sweeping panoramas from the viewing platform at one end, accessed by a metal ladder. I climb the rungs, not realizing this was just a taste of things to come.

Ten minutes further through the forest we stumble across Šaunštejn Castle, a fortification chiseled into the rock in the 14th century. Today the ruins are a veritable climbing frame, with more ladders and walkways allowing you to clamber all over the site (and to stop you falling off). From the top of the rock castle's high perch, the views of the surrounding hills are magnificent, stretching as far as the Ore Mountains on clear days.

More crazy rock structures follow, all bearing imaginative names, such as Grouse View, the Golem, the Spa Dandy and Pavla's Tower. I glimpse a view of the almost impenetrable area north of here, and see what must be hundreds of cliffs, rocks and formations puncturing the tree canopy.

The going is easy for the next 2km (1.2 miles), the path hugging the contours of the landscape. I relax in to a gentle amble, saving my energy; I've heard the last section is something of a rollercoaster.

From here the hike is more like a rock-climbing expedition than a walk. Over the centuries, ladders, chains, railings and bridges have been installed on the rock stacks for hikers to reach some truly bird's eye vantage points. The first ascent I encounter comes at Rudolfův kámen (Rudolf's Stone), a hut built in 1824 by a local nobleman who particularly loved the view. To see it for yourself, there's a slightly challenging climb up and over some rather precarious ladders and bridges, and up steps carved into the rock. The hut – equipped with openable windows for 360° vistas – stands on a sloping chunk of rock with sheer drops on most sides and could be used as an overnight refuge if the weather turned bad.

Next stop – Vilemínina stěna (Vilemina's Wall), a short, there-and-back detour from the main path. From this vantage point at 439m (1440ft) I take in a panorama of the park's peaks through the haze.

HIKING FRENZY

It's a little-known fact outside the country that the Czechs are mad about hiking. In fact, the country has the densest network of hiking trails in the world, many dating back to the early 20th century, and well-maintained even during the communist decades. Czech Hiking Club (Klub českých turistů) volunteers spend their summers maintaining markings on an incredible 44,000km (over 27,340 miles) of trails that link every town, village and place of interest in the country.

Clockwise from top: sunset from a rocky viewpoint in Czech Switzerland National Park; bring a head for heights to make the most of the park; Kamenice: the gateway town to Czech Switzerland. Previous page: the bizarre pinnacles and pillars of the landscape

© CzechTourism; © Bertbeug | Alamy Stock Photo; © dpa-Zentralbild | Getty Images

By now I'm feeling all the climbing in my legs, so take a welcome pause at the carved wooden bench at Balzerovo ležení cave. It turns out to be a lovely spot for a muesli bar and a cup of Thermos tea, if the brain-confusingly supersized boulders didn't look ready to come crashing down on me at any moment.

The last climbable tower is Mariina skála (Maria's Rock), a lonesome cabin atop a stack of stone. A forest fire in 2006 cleared

> "*Each formation bears its own descriptive name and each turn reveals ever more unlikely shapes in grey sandstone.*"

the forests around, and grow-back has been slow. Access is up narrow ladders that almost tunnel through the stone, across precarious bridges and along chains. It's not for the faint-hearted but the view from the hut is one of the best in the national park, with other Czech mountain ranges clearly visible in the distance. The hut, first built in 1856, served as a fire watchtower – somewhat ironically, it burnt down in the forest fire so what you see today is a replica.

Before our short descent into the village of Jetřichovice and the end of our hike, I take a moment to appreciate the national park one last time. I think about the robber barons who hid out here in medieval times, and the Romantic-era artists who drew inspiration from the dramatic beauty of the landscape. Ladders and chains there may be, I realise, but nothing can truly tame this wild place. **MDD**

ORIENTATION

Start // Hřensko
Finish // Jetřichovice
Distance // 20km (12.4 miles)
Duration // Six to eight hours
Getting there // Mainline trains run from Prague to Děčín from where local buses serve Hřensko and Jetřichovice.
When to go // Avoid high summer, and visit April to June and September to November.
More info // www.ceskesvycarsko.cz

*Opposite from top: Baroque statues
lining the way to Hrubá Skála; the
Bastei bridge and views over the
Elbe Valley*

MORE LIKE THIS
SANDSTONE LANDSCAPES

BASTEI HIKE IN SAXON SWITZERLAND, GERMANY

On the opposite side of the border to the main walk, in Saxon Switzerland National Park, this short and much-frequented circuit takes in the Bastei, a 76m- (249ft)-long bridge built in 1851 as a tourist attraction. It spans several rock towers and provides extraordinary views of the Elbe Valley. The rest of the loop twists and turns through weird-and-wonderful formations, a labyrinth of eroded sandstone pinnacles stacked high above the mighty river. Viewing points, information boards and countless attractions line the route. The return is along the Elbe River with views up to the stern rock formations and along the forested valley.
Start/Finish // Wehlen
Distance // 10km (6.2 miles)
More info // www.saechsische-schweiz. de

ADRŠPAŠSKO-TEPLICKÉ ROCKS, CZECH REPUBLIC

The most famous 'rock town', as the Czechs call their famous formations, are the tricky-to-pronounce Adrspaško-Teplické Rocks, a 2½-hour drive northeast of Prague on the border with Poland. Be warned that some of this route is a must-see for every Czech family and is very busy between June and August. It's the only hike in the entire country where admission is paid, but don't let that put you off. A circuit from the train station in Janovice takes walkers along sandy paths and walkways that delve into warrens of rock, burrow through deep valleys, squeeze through slender gorges, pass splashing waterfalls and skirt castle ruins on what must be one of the most action-packed hikes in the country.
Start/Finish // Janovice
Distance // 20km (12 miles)
More info // www.skalyadrspach.cz

BOHEMIAN PARADISE, CZECH REPUBLIC

Just over an hour's drive northeast of Prague, the protected Český ráj (Bohemian Paradise) is a little piece of gentle hiking nirvana within easy striking distance of the capital. In theory, you could breakfast at your hotel in Prague and make it back for a late dinner on the famous Old Town Square. The highlights of this route are places to avoid in the warmer months, though any time between late September and June you can have the forests, rock towers, canyons, viewing points, castle ruins and cliffs all to yourself. The route follows the Zlatá Stezka (Golden Path), which links the two historical towns of Jičín and Turnov, interesting day-trip destinations in themselves. Along the way rise countless rock formations for which the Czech north is known, as well as the iconic castles of Trosky and Hrubá Skála.
Start // Jičín
Finish // Turnov
Distance // 31km (19.2 miles)
More info // www.cesky-raj.cz

INDEX

Epic Hikes of Europe
May 2021
Published by Lonely Planet Global Limited
CRN 554153
www.lonelyplanet.com
10 9 8 7 6 5 4 3 2 1

Printed in Malaysia
ISBN 978 1 83869 428 9
© Lonely Planet 2021
© photographers as indicated 2021

Managing Director, Publishing Piers Pickard
Associate Publisher Robin Barton
Commissioning Editor Dora Whitaker
Designer Kristina Juodenas
Cartography James Leversha
Picture Research Ceri James
Editors Karyn Noble, Dora Whitaker
Index Anna Tyler
Print Production Nigel Longuet

Lonely Planet Offices

Ireland
Digital Depot, Roe Lane (off Thomas St),
Digital Hub, Dublin 8,
D08 TCV4

USA
230 Franklin Road, Building 2B,
Franklin, TN 37064
T: 615-988-9713

STAY IN TOUCH lonelyplanet.com/contact

Authors Alex Bescoby (**AB**), Over the Pyrenees on the Chemin de la Liberté; Alex Crevar (**AC**); Andrew Bain (**AB**), Four Days on the Alpine Pass Route, Tour de Monte Rosa; Ash Bhardwaj (**AB**), Poland to Belarus along the Augustów Canal; Ben Lerwill (**BL**); Brandon Presser (**BP**); Brendan Sainsbury (**BS**); James Bainbridge (**JB**); Jacqueline Kehoe (**JK**); Jasper Winn (**JW**); Jini Reddy (**JR**); Kate Armstrong (**KA**); Kerry Walker (**KW**); Laura Itzkowitz (**LI**); Luke Waterson (**LW**); Marc di Duca (**MDD**); Mark Elliott (**ME**); Mark Stratton (**MS**); Oli Reed (**OR**); Oliver Berry (**OB**); Oliver Smith (**OS**); Paul Bloomfield (**PB**); Piers Pickard (**PP**); Phoebe Smith (**PS**); Rory Goulding (**RG**); Sarah Baxter (**SB**), High Drama in the Cares Gorge, Portuguese Coastal Way, Steps and Ladders: The Kaiserjäger, A Hop-On, Hop-Off Tour of the Heart of Wales Line; Stuart Butler (**SB**), Wild North: The Karhunkierros Trail; Stuart Maconie (**SM**); Zora O'Neill (**ZO**).

Cover illustration by Ross Murray (www.rossmurray.com).